Proxy Warriors

# Proxy Warriors

## THE RISE AND FALL OF STATE-SPONSORED MILITIAS

Ariel I. Ahram

Stanford Security Studies
An Imprint of Stanford University Press
Stanford, California

Stanford University Press
Stanford, California

Printed in the United States of America on acid-free, archival-quality paper

Library of Congress Cataloging-in-Publication Data

Ahram, Ariel I. (Ariel Ira)
  Proxy warriors : the rise and fall of state-sponsored militias / Ariel I. Ahram.
     p. cm.
  Includes bibliographical references and index.
     ISBN 978-0-8047-7358-4 (cloth : alk. paper) — ISBN 978-0-8047-7359-1 (pbk. : alk. paper)
  1. Developing countries—Militia. 2. Paramilitary forces—Developing countries.
3. Developing countries—History, Military.  I. Title.
  UA13.A35 2011
  355.3'5—dc22                                                                    2010023018

Special discounts for bulk quantities of Stanford Security Studies are available to corporations, professional associations, and other organizations. For details and discount information, contact the special sales department of Stanford University Press. Tel: (650) 736-1782, Fax: (650) 736-1784

Typeset by Thompson Type in 10/14 Minion

# CONTENTS

## FIGURES AND TABLES

**Figures**

**Tables**

# ACKNOWLEDGMENTS

I have accumulated debts both professional and personal in the process of completing this project. Andy Bennett took me on as an advisee under some very inclement circumstances, but I am glad and thankful that he did, as he offered me valuable critique and advice throughout the project. Debbie Avant, Dan Brumberg, Jack Goldstone, Steve Heydemann, Marc Howard, and Charles King pushed me to consider realms of inquiry I would otherwise have neglected. In addition, I am grateful to John Gledhill, Sara Goodman, Gabe Rubin, Ryan Saylor, and Rachel Templer for their friendship, advice, and commiseration. Since coming to the University of Oklahoma, Mark Frazier, Zach Messitte, and Greg Russell and have offered me an extraordinary home in which to make the transition from student to professor.

A number of people offered comments and suggestions on various facets of this project. I gained a great deal of knowledge about the Middle East through my discussions with Amatzia Baram, Adeed Dawisha, Michael Hudson, Kanan Makiya, Phebe Marr, Yitzhak Nakash, and Ken Pollack. David Steinberg and Fred Von Der Mehden indulged me as an interloper in Southeast Asia. Sunil Dasgupta, John Fishel, Hillel Frisch, and Meyer Kestnbaum gave me the value of their insights on militias around the world. Any mistakes are mine, not theirs.

The project benefited from a number of sources of institutional support, notably the Foreign Language and Area Studies Program, the Boren National Security Education Program, the Institute for Qualitative and Mixed Method Research, Georgetown University Graduate School, Georgetown's Center for Democracy and Civil Society, and the University of Oklahoma Vice President for Research's Junior Faculty Grant. I also thank the staffs at the libraries of Georgetown and Oklahoma, as well as those at the Africa and Middle East Reading Room at the Library of Congress and the U.S. National Archives. Geoffrey Burn at Stanford University Press believed in this project since I first mentioned it and shepherded it through to completion with patience and expertise.

Outside the academy, I wish to acknowledge a number of people whose role was no less important. Jacob Ebin, Yunsung Hong, Kathryn Hinkle, Jason Kohn, and Joe Neumann served as role models and sounding boards. I can only hope I was as supportive for my mother, Judi; father, Yossi; brother, Roey; and sister, Sharon, as they were for me. I thank my wife, Marni, who has listened to and read so much about this project that words now escape me to express my gratitude; and finally, my daughter, Leonie Emilia, who arrived an hour before the page proofs. May this book contribute in some way to improving the world in which she grows up.

*Are not men strongest, who rule over land and sea and all that is in them? But the king is stronger; he is their lord and master, and whatever he says to them they obey. If he tells them to make war on one another, they do it; and if he sends them out against the enemy, they go, and conquer mountains, walls, and towers. They kill and are killed, and do not disobey the king's command; if they win the victory, they bring everything to the king—whatever spoil they take and everything else. Likewise those who do not serve in the army or make war but till the soil; whenever they sow and reap, they bring some to the king; and they compel one another to pay taxes to the king. And yet he is only one man! If he tells them to kill, they kill; if he tells them to release, they release; if he tells them to attack, they attack; if he tells them to lay waste, they lay waste . . .*

**—I Esdras 4**

# INTRODUCTION

IN 2003, A NEW WORD entered Western parlance, drawn from colloquial Arabic—
*janjaweed* (devil-horsemen). The term connoted a phenomenon that had suddenly caught the world's attention: nomadic tribal bands rampaging through
Sudan's Darfur region, attacking villages and destroying the crops of the seden-
tary population. Notwithstanding protestations by the Sudanese defense minister that the *janjaweed* are nothing but "gangs of armed bandits" whom the
government is unfortunately powerless to stop, a U.N. commission of inquiry
documented the way these militias acted "under the authority, with the support, complicity or tolerance of the Sudanese State authorities, and who benefit
from impunity for their actions."[1]

Groups like these are becoming ever more common on the global stage.
As Mary Kaldor observes, contemporary warfare tends to involve a host of
"paramilitary units, local warlords, criminal gangs, police forces, mercenary
groups, and also regular armies including break away units . . . operat[ing]
through a mixture of confrontation and cooperation even when on opposing
sides."[2] Concurrently, John Mueller and Martin Van Creveld each argue that
conventional armies are being replaced by a sundry mix of thugs and mercenaries whose allegiances to the state and adherence to long-established norms
of conduct are weak.[3]

Underlying this jeremiad is the fear that states, the entities that have been the
authoritative arbiters of violence in and between societies for over three centuries, are similarly becoming obsolete.[4] A 1999 U.N. report noted that violence is
frequently perpetrated by such nonstate actors. The greatest dangers to human
security—ethnic cleansing, civilian massacres, banditry, enslavement, and child

soldiers—stem from the incapacity of states to secure and maintain order.[5] Following the terrorist attacks of September 11, 2001, U.S. national security doctrine identified weak states as posing as grave a danger as strong ones.[6] In 2010, U.S. Defense Secretary Robert Gates reiterated that dealing with "fractured or failing states is, in many ways, the main security challenge of our time."[7] Of course, no state is without some illicit or criminal use of violence. Rebellions and insurgencies challenge many states. But the possibility that a state would encourage a vigilante group like the *janjaweed*, the Colombian *autodefensas*, or the Rwandan *interahamwe* to deploy violence on its behalf seems to indicate a novel and dramatic degradation of the most fundamental of state functions.[8]

This study contends that the devolution of state control over violence to nonstate actors, like many features of the so-called new wars, is hardly new and does not necessarily presage a descent into chaos.[9] It follows Michael Mann in recognizing that "most historic states have not possessed a monopoly of organized military force and many have not even claimed it."[10] Indeed, key features of statehood—including the monopoly over force—are empirically variant, not ontologically given. In other words, we should not mistake the ideal type for a representation of actual states.[11] Rather than begin with a normative premise about the qualities of "weak" versus "strong" states, this study seeks to answer a series of empirical questions about military development and the ways states historically have come to organize institutions of coercion.[12] Why do some states enjoy centralized and bureaucratized control over violence in the form of conventional armed forces, whereas others rely on militia and paramilitary units whose allegiance extends not to the state but to individual leaders, tribes or ethnic factions, or local strongmen? Are states that collude with nonstate violence wielders necessarily doomed to fail, as many allege? If so, how do so many devolved states survive? Finally, what is the impact of militias on international and human security?

## EXPLAINING MILITARY DEVELOPMENT IN THE THIRD WORLD

There is a long strand of inquiry into the origins of social order and the drivers of state formation.[13] Max Weber couched his famous conceptualization of the state as the holder of a monopoly over the use of force within a wider attempt to explain Europe's unique course from feudalism to modernity. Over the course of a millennium, Europe witnessed the gradual replacement of the feudal lords' small, decentralized, locally raised militias with large, centrally controlled national armies.[14] While emphasizing different combinations of political, technological, social, and economic factors as the primary catalysts, historical sociologists tend to agree that European states that could not manage the transition to military centralization—such as the kingdom of Poland or the Italian city-states—suffered predation and dismemberment at the hands of their more powerful neighbors. As articulated by Charles Tilly and others, Europe's hypercompetitive, neo-Darwinian environment led to an isomorphic process of military development and state formation. Political entities had to adopt the irresistible trappings of a bureaucratic state combined with a large, centralized military in order to survive.[15]

Despite the explanatory power of these mechanisms in accounting for the trajectory of European state formation, the same theories have not been applied with equal vigor to the developing world.[16] Certainly violence has been no less intrinsic to the formation of late-developing states (LDSs) than it has been in Europe.[17] But most scholars come to reiterate some variant of Miguel Centeno's conclusion that if war made the state in Europe, then limited war in the developing world contributed to the emergence of limited states.[18] Subordination to Western control, first as colonies and then as dependents within the international system, distorted the process of interstate competition in the Third World. Postcolonial elites eagerly appropriated the juridical and normative concepts of statehood, even as decolonization left states bereft of the coercive and infrastructural capacity needed to actually govern their own territory.[19] After independence, the provision of superpower protection and international norms guaranteeing the sanctity of state boundaries combined with the weakness of any potential regional rival to diminish LDSs' need to engage in more thorough forms of centralization over force of administration. LDSs avoided the difficulties of building up conventional armed forces akin to what was seen in Europe. Instead, they focused on challenges of internal security and domestic pacification. The isomorphism prevailing in the developing world is the opposite of what was witnessed in Europe: LDSs could deal with internal challengers in a manner similar to premodern European lords, building up local militias through a combination of coercion and enticements directed at local strongmen and other peripheral agents.[20] This technique of violence devolution represents a fundamental abandonment of the state's monopoly over violence and a turn toward what Robert Holden calls a reliance on parainstitutional violence wielders.[21]

The problem with such a broad generalization, however, is that it fails to explain the differences in military development *within* the Third World.

Not all LDSs have adopted violence devolution and or used state-sponsored militias to the same extent. Indeed, even a cursory glance reveals profound variation in the size of military forces, the degree of technological sophistication, and levels of centralization, as well as the intensity, frequency, and types of conflict seen by various states in different regions. The Middle East, for instance, has seen numerous international wars and much higher levels of military spending than any other developing region. The region's armies are highly mechanized, technologically advanced, and organized along a more or less centralized basis akin to the militaries of the West. Regional states uses these armies to eliminate rivals to their presumptive monopoly over the use of force.[22] By comparison, interstate relations in other developing regions have been generally peaceful, with national armies small and technologically unsophisticated. In response to ongoing internal crises, states have had frequent resort to the devolution of violence, recruiting parainstitutional forces instead of centralizing military control.

This study builds and tests a theory to account for variation in the use of state-sponsored militias versus conventional armed forces among LDSs. The theory follows Eliot Cohen in finding the roots of different modes of Third World military organization in the impact of threat, distant battles, and inherited models of military organizations.[23] It offers a more concrete, historical explanation of Third World military development by situating generic mechanisms of institutional change in specific contextual space.[24] As such, it makes two interrelated arguments about the conditions that generate and sustain state devolution of violence to nonstate actors. First, the origin of state devolution of violence depends on different legacies of decolonization, particularly whether decolonization occurred through violent revolution or through negotiation. If guerrillas were active around the time of decolonization, newborn states tended to appropriate the networks of local violence-wielders, converting them from anticolonial insurgents into pro-state militias. If, on the other hand, decolonization occurred through negotiation, new states inherited the bureaucratic military organizational format of the departing colonial powers. Second, the persistence of these differing forms of coercive institutions depends on the permissive conditions of the international environment. If states face strong external competitors and the threat of war, then they are forced to adopt (or retain) centralized military formats to defend against external predation. If, on the other hand, the environment is pacific, either because of ongoing intervention by great powers or the relative impotence of regional rivals, then these states can persist in devolution. Forgoing military centralization, such states deal with internal threats by relying mainly on state-sponsored militias.

Shedding new light on the dynamics of military development also offers a new set of policy recommendations for dealing with frail states that seem unable or unwilling to assert control over violence within their territories. These unorthodox prescriptions stand in direct contradiction of the presumed "imperative" state building that has guided the international community in recent decades.[25] On one hand, both violence devolution and centralization are systemic outcomes that can scarcely be addressed by the international community through the provision of aid, advice, and troops. Only revisiting the international system's fundamental components—the norms of international sovereignty and the structure of international hierarchy—can avert the proliferation of state-sponsored militias. On the other hand, while nonstate actors have been implicated in atrocities, in many circumstances they have also provided levels of stability and security superior to a failing state. Instead of privileging state over nonstate violence wielders, a better way to promote human and regional security is to bypass frail states and instead integrate realms of limited state control directly into the international system. In sum, the international community must learn to live with militias rather than trying in vain to displace them.

## PLAN OF THE BOOK

This study applies the logic of historical institutionalism and comparative historical analysis to examine violence devolution and military centralization.[26] It employs large-scale macrohistorical comparisons to achieve what Theda Skocpol and Margaret Somers call the parallel demonstration of theory.[27] Chapter 1 begins by sketching the concepts of state-sponsored militias and violence devolution. It offers a concrete historical theory to explain how different military formats originated in periods of decolonization and how conditions of internal and external threat determine the persistence of these formats over time.

Chapters 2, 3, and 4 provide empirical testing of these hypotheses using comparative case studies of Indonesia, Iraq, and Iran, respectively. Despite having similarly weak central state institutions at the beginning of the twentieth century, each of these countries followed different courses of military development. Following its revolution, Indonesia emerged heavily dependent on militias and has continued to rely on nonstate actors until today. While this form of violence devolution has been effective at maintaining control across the far-flung archipelago, it has also proved to have significant liabilities in Indonesia's efforts to exert power abroad. Iraq, in contrast, was endowed with a centralized and conventional military force due to its position under the British mandate. The Iraqi state quickly deployed this military apparatus both to compete with other regional powers and to control its own population. Since the American invasion of 2003, however, Iraq has seen a reversion to negotiation with armed tribal, religious, and other militia factions to gain a modicum of internal security. Finally, Iran initially took a course of military centralization by importing Western military technologies roughly comparable to Iraq's path of military development. After the revolution of 1979, Khomeini and the regime of the Islamic Republic tried to replace the conventional army with part-time militia-based units. The persistence of significant foreign threat, however, has forced Iran to reconsider its commitment to violence devolution and find new ways to join a conventional military force with state-sponsored militias.

In technical terms, these empirical chapters aim to facilitate both latitudinal (between cases) and longitudinal (within cases) comparisons.[28] They are therefore written with an eye toward capturing ideographic details while linking to general explanations of how and why these countries took such different courses.[29] Secondary sources, newspaper accounts, and U.S. and British government archival material provide the bulk of the data. To avoid biases of interpretation, significant care is taken to triangulate from diverse sources and to highlight contention within the relevant historiographies.[30]

Finally, Chapter 5 concludes by applying these insights to contemporary policy dilemmas stemming from frail and failing states. Demonstrating the impact of deep-seated historical processes on the formation of centralized or devolved forms of coercive institutions calls into question some of the most important assumptions about state formation in the Third World. The alternative to intervening to augment state power, seeking to establish a monopoly of violence where it never truly existed, is to embrace violence devolution and find ways to recruit nonstate actors in lieu of defunct or rapacious states.

# 1 THE ORIGINS AND PERSISTENCE OF STATE-SPONSORED MILITIAS

MAX WEBER'S FAMOUS DEFINITION of the state as "a human community that (successfully) claims the *monopoly of the legitimate use of physical force* within a given territory" is the touchstone for contemporary understanding of the entities typically considered to be the ultimate arbiters of political life.[1] While scholars have since amended and revised its dimensions, the core emphasis on a state's ability to control violence remains unaltered.[2] Of course, empirical cases always fall short of this ideal type. Weber himself notes that force is a means specific—not exclusive—to the state. States enjoy, at best, only a comparative advantage in its application.[3] Where the 1980s saw efforts to bring the state back to the forefront of social science, the 1990s saw a countermovement questioning the elusive contours of the state as an ideal type.[4] Refusing to reify the state, however, does not necessarily banish it from the conceptual lexicon. What is needed is a more nuanced schema for appreciating and categorizing the counters of actual existing states.

Few states have ever actually sought a complete monopoly over military force, much less possessed it. States engage continuously in negotiation, collaboration, and domination of external and internal challengers to assert and maintain a hold on power.[5] Michael Mann notes that institutions of coercion rest somewhere along a continuum between absolute domination of force and the equally hypothetical Hobbesian ideal type of total anarchy. In medieval Europe, states organized large numbers of people over far-flung territories, engaging in minimally stable coercive exercises but with limited mobilization or coordination. Chains of command were mediated and indirect, with weak oversight and monitoring of those who ruled on the king's behalf. No matter how vast a king's domain, he still had to negotiate for the services of dukes and barons who retained their own independent forces. On the other hand, modern states incorporate coercion as part of their infrastructural bureaucratic power. Direct, linear chains of command extended from the sovereign to the lowest violence-wielding subaltern without the need for collaboration with such nonstate elements.[6] The transition to modernity in Europe, then, entailed a move from small, decentralized, self-equipped militias raised by feudal lords to "large, centrally-financed and supplied armies."[7] Such a centralized force structure was adept at what Charles Tilly calls the dual tasks of state formation: *war making*, the elimination or neutralization of external rivals; and *state making*, the elimination or neutralizing of rivals inside the territory who possess autonomous means of deploying violence.[8]

In much of the Third World, however, competition and cooperation between the state and embedded societal elites for control of coercion remains ongoing and unresolved.[9] This chapter articulates a theory to explain the outcome of these struggles and the variety of forms of control late-developing states (LDSs) exert over coercion. First, it sketches the concept of violence devolution as a mode of military development involving cooperation and collusion between a state and state-sponsored militias. Violence devolution is thus an alternative to central control over the use of force. Second, it uses insights from organizational theory to describe the interaction among states, insurgents, and militias and explains how the survival of different forms of military organization depends on the nature of the threat environment states inhabit. Finally, it links these general theories with a specific account of the origins of different military forms at moments of decolonization and combines these hypotheses into a typological theory that accounts for distinctive trajectories of LDSs' military development. Ultimately, it elaborates a more concrete historical explanation about the emergence of both violence devolution and centralization in the postcolonial world.

## STATES, INSURGENTS, AND MILITIAS

Studies of civil war tend to depict internal conflict as dyadic engagements between the state and rebel groups, two-player games of incumbent versus challenger.[10] Yet closer examination belies such simplification. In a detailed study of the Greek civil war, Stathis Kalyvas argues that microlevel conflicts of personal and family ambitions motivate belligerent action more than abstract political ideology. Local militias often function as free agents, variously fighting on behalf of the state or of the rebels.[11]

Indeed, studies of violence in Latin America richly describe patterns of cooperation between states and nonstate actors, calling such activity *parainstitutional* violence (*la violencia parainstitucional*).[12] In Colombia, for instance, the mobilization of civilians into so-called self-defense forces was an explicit state strategy to help fight leftist insurgents since at least the 1950s. The Colombian army encouraged landowners to take protection into their own hands. Said one paramilitary leader, "The struggle against the same enemy converted us into allies of the army."[13] These nonstate actors retained considerable autonomy to use force at their own accord. In fact, by the 1980s groups like Autodefensas Unidas de Colombia, originally formed to assist the army against leftist insurgents, were in alliance with drug cartels. Despite professing loyalty to the state, they refused to disarm.[14] Similar phenomena of state-sponsored nonstate militias are visible in the likes of the Sudanese *janjaweed*, the Ulster loyalists, the Sierra Leonean Kamajors, armed wings of ruling political parties, plus all manner of bandits, privateers, and vigilantes with whom the state makes accommodations, however temporary.

Recognizing the ubiquity of state-sponsored militia forces complicates our understanding of civil conflict and the processes by which states pursue and accumulate power over society. Instead of a simple dichotomy, a trilateral relationship exists among state, antistate, and state-sponsored elements, as depicted in Figure 1.1. In the upper left, the state is a purveyor of violence through agents—the army, police, judges, and so forth—deemed legally entitled to enact coercion and formally part of the state apparatus.[15] This entitlement has both domestic and international dimensions: Even if tens of thousands of their own citizens take up arms independently, states enjoy the imprimatur of international norms of sovereignty and the domestic legal system on its side. Moreover, reliance on international standards for validation of sovereignty has led to the diffusion of common patterns in the formal institutions of coercion. In particular, the rituals of militarism—parade ground marches, salutes of submission, the changing of the guard—are known the world over. Soldiers and police wear uniforms bearing epaulettes and insignias indicating their positions in the bureaucracy of violence. Armed forces are divided into the familiar army, navy, and air forces. Ministers of war and

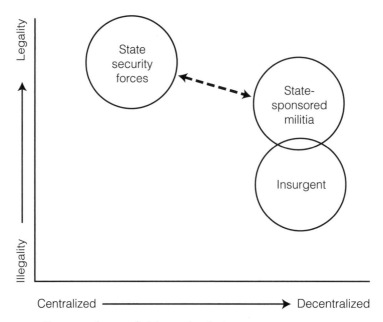

**Figure 1.1.** Conceptual map of violence devolution.

interior meet regularly, mutually acknowledging and reinforcing each other's standing as the sole legal purveyors of violence within their designated territories. Even clandestine security services or praetorian guards qualify as part of the state apparatus, although they also represent a limited decentralization of the state's coercive power.[16]

In the lower right of Figure 1.1 are the counterstate actors—coup plotters, guerrillas, insurgents, and criminals. They specifically seek to displace or replace the state's authoritative position and use violence to compel changes in state behavior. As the state monopolizes the juridical claim to violence, the actions of this second class of violence wielders are necessarily illegal. Again, the level of domestic support or actual coercive power held by insurgents must be weighed against the normative bias in favor of states. Even when the guerrillas control large swaths of territory, the international community tends to deny recognition and authority to any entity that fractures existing designs of sovereignty.[17]

Between these two poles, parainstitutional agents share characteristics of both the state and counterstate actors.[18] Parainstitutional agents collaborate in intimidating or eliminating the state's enemies but remain outside the state's legal bureaucratic boundaries. Their affiliation with the state is loose or covert. They do not enjoy the recognition offered by international norms or domestic law. While there can be some ambiguity in the distinction between the extralegal components of militia behavior and those of state organs, there remain strong normative grounds to differentiate what is sovereign and what is not. Parainstitutional relationships exemplify what William Chambliss calls state-organized crime, where the state is complicit as an accessory before or after the fact in acts defined by law as criminal.[19] As a leader of the striking teacher's union in Oaxaca, Mexico, expressed,

> Sicarios [hired gunmen] paid by the PRI [the ruling Institutional Revolutionary Party] could do things the police legally couldn't do—grab people without cause, beat them, torture them . . . The only authority they had was the money they were getting, but who was to stop them? The government? The government was paying them![20]

Understandably, the nomenclature attached to parainstitutional groups and their leaders is subjective, veering from derogatory or euphemistic. What could be called a "warlord army" can just as easily be dubbed a "village protection force."[21] The origins of these groups also vary. Robert Bates notes that in Africa's civil wars the youth wings of political parties, regional coalitions, and ethnic groups have all been known to "transmute into militias" under the right conditions.[22] As Eric Hobsbawm observes, every bandit will "sooner or later be tempted to take the easy road . . . [becoming] a retainer of the lords, a member of some strong-arm squad which comes to terms with the structures of official power."[23] Their activities, however, remain outside a formal legal framework. This is a crucial distinction between parainstitutional forces and private military contractors, whose role as purveyors of violence is explicitly set out in a legal contract between the state and the firm.[24]

## ORGANIZATION FORMATS
## AND INSTITUTIONAL PERFORMANCE

Why do states—assumed to jealously guard the prerogative of violence—rely on nonstate actors? How do those engaging in violence devolution survive this three-way competition? Both cooperative and competitive interactions among states, insurgents, and parainstitutional militias depend critically on their respective organizational structures and cultures. Abdelkader Sinno

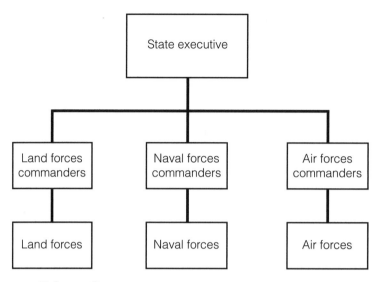

**Figure 1.2.** U-form military organization.

observes that organizational structure limits the range of coercive strategies that can be initiated or countered by insurgents.[25] Similarly, Jeremy Weinstein argues that different organizational formats provide different incentives and constraints for coordination, monitoring, and discipline of individuals within the group, which in turn have an impact on the functional capacity of these organizations to vie with one another.[26] The same consequences stem from a state's organization of coercive institutions.

In Oliver Williamson's schema of organizational forms, conventional state militaries represent a unitary-form (U-form) organization, while paramilitary units map onto a multidivisional (M-form) organizational structure. The differences between these forms are shown visually in Figures 2 and 3. U-form organizations are characterized by a hierarchical chain of command and division of units by functional specialization. Military organizations following this pattern adopt the familiar tripartite functional division of army, navy, and air force, differentiated by their specialization in inflicting violence through different means. M-form organizations, in contrast, are characterized by a weblike command structure built around a number of ter-

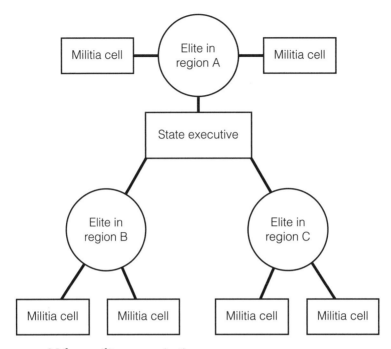

**Figure 1.3.** M-form military organization.

ritorially specific and self-contained units. In an M-form organization, each unit is quasi-autonomous, responsible for overseeing every operation within its given territory. Militarily, this means that the state maintains contact with various redundant cells that are differentiated by geography rather than specialization.

The different organizational forms and different divisions of labor introduce specific constraints on supervision and, conversely, opportunities for deception at different levels of M-form and U-form organizations. Table 1 summarizes these effects. M-form organizations give the subunit director the ability and incentive to innovate. Their decentralization, however, makes it harder for the state to monitor and control independent militia leaders, thus exacerbating the tensions between principal and agent. To incite better performance, states often promote competition between subunits. U-form organizations, in contrast, are easier to control because each unit is responsible for only

**Table 1.1.** Comparison between conventional (unitary form) and militia-based (multidivisional form) military organizations.

|  | Conventional armies: U-form | State-sponsored militias: M-form |
|---|---|---|
| Informational and command flows | Linear and hierarchical | Weblike |
| Organizational principle | Units organized by function | Units organized by territory |
| Governance cost | High | Low |
| Specific capabilities | Coordinated operations, especially in large scale | Minimally stable cooperation for small-scale operations |

SOURCE: Adopted from Alexander Cooley, *The Logics of Hierarchy: The Organization of Empires, States, and Military Occupations* (Ithaca, NY: Cornell University Press, 2005), 51; Michael Mann, *The Sources of Social Power, Volume 1: A History of Power from the Beginning to A.D. 1760* (New York: Cambridge University Press, 1986), 7–8.

one operational task. But U-form organizations are also less flexible because a unit leader can become myopic and focus solely on a particular task rather than on the larger organizational goal.[27]

The devolution of command and control gives militia commanders latitude to improvise techniques of repression and surveillance specifically suited to their environments. Raised and retained on a part-time and ad hoc basis, they are also cheaper than regular militaries to deploy for protracted engagements in low-intensity warfare.[28] Because militia commanders are local elites, they have superior knowledge of the physical and cultural terrain in their respective territories.[29] There are additionally normative or cultural reasons for states to rely on militias. Revolutionary states often adopt military doctrines emphasizing popular participation in military affairs and thus encourage the formation of civilian militias.[30] By colluding with nonstate actors, states gain plausible deniability for flagrant violence committed against civilians in the course of often brutal counterinsurgency campaigns.[31]

The use of state-sponsored militias, however, also entails some significant trade-offs stemming from the state's loss of control over its agents. As Kalyvas notes, militias may not share the state's ideological goals or owe it much allegiance; their fighters might seek economic gain or local status more than any particular political agenda. This contributes to the use of violence in a manner that is counterproductive to the state's ends.[32] Militia leaders can subvert central authority in a number of ways. They can refuse to comply with the state's demands, either by neglecting to target those the state identifies as dangerous or by attacking those groups the state identifies as friendly. They can amass their own power base by setting up a "state-within-a-state," by seceding, or even by marching on the capital to depose the regime. This danger increases when militias can collaborate with one another and when they have an independent source of revenue or support. Colombia is just one of a myriad of countries in which both insurgents and militias gained untold autonomy by embedding themselves in a black-market economy of narcotics and other illicit goods. Still, it is important to note that for some groups the economic threshold for self-sufficiency is relatively low.[33]

To manage these risks, LDSs rely on techniques familiar to any sixteenth-century European monarch beset by unruly vassals. Joel Migdal identifies three critical tactics of state survival. The first is to remove and relocate the local elites involved in raising militias. Those with too strong a foothold in a particular region or group are co-opted to serve in higher office, where they can be isolated from their domestic constituency. Second, and closely related, is to grant nonmerit appointments to those with kinship or patronage ties to state elites over those with greater expertise or competence. This ensures that the local agents have an incentive to remain loyal to the central government.[34] In the Middle East, for instance, states replace tribal chiefs they consider too autonomous with more pliable brothers, uncles, cousins, or other kin. If one clan becomes too powerful, the state sanctions the creation of a rival tribe.[35] The third tool is what Migdal calls "dirty tricks": turning state coercive organs or other militia groups against one another. This in effect fosters a small-scale civil war between two erstwhile state agents. Collectively, these techniques allow states to function as brokers, maintaining exclusive ties with local nonstate actors while blocking any individual militia leader's attempt to unite with other forces in collective action against the state.[36]

Although these techniques may be effective for state making and internal pacification, the needs of war making and external defense dictate the exact opposite approach. In U-form coercive institutions, internal hierarchy and centralized chains of command allow for coordination among different functional units. This coordination is crucial to allowing large-scale mechanized armies to train and operate at maximum military effectiveness.[37] In contrast, indirect control among M-form organizations prevents interunit coordination and hinders coercive capacity. Unlike conventional military units, militia groups are not interchangeable. Fighters who serve on a part-time or semivoluntary basis tend to lack the logistical capability and training necessary to operate far from their homes or with advanced technology. Additionally, their loyalties are primarily to a single local leader, and they may refuse to be integrated under a conventional chain of command. Ultimately, these limitations mean that militias may be able to hunt down subversives in the rear echelons but not capture strategic positions or withstand a concentrated attack.[38] The practices that provide internal stability by violence devolution exacerbate a state's susceptibility to external attack.

Many studies point precisely to differences in the threat environment to explain the differences between the centralized armies that emerged in Europe and the more decentralized forces common in the Third World.[39] War, after all, is a very effective auditor of institutional performance. In Europe, states that failed to match their neighbors' military prowess were defeated, dismembered, and eliminated from the international system, propelling the transition from militias to professional armies. The process of military centralization became a self-reinforcing pathway, rewarding those states that could continually improve their coercive capacities. Yet, in the developing world, the protection of client states by superpowers and the existence of international norms preserving the inviolability of international borders combine to mitigate the pressures of external threat on LDSs.[40] As Stephen David explains, regimes practice a form of "omni-balancing," focusing equally on keeping internal challengers at bay as well as foreign enemies. Instead of building up the formal military, they can fragment coercive institutions to forestall an internal coup.[41] For many observers, then, the developing world is a zone of "impotent peace": LDSs can safely devolve control over violence to militias because they are surrounded by relatively innocuous neighbors. Lacking the capacity to conduct aggression against one another, there is no reason for LDSs to adopt military centralization.[42]

Such broad generalizations, however, suffer from a number of theoretical and empirical shortcomings. First, the impact of subordination in the international system is inconsistent. On one hand, dependence on superpowers could yield protections that allow a state to concentrate exclusively on internal security and adopt violence devolution.[43] On the other hand, the guarantees offered by great powers to client states are never absolute. In fact, the goal of

Table 1.2. Conflict by type and region, 1945–2006 (tally and crosstab by row).

|  | Extraterritorial (decolonization) | Interstate | Internal | Internationalized internal | Total |
|---|---|---|---|---|---|
| Africa | 11 (15%) | 8 (11%) | 36 (49%) | 19 (26%) | 74 |
| Asia | 6 (9%) | 15 (22%) | 38 (56%) | 9 (13%) | 68 |
| Middle East | 2 (6%) | 11 (34%) | 12 (38%) | 7 (22%) | 32 |
| Latin America | 1 (4%) | 5 (19%) | 18 (69%) | 2 (8%) | 26 |
| TOTAL | 20 (10%) | 39 (20%) | 104 (52%) | 37 (19%) | 200 |

SOURCE: Uppsala Conflict Dataset/Peace Research Institute-Oslo. See Nils Petter Gleditsch, Peter Wallensteen, Mikael Eriksson, Margareta Sollenberg and Havard Strand, "Armed Conflict 1946–2001: A New Dataset," Journal of Peace Research, 39 (2002).

the sponsor is to use the client to its own advantage. Such interference can just as easily aggravate regional conflicts and push LDSs toward war.[44] Second, regimes and states are often inextricably linked. No ruler can be completely oblivious to the disposition of the state's institutional apparatus. Although the appropriation of the entirety of state territory is rare, losing control of territory to a neighboring state or domestic subversive or suffering diminishment and subjugation in the international system can substantially destabilize the elite itself. This provides strong incentive to remain attentive to the external threats surrounding a state and regime.[45]

Third, and most importantly, empirical evidence belies the notion that all LDSs face an equally pacific and permissive international environment. Tables 2 and 3 show profound regional variation in the incidence of different types of conflicts and the levels of military spending.

The Middle East, for example, has far higher than average rates of interstate and internationalized conflict, and its states devote more resources to military expenditure than do those of any other region. By comparison, internal conflicts predominate in Africa, Asia, and Latin America, where military spending is comparatively low. LDSs in different regions still respond to varying military threat by adapting different organizational models.[46] While states in some regions can survive without a powerful military, in other regions high military threat compels a constant struggle to build and equip a large conventional army. A more complete theory of military development must not stop at explaining variations between Europe and the non-Western

**Table 1.3.** Military spending among LDSs, 1999.

| Region and country | Military expenditures/GDP | Region and country | Military expenditures/GDP |
|---|---|---|---|
| Africa | | Latin America | |
| Angola | 16.5 | Argentina | 1.9 |
| Congo | 7.8 | Brazil | 2.7 |
| Ethiopia | 6.0 | Chile | 4.0 |
| Kenya | 3.1 | Mexico | 0.9 |
| Nigeria | 4.4 | Peru | 1.6 |
| S. Africa | 1.3 | Venezuela | 1.5 |
| Sudan | 4.9 | *Average* | *2.1* |
| Zimbabwe | 4.5 | | |
| *Average* | *6.0* | Middle East and North Africa | |
| Asia | | Algeria | 6.6 |
| Indonesia | 1.1 | Egypt | 7.7 |
| Malaysia | 4.0 | Iran | 6.2 |
| N. Korea | 14 | Israel | 8.9 |
| Pakistan | 5.7 | Jordan | 7.7 |
| Philippines | 2.1 | Morocco | 5.0 |
| Singapore | 5.6 | Saudi Arabia | 15.5 |
| South Korea | 3.0 | Syria | 5.6 |
| Taiwan | 5.2 | Yemen | 6.7 |
| Thailand | 1.9 | *Average* | *7.8* |
| *Average* | *4.7* | | |

SOURCE: *The Military Balance* (London: International Institute for Strategic Studies, 2001)

world but must also account for this disparity in military development *among* postcolonial states.

## A TYPOLOGICAL THEORY OF
## THIRD WORLD MILITARY DEVELOPMENT

Although the persistence of centralized and decentralized military formats may depend on the balance of internal and external threats an individual state faces, this alone does not account for the specific distribution of military capacity across developing regions. Why did states initially adopt military centralization or decentralization? What explains regional clustering of military formats?

How did these particularly institutional formats emerge in the first place? Among the core insights of historical institutionalism is that institutional origins do not necessarily correspond to their subsequent functions. Rather, after their establishment, institutions often adapt to fill roles that were only dimly perceived at their inception. Simply because a state employs state-sponsored militias to fight internal subversives does not mean that counterinsurgency was the original motive for violence devolution. Similarly, the use of conventional military forces in interstate war does not mean these institutions were intended as such from the outset.

To explain the geographical and historical variation in the appearance of violence devolution and centralization in the Third World requires a more concrete theory. This theory must be sensitive to variation in the initial conditions that propel LDSs on different trajectories of military development as well as subsequent threat conditions that account for institutional persistence and change.[47] Underpinning such a theory is the notion of path dependence, which emphasizes how specific institutional formats and rubrics become locked in after critical junctures of institutional creation.[48] Among LDSs, decolonization has provided the new state elites the opportunity to redefine the uses of bequeathed colonial institutions and to try to build new ones. Specifically, the initial crystallization of a military's organizational structures, its cultural orientations, and its technological endowmentment has had a number of long-term and often unintended consequences for the way states engaged both in state making internally and war making externally.[49]

Two forms of decolonization are possible. The first type is *revolutionary decolonization* through insurgency. Anticolonial struggles activated locally based networks of coercion and self-defense. Overlapping networks of opportunists and politically motivated ideologues emerged, each with different reason to resist the imposition of the colonial masters. Mingling criminal and political motives, local actors vied to appropriate the revolutionary mantle, claiming a connection between their own cause and that of the national struggle. Revolutionary leaders acted as brokers who knit together a fabric of local violence wielders into the revolutionary army and bestowed nationalist legitimacy on essentially parochial interests. Thus, both top-down and bottom-up processes in revolutionary decolonization combined to make the ranks of the new revolutionary army a ready-made militia force.[50] Armies that emerged from decolonization wars tended to have the flexibility of M-form organizations. They were well acquainted with the techniques of violence devolution and popular mobilization, possessing a sense of mission different from that of a conventional professional fighting force.

In contrast, nonviolent *negotiated decolonization* involved a bequeathal of institutions modeled directly on European armies. The inheritance of a conventional military was part and parcel of the imperialist legacy, either when directly implanted by a European overlord in the colonial army or when imported by an indigenous elite aiming to stave off foreign domination.[51] Even when poorly equipped and distrusted by its colonial masters, the colonial army was a dedicated career track. Competence and professionalism were valued, at least in theory. The recruitment of soldiers from "martial" races, typically minorities, separated and insulated the colonial military from the masses.[52] Its primary mission was to prevent the bulk of the population from obtaining the means to use violence against the ruling elite.[53] As such, the armies that emerged through negotiated decolonization already resembled European forces in their U-form organizational structure and their resistance to permitting the independent use of force by civilians.

The legacy of these two types of critical junctures established the parameters in which the newly incumbent state elites could use the military institutions that were bequeathed to them at decolonization. After independence, elaborate drilling, training, and repetition contributed to what Elisabeth Wood calls each coercive institution's specific *repertoire* of violence, the kinds of practices in which an armed group routinely engages.[54] The key to military effectiveness, as Risa Brooks notes, is consistency and mutual reinforcement of organizational activities at the strategic, operational, and tactical levels.[55] Once a given repertoire was established, path dependence became stronger and more determinative. The formalization of standard operating procedures, incentive structures, and normative rules made any attempt to replace one institutional format with another progressively harder and duplication easier.[56]

At the same time, though, path dependence was not mere inertia. Bounded innovation within these parameters was still possible by borrowing, imitating, and learning. Strategically minded agents found new applications for old institutional repertoires, manipulating them in ways that were orthogonal or even contradictory to the purposes of their original design.[57] In the military domain, LDSs responded to the constellation of internal and external threats confronting them by learning from their own experiences, by studying their adversar-

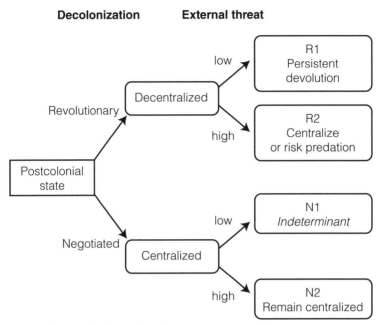

**Figure 1.4.** Pathways of military development.

ies, and by accumulating military expertise and technology from abroad in order to graft new techniques onto their initial institutional endowments.[58]

Typological theorizing offers a way to capture the conjunction between the origins and the persistence of different military organizational formats.[59] Four distinct historical pathways of LDS military development are possible, summarized in Figure 1.4. These pathways depend on whether decolonization was violent or negotiated and whether the regional threat environment was hostile or permissive.

Pathway R1 is typical among LDSs inhabiting the zone of impotent peace. In this pathway, a state gains independence through violent revolution and thus inherits a militia-based force. Shielded from the pressure of interstate competition, leaders focus on internal enemies without subjugating a force to the state's bureaucratic controls. They adopt the techniques to neutralize disloyal militia forces, maintaining a measure of stability despite the lack of a monopoly over the use of force and making violence devolution a persistent military mode. The exact opposite mode prevails in pathway N2, which parallels Europe's course toward military centralization. A state emerges from negotiated decolonization with relatively centralized military organizations and is confronted by similarly endowed neighbors. High external threat pushes the state to continue centralizing and augmenting its forces. Otherwise, it runs the risk of falling prey to its neighbor. Just as in early modern Europe, as one state builds up conventional military capacity, its neighbors are forced to do the same. States in such a regional system are trapped in an escalating arms race that makes decentralization perilous. Leaders innovate within the parameters of the centralized organizational format they inherited to maximize their defense against external aggression.

But what happens when a state bucks the pressures imposed by the international system or when there is a mismatch between the initial endowment of military organization and the demands of the international system? Cases in which a state begins with a centralized military but then faces little external pressure are logically indeterminate. In such conditions, a state might either remain centralized or devolve. The N1 pathway, therefore, is of little analytical value. The R2 pathway—in which a revolutionary state faces strong external threat—is crucial because it shows how the regional environment constrains the impetus to violence devolution. As Jonathan Adelman describes, revolutionary states are especially vulnerable in their early years, when these hastily improvised armies rely "more on revolutionary enthusiasm than professional organization, [placing them] in danger of being defeated by stronger, more cohesive professional armies of the old order."[60] Revolutionary regimes in France and Russia, for instance, initially sought to use popular militias and other civilian forces to fight counterrevolutionary forces at home and abroad. Once confronted by hostile foreign powers, though, they were forced to consolidate and centralize their armies. Similar constraints in the developing world can prompt a revolutionary state to abandon violence devolution and subjugate its militias under central control or risk external attack.[61]

## METHODOLOGY AND CASE SELECTION

To test these hypotheses about the critical junctures, path dependence, and bounded innovation, deductive identification of different pathways of military development must be matched by empirical observation. The chapters that follow consider each of the theoretically relevant pathways one by one through in-depth case studies of Indonesia, Iraq, and Iran. Each of these three countries entered the twentieth century with roughly similar counters of state–society interactions: Attempts to centralize power in state hands were still incipient. Significant military capacity remained in the hands of nonstate actors, such as tribal chiefs, village heads, and other local potentates. The chapters use historical narrative and process tracing to examine the mechanisms that connect the antecedent conditions of decolonization, internal and external threat, and the divergent outcomes of military development. To probe the limits of path dependence, particular attention has been paid to counterfactual reasoning at crucial moments of institutional generation, successful and failed efforts to change institutional models, and exogenous shocks. So-called dogs that didn't bark—changes in military institutions that were considered but never implemented—are instructive for better understanding when and how military development occurs.[62] Beside this longitudinal view of the unfolding of institutional change within a single country, each chapter is laid out to facilitate comparison between countries, offering further leverage to identify causal patterns using the methods of similarity and difference.[63]

Indonesia (Chapter 2) follows pathway R1. Indonesia's revolutionary decolonization following World War II embedded militias and solidified patterns of violence devolution. Indonesia's emergence in a region of low external threat allowed the state to continue relying on nonstate actors, heedless of the risks. Iraq (Chapter 3) represents pathway N2. Though coming close in both 1920 and 1941, anticolonial revolution was never realized in Iraq. Instead, the state directly inherited a European-trained army, which allowed it to begin consolidating control over nonstate actors. This tendency was reinforced by the demands of a highly threatening regional environment, making it impossible for the Iraqi state to countenance violence devolution. Iran (Chapter 4) is a pathway R2 case, where revolution erupted under conditions of high external military threat. As in Iraq, successive Iranian rulers tried to import a Western military model and to monopolize the use of force. With the revolution of 1979, the new government tried to replace the conventional army with popular militia-based forces. Facing severe international pressure, however, the revolutionary regime was forced to return to the model of military centralization while bringing revolutionary militias under state control. Iran is a crucial case, then, for illustrating the ultimate constraints on the devolved military model.[64]

Chapter 5 extrapolates to explain a wider set of historical cases and builds on the theory's implications for contemporary policy debates. The rise and fall of state-sponsored militias are conditioned by deep-seated historical factors originating in decolonization and the structure of the international system. These factors cannot be easily changed given the limits of the current policy toolbox. Instead, the international community must also find ways to accommodate the persistence of nonstate actors and to use them to help improve international and human security.

# 2 INDONESIA

INDONESIA OCCUPIES A PROMINENT PLACE in studies of Third World development. Created by colonial caprice, encapsulating a highly fractious population
spread over an enormous and disparate territory with an economy heavily
dependent on agriculture and natural resource export, Indonesia in some eyes
represents the epitome of late development. Few scholars fail to mention the
singular role of violence in the process of Indonesia's state formation, dividing
Indonesian history into long periods of tranquility punctuated by outbursts
of disorder. Indeed, Clifford Geertz's seminal essay on the dilemmas of "new"
states focuses on the failure of Sukarno's postrevolutionary regime to establish
state authority in the 1950s and 1960s. For over a decade after Indonesia's 1948
revolution against the Dutch, militias spawned of the anticolonial upheaval
thwarted demobilization and integration under state control. It was only with
Suharto's imposition of the so-called New Order in 1966 and its severe curtailment of political openness that stability seemed to return.[1]

Characterizations of Suharto's thirty-year rule diverge wildly.[2] Some consider the installation of GOLKAR (*Partai Golongan Karya*, the Party of Functional Groups) and its military-backed technocracy as a form of bureaucratic
authoritarianism. Ulf Sundhaussen declares emphatically that, in the first decade of the New Order, "effective control over their combat troops transferred
to the center [and] the *panglimas* [regional division commanders] have ceased
to be independent sources of power. Warlordism has thus arrived at its final
conclusion."[3] Yet, as Syarif Hidyat argues more recently, nonstate violence
wielders maintained a hidden autonomy within the New Order. Total bureaucratic control over the use of force may have been the regime's mantra, but

its pursuit conflicted with the regime's entrenched patrimonialism.[4] Indeed, since Suharto's downfall in 1998, the endemic collusion between the state and nonstate violence wielders has gained renewed attention.[5]

This chapter proceeds in three sections to examine the emergence and durability of violence devolution in Indonesia. The first section discusses the conflicting impulses of Dutch colonialism both to suppress and to utilize militias, leading to a systematic herniation of coercive power to nonstate actors. The second section describes how the sudden displacement of the Dutch during World War II and Japanese efforts to mobilize Indonesian society provided a window of opportunity for Indonesian nationalists to activate local networks of violence in resistance to the colonial order. The revolution of 1948 and 1949 thus comprised a critical juncture in which a pattern of violence devolution was solidified. The third section describes how the Indonesian state overcame the inherent centrifugal risks of devolution and managed to make routine the techniques of militia mobilization after the revolution. The state elite became more adept at controlling these nonstate actors by eliminating alternative sources of patronage. Equally important, Suharto assiduously avoided international conflicts that might strain Indonesia's militia-based army. Indeed, the absence of war making and the lack of foreign threats proved crucial factors permitting violence devolution to become a stable organizational form, consolidating the model that had emerged from revolutionary chaos.

## INDIRECT RULE AND THE HERNIATION
## OF COERCIVE POWER, 1602–1941

As has been the case in many imperial endeavors, the Dutch tried to rule Indonesia with as little effort as possible. The practice of indirect rule left minor sultans to serve as vassals in the outer islands. In Java, Madura, and Sumatra, the Dutch claimed direct sovereignty but retained local aristocrats and village heads to serve as the primary agents of colonial administration. The Dutch believed that indigenous people would respond more obediently to a familiar face of authority and also sought to reduce the burden of staffing village administration with European personnel. Even as they tried to build rationalized bureaucratic structures within their domain and to centralize coercive control in state hands, the Dutch system of indirect rule allowed traditional patterns of decentralized coercion to persist at the margins of the colonial state. Indeed, these techniques were invoked by the Dutch themselves when their control was challenged.

The first two centuries of Dutch domination of the East Indies (1602–1798) involved only modest changes in coercive and administrative institutions. Like its counterpart in British India, the Dutch United East Indian Company had a potent but relatively small military arm. The company preserved the indigenous structure of power, using the village headmen and chiefs as vassals in a manner roughly similar to those practiced in the precolonial era.[6] Indonesia's kingdoms retained the shape of a mandala; different strata in the political hierarchy possessed different amounts of power, but they were functionally undifferentiated. The magnitude of the ruler's power varied inversely to the distance from the inner circle of his superior's court. In the outlying villages, local lords and petty kings served as proxies for the sovereign. In return for patronage from a more powerful king, each lord was responsible for supplying his own armed retinue at the behest of the king.[7]

The establishment of the crown colony in 1798 brought a more thorough-going transformation of administrative structures. The successive governorships of Herman Willem Daendels (1808–1811) and Thomas Stamford Raffles (1811–1816) saw the first attempts to centralize power in Batavia (Jakarta). The subjugation of the Indonesian potentates began with the sack of Yogyakarta in 1812 and continued through the Java War (1825–1830), the conquest of Bali (1840), and the successive campaigns against Sumatra, which began in 1873 and culminated in the final suppression of the Muslim rebels at Aceh by 1904. The Dutch forces were outnumbered in most of their battles but had superior technology and organizational and logistical structures. As Gayl Ness and William Stahl note, it was the repeated ability of the Dutch armies to maneuver in small units and then rapidly concentrate firepower that proved critical to success. For instance, during the Java War, a system of fortified outposts backed by small mobile columns was instrumental to defeating the guerrilla-style attacks. During the Sumatra campaigns, the Dutch developed a new mobile rural police force that roamed the countryside intimidating local villages into compliance.[8]

At the cornerstone of colonial control was the Royal Dutch East Indies Army (*Koninklijk Nederlandsch Indisch Leger*, KNIL), established by Governor General Johannes van den Bosch in 1830. By the eve of the twentieth century, KNIL forces numbered 16,000 Europeans and 26,000 Indonesians. Unlike vassalage-based armies of the precolonial period, who were temporarily conscripted to fight under the command of a local lord, the Dutch emphasized the professionalism and distinctiveness of the colonial forces. Where the warriors of the precolonial period were economically dependent on the local community, the Dutch purposefully recruited Ambonese Christians to fill KNIL's ranks, making its soldiers linguistically and ethnically distinct from the population they patrolled and dependent on the colonial administration for salaries and supplies. The police was similarly isolated in barracks under European command.[9]

Despite their clear military predominance over the width and breadth of Indonesian territory, however, co-optation—not domination—remained the ultimate end of Dutch rule. Village chiefs were regarded as crucial bulwarks against popular agitation and nationalist unrest. The Dutch sought to uphold the chief's claim to traditional authority even as administrative rationalization demanded the diminishment of the aristocracy to junior administrators of Batavia's policies.[10] Deprived of the customary right to peasant labor for personal use, to raise an army independently, and to practice hereditary succession, the chiefs' prerogative was steadily circumscribed. Of the seventy-five regents in Java, only thirty-three had succeeded their fathers, and only twenty-four others had aristocratic blood by 1930. The establishment of Dutch-language schools to train the sons of the elite and the installation of Dutch residents to serve as the regents' "elder brothers" further transformed the local aristocracy into adjuncts of the Western bureaucratic apparatus.[11]

Europeans played far more significant and penetrative administrative roles in the Dutch East Indies than in British India. The interior ministry had two to three times as many officials per square mile in Indonesia than did the British in India.[12] The adoption of the "Ethical Policy" in 1901, meant to alleviate the exploitative and impoverishing effect of existing economic policy and tax code, was more successful in embellishing the colonial state's bureaucratic and military domination than in actually helping the masses of Javanese peasants. The Dutch focused on raising agricultural output by expanding irrigation and impounding coolie labor. Tax farming was curtailed and finally abolished in 1915.[13] Suspicious of any inkling of subversion, the Dutch jealously guarded the means of coercion. In 1913 and 1914, as the Dutch readied for a possible attack on the colony by Germany or Japan, they offered Indonesians seats in a newly established legislative council but refused to allow natives to prove their loyalty by forming a home guard to supplement KNIL. While supportive of groups like the Sarekat Islam and Muhammediyah, who provided modernized Islamic education to the masses, the Dutch were keenly aware of the dangers of letting any organization—particularly secular nationalists or the communists—organize a mass-based constituency. Even during the period of administrative devolution and "de-tutelage" of the regents in the 1920s and 1930s, control over the local police force was kept out of the regents' hands. Indeed, this reluctance to permit indigenous control over the means of violence seems well founded, as the eruption of rebellions in southern Sumatra, Java, and Sulawesi during and immediately after World War I demonstrated the continued need for a strong, reliable military presence.[14]

Yet alongside the impressive display of bureaucratized violence, the Dutch also retained the extensive coercive institutions vestigial from the mandala state. Social histories of the Dutch colonial period note the frequent collusion between the aristocracy and local violence wielders known as *jago* (literally, fighting cock). Distinguishing the mythical from the social component of this role is difficult. In popular lure, the *jago* was a warrior-prince, a retainer of the king, and a social bandit shielding his community from intrusion and exploitation. The meaning of the word itself connotes potency and virility. In practice, however, he was just as easily a government enforcer and informant as a resistance leader.[15] Trained in the arts of thievery and cattle rustling, these bandits traded exemption from land tax and the corvée in return for protecting the village from their own ilk, a sort of Mafia-style extortion racket.[16] Robert Cribb notes that in the outskirts of Jakarta, such criminal gangs—deracinated from their rural environs—emerged both as hired muscle for landowners and capitalists and also as leaders in numerous minor labor disturbances and messianic uprisings.[17]

The dual nature of these methods of violence enforcement can be appreciated by considering the Dutch response to the rise of the Indonesian Communist Party (PKI) in the 1920s. PKI specifically drew a mass following by appealing to concepts of social justice drawn from Javanese mythology of the just king (*ratu adil*). In some cities, PKI cadres worked with members of the underworld to organize pickets and strikes. Communist inroads alarmed both the Dutch and the Indonesian aristocracy. The Islamic leadership identified communism as a rival to religious orthodoxy. The Dutch administration and the regents encouraged local clerics to recruit their own bands of local toughs and gangs to disrupt PKI meetings, destroy the homes and property of its members, and target its leaders for intimidation and assassination. During the outbreak of the nationwide communist rebellions of 1926–1927, some 20,000 members of these Islamic vigilante groups engaged in open battle with PKI forces. By the end of the rebellion, 13,000 were arrested, 4,500 imprisoned, and over a thousand exiled to prison camps on the outer islands.[18]

The Dutch colonial administration was renowned for the intensity and scope of its coercive and bureaucratic power, bringing *rust en orden* (tranquility and order) to a volatile and fragmented country. But specialized, modern coercive institutions like KNIL did not replace the diffuse coercive networks comprising the brigand and his indigenous elite patrons. On the contrary, the Dutch co-opted these networks, using the indigenous elite to contract out the enactment of violence to nonstate actors. This herniation of coercion is remarkable because it went against so much official colonial policy and seemed to imperil the stability and legitimacy of the Dutch bureaucratic system. Observed one Muslim leader, the government "was playing with fire in encouraging violence and placing its opponents beyond the protection of the law. In the end, such a course could sabotage all respect for authority."[19]

The availability of state-sponsored militias, even in the limited extent seen in the late colonial order, was made possible by maintaining the traditional social patterns of village life—from the aristocracy to the underworld—alongside a rationalized and specialized colonial administrative structure. Contracting with militias, however, required deliberate and strategic choice about ways to maintain control. The colonial administration had the option to deploy the army and police directly to quell the rebellions of the 1920s and indeed relied on these official arms of the central administration as insurance that vigilantism did not turn to outright anarchy. Yet this colonial-era collaboration proved a harbinger of the model of coercion Indonesia would see in the near future.

## DECOLONIZATION, REVOLUTION, AND RUPTURE, 1941–1949

Harry Benda observes that it is impossible to be "sure that, without the Japanese cataclysm, Dutch colonialism would or could have been forced into far-reaching concessions, let alone seriously challenged, by Indonesian nationalism."[20] On August 17, 1945, two days after the Japanese surrender, Sukarno and Mohammed Hatta, acting as representatives of the Japanese-established Committee for the Preparation of Indonesian Independence, met at the home of a Japanese vice admiral in Jakarta to announce Indonesia's independence. But while the Japanese had sought to recruit locals to participate in their struggle against European colonialists, they had never intended to foment revolutions within the Asian Co-Prosperity Sphere. In the winter of 1941–1942, Japan swept away the colonial armies that had been the defense against local uprisings, as well as other facets of the colonial administration. Assertive nationalists seized the opportunity of Japanese withdrawal to establish new state institutions before the return of the European powers.

Whereas the Dutch saw Indonesian nationalists as intractable enemies and tried to ensure quiescence by blocking mass-based political mobilization, the Japanese treated nationalists as junior partners in their imperial venture. By offering influential leaders like Sukarno and Hatta a role in self-government and the promise of eventual independence, Tokyo stoked anticolonial sentiments among the nationalist elite.[21] Japan made inroads among the masses through a host of paramilitary, youth, and other organizations. The best-trained and most important militia was Volunteer Army for the Defense of the Fatherland (*Tentera Sukarela Pembela Tanah Air*, PETA), which had 40,000 members in Java and 30,000 in Sumatra. PETA soldiers were given arms and basic training by Japanese NCOs and officers and organized regionally, so its members were already serving close to home and could keep watch on behalf of the Japanese. Other less diligently trained groups included Heiho (Auxiliary Forces), Seinendan (Youth Corps), Keibodan (Vigilance Corps), and Barisan Pelopor (Vanguard Corps), which in total may have enlisted over a million people.[22] As the outlook for the war turned bleak in the summer of 1944, the Japanese also allowed Masyumi, the union of Islamic groups, to organize a specifically Islamic militia, called Hizbollah (Troops of God). Led by local preachers using local mosques and Islamic schools as recruitment centers, Hizbollah grew to between 20,000 and 50,000 troops during the war.[23]

The Japanese envisioned Indonesia's militias as a home guard that could relieve Japanese soldiers from the drudgeries of garrison duty. To the Indonesian nationalists who held nominal command responsibilities, however, these forces formed the kernel of the revolutionary army they hoped to use to obtain independence. As Benedict Anderson emphasizes, the advent of these mass movements unleashed a new social force in Indonesian politics—the *pemuda* (youth). Before the war, only a small number of aristocratic Indonesians and even fewer commoners had received secular education at Dutch-language schools. These new forces were younger and less educated but had a prescient if unsophisticated nationalism and a willingness and expertise in the use of violence.[24]

The Indonesian revolution consisted of an untold multitude of violent engagements, acts of varying severity and levels of coordination. The classic historical account by George Kahin, followed by many others, highlights the complex and frequently indistinguishable acts of nationalists, radicals seeking full-on social revolution, restorationists seeking to reinstall aristocratic rule, and opportunists using the outbreak of violence as a cover for settling griev-ances or seizing property.[25] After the surrender announcement, some Japanese units tried to maintain law and order until the Allies arrived. Others simply retired to their barracks, abandoning their weapons to the locals either will-ingly or under duress. Amsterdam lobbied the Allies to establish a European presence in Java quickly to quash the uprising but to no avail. Looting, riot-ing, and assassinations targeted the indigenous Sino-Indonesian landlords, Europeans imprisoned in concentration camps, and the beleaguered Japa-nese. New armed gangs sprang up spontaneously alongside PETA, Hizbollah, and the other militias, contributing to competition for recruits and weapons. These new forces bore the red and white republican standard but frequently mixed criminals and other violence specialists with political entrepreneurs.

At least initially, the republican government existed solely on paper. On August 29, the government announced the formation of a republican army that would incorporate PETA, dissident members of KNIL, and all the new militias. The republican leadership, though, had little ability to monitor or control military actions from the center and relied instead on local revolu-tionary committees. The fact that the republican army repeatedly changed its name over the course of a few years is indicative of the rapidity with which new organs were incorporated and political orientation changed.[26] Abdul Harris Nasution, at twenty-eight years of age already a divisional commander in the new army, describes "hundreds of TKR [militias] had sprung up locally, acting entirely on their own. The leadership of the central headquarters was not felt at all."[27]

The success of a militia leader was not based on his military prowess nec-essarily but the ability to attract young men into service. Lines of command were defined by personal relationships and charisma, not the sanction of ci-vilian leadership. The most powerful forces were associated with established political formations. By early 1946, Hizbollah's ranks had swelled tenfold to 300,000, although its core of fighters was still limited to about 25,000 troops. Other militias had no strong political affiliation but were fiercely nationalist, refusing to abide by the commands of the civilian leadership that they saw as wavering in commitment. Some took on more ethnosectarian dimensions while still expressing ultimate loyalty to the republic, as in the 6,000-man Christian militia in Sulawesi. Militias gained self-sufficiency by smuggling rice, opium, and weapons between the zones of Allied and republic control. Some even established rice boards to ensure adequate food distribution for the local civilian population. Still, it remained difficult to distinguish politically from criminally motivated acts of expropriation.[28]

Recognizing that lack of military preparation and unity had left the republic vulnerable to attack, Prime Minister Sjahrir and Defense Minister Sjarifuddin tried to augment central control by appointing a retired KNIL officer as chief of staff. The defense ministry envisioned an army slimmed from approximately 400,000 to 160,000 men. Individual warlords were offered ranks and salaries within the new army, allowing whole units to integrate into the republican army. Political commissars were dispatched to monitor and indoctrinate these units, and a central headquarters was established to manage logistics, payment, and supply. The central government also devoted new resources to build up an elite corps of shock troops, primarily the West Java Siliwangi Division under Nasution's command, to form the new army's core. These troops—often KNIL veterans—were the best equipped and most professional in the republican arsenal.[29]

Still, conflicts between the center and periphery continued. Divisional commanders refused to demobilize. A month after the chief of staff's appointment, the militias themselves elected Sudirman, a thirty-three-year-old PETA battalion commander, as commander in chief.[30] The split between the civilian leaders in Yogyakarta and the various military units in the field reflected profound generational, ideological, and doctrinal fissures. PETA platoon and squad leaders formed the core of the republican's field officers. In contrast to the ex-KNIL soldiers, the Japanese-trained officers were younger and not Western educated. Japanese training emphasized that a warrior's élan could overcome any advantage in technology or armature and structured the forces in a decentralized, rather than hierarchical, manner. The availability of extrabudgetary resources from smuggling, seizures, extortion, and solicitation of support from the local population allowed individual commanders unprecedented degrees of autonomy.[31] In some instances, radicals kidnapped civilian ministers they perceived as threatening military autonomy or selling out the nationalist cause.[32]

To complicate matters further, the Dutch foothold was growing steadily more menacing, amassing nearly 100,000 troops.[33] The Dutch launched a surprise armor and air assault on Jakarta on July 20, 1947, quickly overrunning the chaotic republican lines. Most of the 400,000-man revolutionary forces melted away in favor of passive guerrilla resistance. To emphasize the return of colonial law and order, the Dutch dubbed their invasion a "police action."

By August the Dutch had seized the agricultural heartlands of Sumatra and Java and in some areas were winning popular support by ameliorating the excesses of the occupying republican militias. Said one Dutch official,

> The gangs have become more numerous and more dangerous, and are equipped with all kinds of weapons which formerly one did not find in their possession, such as hand-grenades, landmines and aerial bombs. In mopping-up operations most victims fall not in open battle, but as a result of all kinds of mechanical devices such as wires stretched across the road, booby-traps, and pitfalls. The *desa* [village] population knows all about this, but has no patriotic sympathy for the bands as is found elsewhere in the case of guerrilla and underground resistance movements; it welcomes our intervention with feelings of great relief and keeps mum![34]

As an alternative political framework to the Republic, the Dutch recruited Indonesian aristocrats to federate into the United States of Indonesia (USI). Republicans denigrated USI as merely a collection of Dutch puppets and collaborators, but the semisovereign rulers enjoyed some real independence of action.[35]

The success of the first police action increased the fragmentation of the republican cause. Sukarno met with Dutch representatives aboard U.S.S. *Renville*, accepting the military fait accompli and agreeing to withdraw republican forces from beyond the Dutch line of control. Many irregulars, however, refused the order and continued the guerrilla war. The republic now faced a multisided conflict, fighting simultaneously the Dutch, USI, and dissidents from within its own camp. In the area of West Java ceded to Dutch control, Kartosuwiryo, a former affiliate of the Islamic militias, declared the republicans infidels for making concessions to the Dutch and turned the Islamic militias into an army for his newly proclaimed Indonesian Islamic State. This movement—called Realm of Islam (*Darul Islam*, DI)—was as fiercely anti-republican as it was anti-Dutch. On several occasions the republican military commanders proposed cease-fires with USI to concentrate their efforts against DI.[36] Inside the republican zone, PKI elements launched major protests, strikes, and land seizures in the hopes of fomenting a social revolution in the midst of the nationalist struggle. The communist insurrection came to a head with the rebellion at Madiun in September and October 1948. When the republic had to redeploy the Siliwangi Division from the front lines to suppress it, it was only the United States—eager to strike a blow against Third World communism—that restrained the Dutch from attacking again. Ultimately, the

Siliwangi Division and the mobile police killed 8,000 PKI-affiliated fighters. For many Indonesians, especially in the military, PKI was indelibly marked as betrayers of Indonesia at the most critical moment.[37]

Believing they could deal a deathblow to the weakened republic, the Dutch launched a second police action on December 18, 1948. Paratroopers landed in the republican capital at Yogyakarta, capturing Sukarno, Hatta, Agus Salim, and Sjahrir, and seized most of the major cities in Java and Sumatra. Fighting, however, continued in the countryside as the revolution became localized in individual acts of sabotage and civil disobedience. Dutch attempts to intimidate the local population only aggravated resentment and drove the population into the arms of the rebellion. On two occasions the republican army raided the heart of Yogyakarta. The war became an embarrassment on the world stage. Impressed that the republican government was sufficiently anticommunist, the United States threatened to cut off Marshall Aid unless the Dutch recognized Indonesian independence. After a year of seemingly fruitless efforts to quell the insurgency and facing increasing international pressure, the Dutch finally agreed to cede sovereignty to the Republic of Indonesia on December 5, 1949.[38]

The republican leadership drew important lessons about the organization of coercion and military forces from the fighting. For the civilian cabinet, reining in and neutralizing the militias was a top priority.[39] Nasution, probably the best-trained and best-regarded republican general, tended to see the militias as unprofessional, undisciplined, and disorganized. However, he also recognized the difficulty of demobilizing them and envisioned a role for them in national defense.[40] While still working to disarm the least reliable units, Nasution developed plans for a military apparatus of two complementary components. The first would be a small mobile strike force, composed of the Siliwangi Division and other highly trained and heavily armed units that could amass force and take offensive action. Alongside it would be three "territorial divisions." These divisions would remain lightly armed (having one weapon for every three soldiers) and function as a kind of nationalized militia, mobilizing the population in mass struggle in case of internal subversion or external attack and offering passive defense until the strike force could arrive.[41]

The type of war the Indonesians waged against the Dutch would have been unthinkable just a decade before, when a small but strong and centralized colonial force remained firmly in place to deter and repress any uprising. In eastern Indonesia, European forces quickly regained control and thus snuffed out the revolution. But in Java and western Indonesia there was no counter-vailing force to forestall the rupture that granted nonstate actors the ability to wield violence. The youth who incited local rebellions and led the militias represent a historical and cultural bridge, linking the *jago*'s parochial role as village protector (and extorter) to a more catholic nationalism. The ability to finance activities through expropriation and smuggling only increased the independence of these militia forces. In his war memoir, Deputy Chief of Staff of the Armed Forces T. B. Simatupang quotes Mao's famous dictum stressing the importance of mass mobilization, saying, "Had the Dutch in fact faced only the TNI [regular republican army], without the territorial organization which allowed it to move everywhere like 'fish in water,' then they might have achieved their goal of eliminating our army." [42] The fact that Indonesian forces would carry on despite a decapitation strike during the second police action is a testament to the resilience and effectiveness of "people's war" as a strategy for mass mobilization. But the functional limitations were also obvious. As Simatupang writes:

> Autonomy and financial independence on the part of troops and regions is to be applauded in a people's war situation. But might it not become a "habit" hard to eliminate once life had returned to normal? [43]

Internally, factional alliances between militias and members of the political elite raised the threat of coups and domestic fragmentation. Lack of coordination and communication and internal rivalries further limited the effectiveness of the militia army. The Indonesians could use their advantage in sheer numbers for low-intensity insurgency but lacked the organizational structure necessary to withstand a concerted Dutch attack, much less launch and offensive themselves. [44] Success came mainly by elevating the diplomatic costs of continuing in occupation, not by attaining outright military victory. In the historical heyday of decolonization, however, that was enough.

## CONSOLIDATION OF MILITIA POWER, 1950–1999

Waging a revolution and building a state are sequentially linked but in many ways contradictory tasks. Fervor and ferment—assets to revolutionary movements—become liabilities in the process of constructing and consolidating state institutions. In Indonesia, the devolution of violence in the militia-based army proved successful in winning independence but was hardly conducive to running the country afterward. From 1949 to the mid-1960s,

Indonesia faced profound instability and social fragmentation as the newly established republic tried to rule over a society that had experienced hyper-mobilization since 1942. Besides the expansion of the DI rebellions, Indonesia faced a string of military mutinies in the outer islands known collectively as the PRRI/Permesta revolts (*Pemerintah Revolusioner Republik Indonesia,* the Revolutionary Government of the Republic of Indonesia), led by officers and warlords who claimed to carry on the revolutionary tradition against the domineering central government. Many regions were essentially outside Jakarta's control. Civilian political parties representing a wide range of ethnic and regional factions vied for the support of the military's various fractious wings. In 1956 Sukarno made a bid to end the infighting and stamp out military mutinies by suspending parliament and establishing Guided Democracy. Yet Sukarno's charismatic and mercurial leadership only deepened the divisions within the society he sought to unite. The military's response to the failed (and perhaps contrived) communist coup on September 30, 1965, culminated in the mass killing of PKI members and sympathizers in 1965 and 1966 and Sukarno's ouster.[45] Speculation abounds about the roots of the conspiracy that brought President (Major General) Suharto and his military cronies to power, establishing a "New Order" of controlled authoritarianism that lasted nearly three decades.[46] But as Ruth McVey aptly puts it, given the profound politicization within the military ranks and the fragmentation within the Indonesian polity, the coup itself was less puzzling than the fact that it took fifteen years after independence to occur.[47] The revolution reinforced cleavages between Javanese and the various outer islanders, between Muslims and Christians, between orthodox and heterodox Muslims, and between the military and civilian politicians. It drastically redistributed power, taking coercive control out of the hands of the state and devolving it to hundreds of smaller local militias, gangs, and paramilitaries. These conflicts and asymmetries of power would have a long-lasting impact on Indonesia's military development.

Moving from the moments of revolutionary political refashioning to the long duration of bounded innovation—institutional reproduction, replication, and maintenance—invites new questions about Indonesia's development. What spurred the military seizure of power in 1965, and how was the New Order able to overcome the centrifugal forces that had dominated the Sukarno era? Why and how did the New Order retain violence devolution as an institutional format after having witnessed the proclivity of local actors to use force at their own volition rather than at the orders of their state?

Four factors, analytically separable but functionally interwoven and temporally concurrent, contributed to the consolidation of violence devolution instead of monopolization. First, at the tactical level, Indonesia's military leadership drew on the revolutionary legacy to offer innovations that continued to stress mutual reliance between state and nonstate violence wielders. Second, at the economic level, the military drew on the revolutionary practice of self-financing to accumulate enormous economic power, which ensured that militias and regional commanders alike had incentive to remain loyal. Third, at the political level, the New Order regime developed political institutions that simultaneously mobilized and isolated the masses, preventing any rival to the state from being able to gain a position of brokerage with local forces. Fourth, at the strategic level, Indonesia's leadership learned the functional limitations of militia mobilization in foreign conflicts and instead free rode on the assurance of regional security. Cumulatively, these practices empowered militias while winnowing down the resources that had permitted them autonomy of action, contributing to the further perfecting of violence devolution.

### The "Fence of Legs": Tactical Basis of Territorial Warfare

The crucial question the Indonesian leadership faced in the 1950s was how to manage the demobilization of the hundreds of thousands who had taken up arms during the revolution. In the early 1950s Prime Minister Wilopo and General Nasution announced plans for force reorganization and downsizing, shrinking the army to about 150,000 men, establishing regular hierarchies and standardized training programs, and formalizing state control over the regional commanders. This plan bore the obvious imprint of the small group of KNIL and (to a lesser extent) PETA-trained officers who possessed the administrative experience to staff the top echelons of the new army. Even before this formal reorganization plan was announced, the army launched programs for retraining and reequipment. A paratrooper regiment was established in 1952. By the mid-1950s a number of Indonesia's top officers, including future army chief of staff General Ahmed Yani, had received infantry and staff training in the United States, and Indonesia's newly established military academies and technical courses had adopted American curricula. [48]

Still, to tens of thousands of revolutionary veterans, particularly outer islanders, the new army appeared an instrument of Javanese domination. Dismissed militiamen were invited to enlist in the new army, but about two-thirds failed the medical and psychological examinations requisite for recommissioning.[49] Some senior military commanders argued that a technology-intensive, professionalized army was inappropriate for an underdeveloped country like Indonesia, especially considering that manpower was the one readily available resource at the country's disposal. Regional commanders were especially reticent to submit to Jakarta and allied with civilian politicians to block expansion of the unitary central government.[50]

In 1953, Nasution published what would be the guiding doctrinal document of the Indonesian army, *Fundamentals of Guerrilla Warfare*. While hardly path-breaking in its reformulation of Maoist doctrines, the book provided an interpretation of the revolution that could accommodate both advocates of force modernization and the integration of nonstate militias for territorial defense. On one hand, he proposed building up a small, mobile, and heavily armed strategic reserve force capable of reaching anywhere in the archipelago. On the other hand, he also planned to incorporate lightly armed local militia groups to act as first responders to foreign attacks or internal disorder.[51] Drawing on the lessons of the revolution, the key for territorial defense was the integration of the army with the people. This was evident as early as the 1950s, when government troops battled DI rebels in Sumatra and organized some 6,000 local PKI fighters in an auxiliary militia. Mohammed Natsir, a leader of the Islamic party Masyumi and former prime minister who joined the rebellion in dismay over Sukarno's growing authoritarian tendencies, observed that

> as long as we were fighting just Javanese troops there was no problem about maintaining our guerilla bases and controlling areas just outside towns such as Padang and Bukittinggi. While I was in the jungle we got food every day from the market in Bukittinggi . . . But the situation was drastically altered when the Javanese troops developed a technique for using members of the local PKI's Pemuda Rakjat [Youth Militia] as scouts to track down guerrillas in the jungle. Being local lads they knew every creek and path just as our people did and could guide the Javanese forces.[52]

Under Guided Democracy, both PKI and various nationalist and ethnic parties all built ties with locally raised militias and paramilitaries.[53]

Innovation in the mobilization of civilians continued into the late 1950s with the tactic called the "fence of legs" (*pagar betis*). The technique first appeared in suppressing the Islamist rebellion in Java. Village heads were forced to submit a number of villagers each day to form a cordon extending every few hundred yards between advancing soldiers. Government troops used the villagers as human shields, forcing the insurgents either to surrender or fire on their own. While obviously brutal, this innovation proved extremely successful in turning the tide against DI. It was soon to be a recurring feature in all of Indonesia's counterinsurgency campaigns, including Aceh, West Papua, and East Timor.[54]

Even after the regional rebellions had been extinguished in the 1960s and 1970, militia mobilization remained a quotidian feature in village life under the New Order. Civil defense corps, night watchmen, and the local branches of the retired servicemen's association were all involved in hunting down thieves, ruffians, sorcerers, and any unsanctioned political activity. In twice-daily tours, the guidance officer—typically an NCO attached to the subdistrict command—met with representatives of various groups, collecting information and providing instructions about the government's expectations for the village's economic and political performance. The state's supremacy in the village did not emanate from the guidance officer's sidearm, though. Rather, the true power stemmed from his ability to co-opt these societal agents, offering political and economic privileges like new roads, electricity, and construction projects in return for compliance.[55] Whereas in the 1950s political parties sent representatives to recruit villagers to join the party armies, under the New Order it was the military itself that played the crucial brokerage role between state and nonstate coercion.

### Dwifungsi: "Off Budgeting" and the Economics of Military Self-Finance

Economic power worked in conjunction with coercive power to ensure that militias remained active but under control. Just as Simatupang had predicted, in the 1950s few revolutionary fighters willingly gave up their ability to engage in racketeering and smuggling. On the natural resource–rich outer islands, regional commanders' revenue from smuggling made them impervious to orders from the high command, which after all could hardly provision them anyway.[56] But in a process similar to the reapplication of territorial warfare techniques, self-financing changed from a liability to an advantage to the state as it sought to manage the devolution of violence.

The 1950s and 1960s saw the military's involvement in economic affairs increase exponentially. In 1957, Sukarno declared martial law and nationalized all Dutch-owned holdings, placing prime agricultural and industrial installations under military control. By 1967 and 1968, after Suharto's ascent, an estimated $200 million in goods was smuggled through military-backed firms.[57] Sino-Indonesians filled the familiar capitalist role they had under Dutch colonialism, making reliable business partners and front men for military enterprises because they were wholly reliant on their military patrons for protection.[58] Spurred by the doctrine of *dwifungsi* (dual civilian–military functionality) and reinforced by American exhortations to use economic measures to counteract the appeal of radicalism to the peasantry, the Indonesian military not only built roads, schools, and mosques but also ran employment-generating ventures like resorts, hotels, and factories.[59]

The need to provide added economic benefits to soldiers and veterans justified further expansion of the military's economic role. In the 1960s, an officer's monthly salary was considered sufficient for just a week of living. The establishment of cooperative societies and veteran's pensions and secondment of officers to private firms brought in much-needed cash. It also increased the domination of the formal sector by military interests. The hodgepodge of charities used to funnel funds from civilians to local militias during the revolution expanded into massive foundations under the control of senior officers.[60]

By the 1970s, it was clear that the military's economic interventions were often at odds with the precepts of expertise and professionalism on which the expansion of the military's economic role was premised. Indeed, one of Suharto's first orders of business was to mollify Indonesia's foreign creditors. But the New Order did not witness a real diminishment in the corruption, but rather its rationalization. Patrimonialism became embedded as a permanent feature of the lucrative natural resource industries. Bulog, the rice logistics board, and Pertamina, the national oil company, were the crown jewels of military-run businesses and served as slush funds for the senior officers through the 1970s. Bulog was established by Suharto immediately after the military coup. It soon expanded from its original mandate to purchase rice for the military and civil service food cooperatives to the more elaborate task of building a national buffer stock. The company used middlemen (typically Sino-Indonesian) to buy up domestic village rice crops while using government credit to speculate on the international market. Similarly, Pertamina was created through the nationalization of Dutch oil and gas holdings in 1957 and was run for years by Major General Ibnu Sutowo. It invested in a wide range of side businesses, including airlines, filling stations, and rice plantations. To the dismay of Suharto's technocrats, Pertamina's revenues were funneled to military coffers without oversight from the treasury. When Pertamina faced a short-term credit run in 1975, Indonesia's treasury found itself liable for an estimated $6 to $11 billion in debt. Only after this meltdown did Suharto allow technocrats to run the oil industry as a state-owned industry rather than a military fief, although still pointedly under the military directorship and with an opaque system of financial reporting.[61] The same pattern of military corruption could be found in Indonesia's other natural resource sectors, whether oil in Aceh, minerals in Papua, or timber in Kalimantan. The location of many of these assets on the restive outer islands complicated further the nexus of political, military, and economic interests. One of the reasons suggested for the unwillingness of the central government to grant regional autonomy is the military high command's refusal to allow civilians to cut in on its largest revenue sources.[62]

Once the senior officers had control over the economic commanding heights, soldiers turned to Jakarta instead of the regional commanders for pay and provisions. Because the generals treated these assets not as public but as prebendal holdings, there was no bureaucratic apparatus with which to systematize and regularize military funding. In the 1970s, the official budget accounted for only about half of the military's funding. By the 1990s, this figure fell to an estimated 30 percent.[63] As recently as 2005, military analysts estimated that a general could add $10,000 to his meager $600 per month salary through sideline businesses.[64]

While the New Order government curbed the most blatant and deleterious abuses of public goods for private ends, grand corruption among the top ranks sanctioned and sustained the petty corruption of small-scale and local military businesses. In fact, one of the high command's main responsibilities was to ensure that the benefits of this extraction were evenly distributed by circulating commanders.[65] Cooperation among active and retired soldiers and organized crime was part of this routine. In the 1960s and 1970s, for instance, the military-sponsored youth group Pemuda Pancisila (PP), originally an association of revolutionary war veterans, was known to control movie theaters and casinos throughout Java, its gangs patrolling city streets after curfew on the pretext of catching criminals and counterrevolutionaries. In the early 1970s, the military outlawed street gangs and dissolved PP, but the group reconstituted in the 1980s with the government's blessing, integrating criminals and ex-convicts under the guise of a military-sponsored youth and sporting association. Other common small-scale military enterprises included shipping and freight (which utilize the military's fleet of trucks), farming, rice milling, and lumber poaching. In regions destabilized by insurgent activities, such as in Aceh and East Timor, the military's footprint was larger, and its business veered further into the illicit realms of prostitution, narcotics, extortion, and contract killing. An enterprising officer could even request posting to an area where he saw an opportunity to build a local network of influence and then retire there to reap the fruits of his labor in uniform.[66]

Military self-financing contributed to the fragmentation of authority in the 1940s and 1950s. When employed on a much grander scale by the high command in the 1960s and 1970s, the same methods provided incentives for junior officers and NCOs to become rent seekers themselves, defying the over-sight of civilians and bureaucrats. It is impossible to determine what propor-tion of a typical subaltern's income consists of a regular salary, "gifts" from his senior patrons, or more localized forms of expropriation by his own hand. Still, it is clear that these economic techniques, once a bane for Indonesia's stability, could be used to solidify and strengthen patrimonial ties between state elites and local militias.

### GOLKAR: Isolating and Mobilizing the Masses

Territorial defense and self-financing drew on the distinctive legacy of revo-lutionary mobilization and applied them in new conditions. In contrast, nar-rowing the space of political contestation to mobilize and to isolate the masses was exactly antithetical to the pluralism of revolutionary legacy. Establishing GOLKAR's hegemony and the insistence on "mono-loyalty" under the New Order seemed the ultimate counterrevolutionary turn. In many ways, though, it was also the logical conclusion of the revolution. The more reliant the state was on mobilizing local militias, the more important it became to find ways to limit the number of national patrons who had clientage relationships with these armed nonstate actors.

Sukarno and the army high command collectively undermined Indone-sia's brief experience with pluralistic democracy in the 1950s. Sukarno's vision of Guided Democracy replaced the fractious and unstable political contesta-tion in parliament with a forty-member committee representing each of Indo-nesian society's "functional groups." The turn to Guided Democracy came as the state faced its most severe challenge since the independence. In Sulawesi and Sumatra, the PRRI/Permesta mutineers continued to resist planned de-mobilization and centralization of forces. Kartusuwiryo's DI movement raged in Java. In Aceh, long the bastion of Muslim orthodoxy, Daud Bereueh joined DI in calling for jihad against the central government and the implementation of Islamic law. The disaffected veterans began to seek contacts with DI. Parliamentarians, including former prime minister Mohammed Natsir, actually encouraged the rebellions to coordinate their resistance to the republic.[67] Many feared that if these four localized rebellions coalesced, their combined power would outmatch that of the state itself.

Unfettered by parliamentary opposition, Sukarno responded with a classic divide-and-rule strategy. The military rebellions were more limited in their goals and less expansive in their mobilization. When offered induction as territorial troops, many veterans simply surrendered. The interlocking DI rebellions posed a more serious threat, both militarily and ideologically. Again, the state's strategy was to isolate each of the DI branches and draw independent armed groups into its orbit. An offer of amnesty in 1959 persuaded most DI fighters to give up their struggle. Only Beureuh and a small hard core rejected the autonomy plan and continued to fight until exhaustion and surrender in 1962. In Java, where the "fence of legs" technique and other tools of civilian mobilization were first introduced, Kartosuwiryo was hunted down and executed that same year. In total, the suppression these interlinked uprisings cost 70,000 lives.[68]

Even after these rebellions succumbed, however, Guided Democracy proved an impossible balancing act. The greater the army's successes in suppressing insurgencies and the more economic resources at its disposal, the more Sukarno came to rely on PKI, a group held anathema by the nationalist army and heretical by Islamic groups. With Sukarno's backing, PKI attracted an estimated 3,000,000 members to various youth and mass organization. In 1965 Sukarno announced his support for the establishment of civil militias as the "fifth force" (alongside the army, navy, air force, and police) that could launch a perpetual campaign against counterrevolutionaries without obstruction from parliament or bureaucracy. Consciously paraphrasing Mao, Sukarno said in an Independence Day speech on August 17 that

> the Armed Forces of the Republic of Indonesia will form an invincible power if they unite with the people like fish in water. Remember—water can exist without fish, but fish cannot exist without water. Integrate with the people because the armed services of the Republic of Indonesia are revolutionary armed services . . . we cannot maintain the sovereignty of our State without a people who, if necessary, are also armed—the people, workers, and farmers, and other groups, who continue to work in the productive sector but who, if necessary, also bear arms.[69]

As Sukarno was well aware, from the perspective of the high command, the danger was not in arming civilians—already a doctrinal tenet of territorial warfare—but in offering PKI the ability to mobilize force independently.[70]

On September 30, 1965, troops affiliated with Lieutenant Colonel Untung and low-level PKI cadres, claiming to have uncovered a plot against the president, kidnapped and killed eight top generals in Jakarta and the garrison commander of Yogyakarta. General Suharto, commander of the Strategic Reserve, used the assassinations as an opportunity to reimpose order and eliminate the rival PKI. Citizens were instructed to stay in their homes, while the military began to mobilize anticommunist elements from among the leading Islamic movements. With the advice of Western propaganda experts, military-controlled media disseminated rumors about a treacherous communist plot.[71] On Bali, local organizations opposed to PKI received weapons, ammunition, trucks, and access to detention facilities.[72] As tensions between PKI supporters and Muslim groups escalated, the military encouraged and assisted machete-wielding vigilantes to hunt down communist sympathizers. Villagers took to settling scores with neighbors over property disputes and local religious authority. Some were given the choice of killing their neighbors or themselves becoming targets. The violence lasted over half a year, claiming between 500,000 and 2,000,000 lives, mainly in Java, Sumatra, and Bali.[73] Even after a formal military investigation, it is difficult to estimate the death toll given the extent to which violence occurred on a local scale, with neighbors killing neighbors, village against village.

To see the bloodshed simply as an example of Indonesians running amok, the instinctive response of a harmony and hierarchy-loving people against the destabilizing social force of communism, however, is to ignore the deliberate and planned actions used both to induce and control the violence.[74] Lieutenant Colonel Sarwo Edhie, who had trained and coordinated the militia's actions, relates that

> the situation in Bali is different from the situation in Central Java. Whereas in Java I was concerned to encourage people to crush Gestapu [the Communist plot], on the other hand, [in Bali] the people were already eager to crush Gestapu to the roots. The important thing was not to let that enthusiasm be misused by certain people, leading to anarchy. That is what we had to prevent.[75]

Although some of the violence may have been exorbitant and gratuitous, in most locations the military was in a position to restrain it, particularly when

Muslim leaders tried to turn the campaign into a wider effort to purify Indonesia of secular and Christian influence.[76]

With PKI's elimination, Sukarno's role as balancer was finished. On March 11, 1966, Sukarno declared a state of emergency and turned over governmental authority to Suharto. Suharto, however, was able to capitalize on the groundwork Sukarno had laid by shifting from party and parliamentary politics to functional groups. Without national political parties to provide patronage and brokerage, the power to mobilize (or demobilize) violence on a large scale defaulted to the military high command. There was no longer need, therefore, for such flagrant coercion. Under Suharto, GOLKAR, the official organizational representative of all Indonesia's functional groups, did not offer an ideological alternative so much as a link to the military–economic nexus.[77] The Islamists, nationalist, and leftist parties that survived after 1965–1966 were forced to merge into one of two government-approved parties in 1973 and were systematically blocked from campaigning or organizing below the district level. In their stead, village guidance officers and their GOLKAR adjuncts were constantly in contact with the masses. Electoral procedures were scrupulously free and fair, but voters are given few and unattractive options.[78]

For thirty years under the New Order's autocratic control, Indonesia experienced nearly unadulterated economic growth and unprecedented levels of stability. Whenever a return to the disorder of the 1950s seemed imminent, though, the state's first response was to activate the militias that lurked in the shadows. When secessionist agitation reappeared in Aceh in the late 1980s, the military began to organize village militias, armed with bamboo spears and other primitive weapons, to form the "fence of legs." By the early 1990s, the militias enrolled around 60,000 people.[79] Of course, there were serious drawbacks to this approach: Reliance on the local economy for sustenance drew soldiers into the black market for drugs and hired muscle, making them doubly unpopular with the local population. Police and soldiers were known to sell weapons to rebels. By some estimates, 20 to 50 percent of government-funded development projects in Aceh, from rice distribution to teachers' salaries, were funneled to insurgents.[80] A similar picture of localized rebellions combated through a combination of specialized troops dispatched from Java alongside organic forces of dubious fidelity emerged in West Papua, Kalimantan, and East Timor (see the following section). What was different about the New Order militias, however, was that no alternative source of sponsorship or brokerage could connect armed men in Aceh with those from another region. So long as their uprisings were isolated, militias did not pose a risk to the state.

## STRATEGIC FREE RIDING:
## INDONESIA IN THE REGIONAL AND WORLD ORDER

While violence devolution was successful in responding to Indonesia's internal challengers, external threat also played an important role in facilitating this trajectory of military development. As Benedict Anderson argues, because Indonesia faced no credible military threat "from the state's point of view, then, there is no point in a large conventional arms buildup."[81] Yet behind this simple logic is a deeper question of the functional capabilities and limitations of Indonesia's militia-based model. The techniques of militia mobilization that proved valuable for internal pacification were ineffective if not counter-productive in Indonesia's external confrontations. War making, the concerted application of power abroad, was made nearly impossible. Consequently, Indonesia was profoundly vulnerable to foreign attack and had to learn to avoid military confrontations and to free ride on the security guarantees offered by superpowers and regional organizations. Stated counterfactually, had Indonesia's regional environment *not* been so benign, the viability of violence devolution would have been in jeopardy.

For its first decade, Indonesia teetered on the brink of dismemberment, but none of its regional neighbors could seize on Indonesia's weakness. In part, this was because the states surrounding Indonesia endured the same turbulence in the post–World War II era. To the west, Malaya and Singapore, still under British tutelage, faced a communist insurgency that had its roots in the anti-Japanese movement of the war. To the east, the Philippines, working with considerable American assistance, struggled to suppress the Huk rebellion, another anti-Japanese guerrilla army. While Communist China loomed as a distant threat, its most immediate impact on Indonesia was through PKI, not direct military action.[82] During the PRRI/Permesta and DI crises of the 1950s, Singapore, Malaya, the Philippines, Taiwan, and South Korea were all supportive of the rebels. The United States and Britain, apprehensive about Sukarno's leftward tilt, secretly provided bomber and air resupply support to the rebels and even considered landing troops to protect the Sumatran oil installations. Yet when the Indonesian military finally deployed against the rebellions, no outside power offered any military resistance, allowing the state to reassert its control over these restive provinces relatively easily.[83]

Indonesia's leaders were aware of the country's subordinate global position and sensitive to any impingement by neoimperialist forces on Indonesia's newfound sovereignty. All agreed that Indonesia should play a leading role in Southeast Asia, but they had no agreement about how to achieve such an objective.[84] The geostrategic competition between the United States and Soviet Union was refracted in the prism of domestic politics. Emboldened by his apparent success in defeating a foreign-backed insurrection in 1957 and 1958, Sukarno hoped that the campaign of what he dubbed the "new emerging forces" (NEFO) against the "old establishment forces" (ODEFO) would provide a focal point for national unity.[85] In two virtually consecutive campaigns, first over West Papua and then over British plans for Malaysia's integration, Sukarno instructed the military to adopt a new "offensive-revolutionary" strategy for confronting ODEFO. What the military devised, however, was a retread of the doctrines learned during the revolution, recruiting local actors as proxies to wage sustained guerrilla warfare.[86] Where the Papua campaign succeeded by combining provocative military feints with skillful diplomatic maneuvers, the much larger confrontation with Malaysia proved an utter failure and ultimately contributed to Sukarno's downfall.

Sukarno placed West Papua on the national agenda at the inauguration of Guided Democracy in 1958. West Papua had been under Dutch control but was not ceded to Indonesia in 1949 and was instead held under Dutch trusteeship while negotiations were held with Papuan nationalists about independence. Sukarno, however, insisted that Papua was integral to Indonesia and demanded immediate evacuation. Sukarno made a series of provocative moves, expropriating Dutch assets in 1957 and beginning to purchase submarines, warships, and combat aircraft from the Soviet Union. By 1961, Indonesia was the largest noncommunist recipient of Soviet military aid. On the anniversary of the second Dutch police action in December 1961, Sukarno established a new military command and called for volunteers to help liberate West Papua.

Indonesia's military tactics during this escalating crisis basically replicated the techniques of mass mobilization used during the revolution, despite the acquisition of heavy weaponry. About 3,000 Indonesian volunteers—mainly drawn from PKI—and army commandos infiltrated West Papua in small boats and planes. Playing off existing rivalries among the Papuan tribes, Indonesia recruited small bands of guerrillas to raid Dutch police and administrative stations scattered in the territory. The effect was less militarily significant than diplomatically troublesome to Amsterdam and its Papuan allies. Against the small Indonesian force, the Dutch had three destroyers, eight patrol boats, a jet squadron, and two infantry battalions. As in the revolution, though, the United States reined in the Dutch for fear of pushing Indonesia closer to the Soviets. Amsterdam agreed to a U.N. trusteeship in 1963, allowing Indonesia to assume administrative control. Seven years later, Jakarta simply bypassed the United Nations' mandated plebiscite by holding "consultation" with a select group of village elders who unanimously approved integration.[87]

After gaining West Papua by bluff, Sukarno set his sights on seeking to block the "neocolonialist" plan for the integration of Malaysia.[88] Just as in the Papuan gambit, *Konfrontasi*, as the campaign was called, combined diplomatic bombast with military impoverishment. Again, Indonesia sought to co-opt local guerrillas to wreak enough havoc and demonstrate popular antipathy toward integration. This time, however, Indonesia faced stiffer resistance. While Malaysia alone had only a few thousand native troops, the British had 10,000 troops in Malaysia and 30,000 others in Southeast Asia as a whole (not counting Commonwealth forces). At its peak strength in 1965, Indonesia was able to devote only 20,000 to 30,000 men to the fight, many of whom were poorly trained volunteers. As tensions intensified, so did Sukarno's rhetoric, even going so far as to express an interest in acquiring nuclear weapons.[89] Yet Indonesia's military remained reliant on the labor-intensive techniques of territorial warfare. It lacked the technological and logistical bureaucracy to do otherwise. Conflicts between operational and regional commanders were endemic; some units refused or could not be seconded beyond their territorial base. The Malayan nationalist leader Ibrahim Yaacob, himself a Japanese protégé during the war, promised that Malays would rise up against British imperialism, but these masses never materialized.[90] British patrols repelled most Indonesian infiltrators. Attempts to coordinate paratrooper landings in Johore with a local uprising in Singapore in September 1964 were botched. Indonesian generals were concerned that Sukarno was purposefully drawing the army into a quagmire in Kalimantan while PKI was gaining strength in Java. Moreover, the high command knew that Indonesia had no defense if Britain retaliated. As the high command became more dissatisfied with Sukarno's leadership, they even had smugglers (their long-time business associates) relay messages of reassurance to the Malaysian and British leadership to avert escalation.[91]

By this time the geostrategic environment had turned decidedly against Sukarno. The Soviet Union was cool in its support, unwilling to endanger détente with the United States and wary of Sukarno's courtship of Beijing.

The United States was more suspicious of Sukarno and less sympathetic to claims against another sovereign country. Whereas Sukarno had masterfully garnered support for Indonesia's cause among nonaligned states during the West Papua adventure, this time the United Nations accepted Malaysia's integration and granted it a seat in the security council in 1965.[92]

In removing Sukarno in 1966, Suharto and the military acted in part to reduce the risk of further international entanglements for which the military was not equipped or capable. In fact, both before and during the 1965–1966 mass killings the military sought (and received) assurances that the British would not seize the opportunity to strike while the army was preoccupied with internal operations.[93] Once he came to power, Suharto repudiated *Konfrontasi* and immediately set out to repair ties with Indonesia's neighbors and the United States. In 1967, Indonesia joined Malaysia, Thailand, Singapore, and the Philippines in establishing the Association of Southeast Asian Nations (ASEAN) in 1967. The ASEAN framework further diminished Indonesia's external insecurity by banning domestic interference by member states and providing that foreign bases would not be allowed to be used to threaten a fellow ASEAN member.[94]

In contrast to Sukarno, Suharto's government for the most part steered away from entanglements beyond Indonesia's border. Suharto knew that Indonesia's military was unsuited for regional power projection. In East Timor, however, trouble found Indonesia. With the abrupt withdrawal of Portuguese imperial forces in November 1975, Indonesia feared that the tiny island would emerge as a communist outpost at Indonesia's flank. Tactfully, Suharto made sure of U.S. support before moving against the communist threat.[95]

From the outset, Indonesia's military campaign in East Timor bore all the hallmarks of earlier Indonesian efforts to stimulate and simulate people's war. Even before the Portuguese withdrawal, Indonesian infiltrators set up prointegration, anticommunist militias in East Timor. When the left-wing Revolutionary Front for an Independent East Timor (FRETILIN) prevailed in the internecine struggle, Suharto launched an outright invasion in support of these proxies. Indonesia's forces, however, were again ill equipped for the transition from guerrilla to conventional war. Organizational decentralization contributed to the breakdown of tactical command. Troops fired indiscriminately at FRETILIIN fighters, civilians, and their own units. There was massive looting of homes and property, driving the population away from the cities. Just as in the botched landing at Johore in September 1964, attempts to land paratroopers to block FRETILIN's retreat proved off the mark, allowing the guerrillas to escape to the mountains.[96] The first five years of Indonesia's occupation were extremely bloody, with an estimated 120,000 Timorese (about a quarter of the total population) killed. This violence, however, did not emerge from genocidal intent but rather as a result of the attempts of the militia-based army to overcome the limitations of its organization and achieve the pacification of a population in which it was decidedly unpopular and unwelcome.[97]

Over time, every one of Indonesia's attempts to mobilize militias led to similar long-term challenges, as the forces Jakarta had treated as proxies eventually slipped away from central control. The leader of the Free Papuan movement was a Papuan-born enlistee in the Indonesian army, trained as an intelligence officer at the Bandung military academy.[98] In Kalimantan, the ethnic Chinese guerrillas Jakarta had recruited during Konfrontasi continued to launch attacks against both Indonesian and Malaysian forces. In response, the Indonesian military began to rely on the autochthonous Dayak, resentful of the recent migrants to the region, to counter the insurgents.[99]

In East Timor, the locally raised garrison was deeply enmeshed in side businesses and racketeering. By the late 1980s, Jakarta came to augment its occupation force with several thousand ex-guerrillas, thugs, and petty criminals serving as auxiliary or "traditional" forces. Yet military intelligence remained keenly aware that Timorese soldiers, civil servants, and militias were unreliable and prone to defection.[100] In 1983, for instance, units from the Jakarta-sponsored Timorese militia turned on a group of Indonesian soldiers, killing fourteen before fleeing into the jungle to join FRETILIN. The attacked provoked brutal reprisals, with as many as 300 villagers killed in the following months.[101]

When the United States and other Western powers finally ceased their subornation of the Indonesian occupation their 1999, the Indonesian military activated precisely the same militia networks to intimidate the population. Jakarta depicted the violence as an unfortunate but spontaneous popular reaction, but government documents and witness interviews obtained by human rights organizations portray a different story. They demonstrate that at least 7,800 men divided among eleven different militia groups were responsible for killing thousands of Timorese and destroying 70 percent of the country's infrastructure in a matter of weeks. These lightly armed militias proved brutally effective against civilians but were no match for the small contingent of Australian and New Zealander light infantry.[102]

Overall, Indonesia has been a disappointing regional power. When the diplomatic environment was unfriendly, Indonesia's efforts at coercive diplomacy fell flat. Yet Indonesia seldom faced such constraints. As Dewi Fortuna Anwar notes, ending Konfrontasi and joining ASEAN freed Indonesia of the burden

> of having to station large numbers of troops to defend the Indonesian border . . . Security from immediate external threat allowed the government to keep relatively small armed forces and facilitated the Indonesian military's pursuance of an inward-looking defense doctrine.[103]

There was seldom need for Indonesia to engage in protracted efforts as war making against its neighbors. Indonesia's militia-model was sustained by the weakness of its neighbors. Had Indonesia been situated in a less innocuous international environment, the results would have been disastrous.

## CONCLUSION: RETURN TO UNGUIDED DEMOCRACY?

Suharto's New Order ended abruptly in 1998 in the midst of the Asian financial meltdown. Indonesia's decade-long economic miracle, which Suharto claimed was his own making, seemed suddenly in peril. Domestic opposition rose precipitously. On Suharto's resignation, the military high commanded withdraw from politics, leading to the first free election in Indonesia since the 1950s.[104]

Patterns of violence devolution, however, remained deeply entrenched. As Romain Bertrand relates, at the moment of this promising democratic transition, the army chief of staff announced the formation of a new 40,000-man auxiliary called *kamra* to augment police efforts in "protecting" highways and "keeping a check on wandering salesmen, prostitutes, and street musicians." Named after a militia deployed during the campaign against DI in the 1950s, this new force drew from criminal gangs that had roamed city streets since the 1980s. The *kamra* promptly began beating up student protesters with government-issued rattan canes.[105] Contemporaneously with the mobilization of militias in East Timor, alliances among local military units, militias, and gangs became a common feature in post-Suharto Indonesia, from the Islamic militants fighting Christian militias in Sulawesi to the Dayak tribesmen attacking Sino-Indonesians and Madurese migrants in Kalimantan.[106]

Breaking GOLKAR's monopoly returned Indonesia to face the dilemmas of political order witnessed in the country's first two decades. National political parties once again competed with the military for the allegiance and service of armed nonstate actors. Administrative decentralization further confounds this problem, empowering yet more local players and multiply the network of patronage and brokerage ties between state and society.[107] The collapse of internal order contributed to Indonesia's plummet from its status as a Western-backed developmental success story to the ranks of corrupt and frail states.

Such collusion between state and bandit has not occurred spontaneously, however. Rather, it represents the activation under new circumstance of the repertoire of brokerage and patronage that was practiced furtively but routinely in the New Order.[108] The dynamics of these relationships are familiar. Civilian politicians like Abdurahman Wahid, the country's first democratically elected president, at once complained of imminent conspiracies among regional commanders and pleaded for the military's help against his biggest political rival, Megawati Sukarnoputri.[109] Secessionism, successful in East Timor, remains a concern in Aceh, Papua, and even tiny Riau and Bali. At the local level, intercommunal and ethnic violence has skyrocketed, as have incidences of highly ritualized vigilantism against suspected sorcerers.[110] The discipline and professionalism of security forces remain abysmal. The police and military continue to be involved in the black market, giving them the perverse incentive to prolong conflicts that afford them the opportunity for more predatory economic gain. The *kamra*, for instance, extorted local government and businesses to give them employment as police or private security guards or else be "subjected to fire and sword."[111]

This repertoire has a long cultural lineage, extending back to the *jago* and his *pemuda* successor, strongmen who placed their expertise in coercion in the service of the state on a temporary and ad hoc basis while remaining distinctly beyond the boundary of the law. Later incarnations of urban criminals doubling as security agents carry on this tradition.[112] It seems almost natural to revert to having local satraps loosely connected to a central power. But as Geoffrey Robinson asks, if local violence wielders are ubiquitous in Indonesia, why are they more readily controlled at certain moments and by certain actors than others? What triggers the enactment of this particular script at these particular historical points?[113]

Certainly, the Dutch knew and made use of nonstate actors to inflict violence. The paradoxical subversion of the legal order by colonial authorities was a result of the contradictions inherent in the system of indirect rule, which maintained an indigenous façade for the penetrative colonial bureaucratic apparatus. While it is impossible to determine the extent or frequency in which the Dutch resorted to using state-sponsored militias, it is clear that they also recognized the peril in authorizing extralegal violence and were careful to maintain strong and centralized military and police forces as bulwarks against anarchy.

The Japanese occupation enlarged the scope of Indonesian nationalism from the elite to the masses, linking enactments of local violence to a nation-wide cause, allowing mobilization of violence on a mass scale. The new Indonesian state quickly found itself struggling to coordinate and control agents who professed loyalty but had gained considerable autonomy by embedding themselves in the local economy of violence and extraction. Flexibility, low cost, and connections to the local population made militias extremely useful but also exceedingly difficult to disarm, demobilize, or organize into a cohesive professional army

The process that led to the stabilization and consolidation in the use of state-sponsored militias could not have occurred in a more hostile regional environment. Even with its strategic reserve force, Indonesia remained profoundly weak militarily, incapable of defending its territory, much less projecting power abroad. The acquisitions of West Papua in 1961 and East Timor in 1975 were more dependent on diplomatic maneuvering than military success. The confrontation with Malaysia and attempts to block East Timor's secession in 1999 laid bare the army's inability to conduct sophisticated, coordinated, large-scale operations given its reliance on diffused, guerrilla-based tactics. Though certain senior military and civilian figures wished to emulate the European model by building a better-trained, better-supplied, and centrally controlled professional army, the regional environment did not necessitate the difficult and painful efforts of trying to disband the militias.

Rather, the revolutionary legacy provided the raw materials for making violence devolution work. The country's new leaders were aware of their vulnerability to internal subversion arising from coalitions of regional forces acting against the state and to predation by a stronger outside power. The enlargement of off-budgeting used to finance individual units during the revolution gave the central command the resources to reward compliance by its regional forces, even as these forces also remained embedded in the local political economy. The buildup of the strategic reserve force, already underway during the revolution, provided enough coercive might to subdue smaller violence-wielding institutions if they became too restive. The military's own doctrinal innovations sanctioned and deepened the already expansive agenda for socioeconomic intervention. The narrowing of the national political space eliminated alternative political brokers who could retain the support of local militias.

While driven by powerful and willful actors, these innovations were at best incidental results of competition, accommodation, and improvisation. In the 1940s, Japan never sought to be midwife to an independent Indonesia, nor did the United States aim to be a prop to an Indonesian leadership that would tilt precariously toward communism. In the 1950s, Nasution and the military high command saw unit self-financing as a threat to unit discipline, yet they utilized it fully to achieve the hegemony of the central command. Furthermore, Nasution's own engagement in politics in the 1950s and 1960s provided an opening to his rivals and subordinates within the ranks. Sukarno initiated the emasculation of political parties and empowerment of the military to break the peripheral alliances between politicians and dissident officers, but this ultimately hastened his own doom by upsetting the delicate balance between the military and PKI. Finally, Suharto's rule seemed to be the ultimate example of how the aim of personal aggrandizement contributed inadvertently to political stability and economic expansion.[114] The unique opportunities and constrains present in the domestic and international context allowed Indonesia to survive by domesticating, rather than disarming, non-state militias.

# 3 IRAQ

VIOLENCE HAS ALWAYS BEEN INTRINSIC to state formation, especially where state structures are transplanted and imposed by colonial and imperial power. Yet, even by these standards, violence has been particularly prominent in Iraq. Indeed, the history of Iraq from its establishment under British mandatory rule until at least the late 1980s has been an immensely aggressive effort at state making, centralizing coercive control, and eliminating domestic competitors. Kanan Makiya goes so far as to aver that at its apex in the 1970s and 1980s, Saddam Husayn's Ba'th Party transformed Iraq into a totalitarian regime whose very ideological premise was the domination of society by violence. The salience of coercion within the Iraqi state augmented the projection of force on Iraq's neighbors. War making, efforts to combat and compete with other states within the regional and international system, had a ratchet effect on military developing, requiring even more commitment to conventional forces while blocking any attempt devolve violence to nonstate actors.[1]

The period of Ba'th rule from the mid-1970s to the late 1980s represent a vast maturation from Iraq's feeble birth, when Britain's High Commissioner Percy Cox supposedly told Iraq's first defense minister, Jafar al-'Askari, "There is nothing to defend it and nothing to be defended."[2] Equally remarkable as the rise of the state's coercive power has been its profound degradation in the last two decades. The data presented in Table 1 show the dramatic reversal in state's coercive power since the 1991 Gulf War, accelerating after the 2003 American occupation. The beleaguered Iraqi state now resorts to co-opting tribal and sectarian militias, some barely distinguishable from criminal gangs, and continues to rely on American military support.

**Table 3.1.** Change in the size of the Iraqi military, 1932–2008.

|  | Size of state security forces | Security forces as percentage of population |
|---|---|---|
| 1932 | 12,000 | 0.36 |
| 1936 | 20,000 | 0.56 |
| 1941 | 46,000 | 1.12 |
| 1943 | 30,000 | 0.68 |
| 1949 | 45,000 | 0.82 |
| 1963 | 50,000 | 0.88 |
| 1967 | 82,000 | 0.92 |
| 1972 | 102,000 | 1.02 |
| 1977 | 188,000 | 1.57 |
| 1980 | 242,000 | 1.83 |
| 1982 | 342,000 | 2.44 |
| 1984 | 607,000 | 4.16 |
| 1990 | 1,000,000 | 5.56 |
| 1994 | 382,500 | 1.91 |
| 2004 | 125,000 | 0.43 |
| 2006 | 232,100 | 0.80 |
| 2008 | 425,345 | 1.47 |

SOURCE: For 1933 to 1994, see Aqil al-Nasri, *Al-Jaysh wa al-Sultah fi'l-'Iraq al-Maliki, 1921–1958* (Beirut: Dar al-Hisad l'il Nasr wa' al-Tawziya' wa al-Tiba'ah, 2000). See also Malik Mufti, *Sovereign Creation: Pan-Arabism and Political Order in Syria and Iraq* (Ithaca, NY: Cornell University Press, 1996), 212. For 2004 to 2008, see Brookings Institution Saban Center Iraq Index (www.brookings.edu/saban/~/media/Files/Centers/Saban/Iraq%20Index/index20080131.pdf).

This chapter examines the interplay between the endowment of colonial institutions, the progress of war making and state making, and the rise and fall of the Iraqi military behemoth. It proceeds in four sections. The first section discusses British attempts to imprint Mesopotamia with a modern military apparatus and how contradictions within the imperial agenda led to the construction of the army as a bastardization of both British and Iraqi ambitions. The second section describes how the combination of internal foes and regional rivals forced the state to redouble its commitment to military centralization as Iraq's postcolonial elite innovated within the inherited conventional military framework. The third section details efforts following the 1958 revolution to veer from the path of military centralization by empowering local violence-wielders through party and tribal militias that stood outside the armed forces. While successive regimes tried to incorporate paramilitaries as a substitute or supplement for conventional military force, each eventually failed under incessant pressure of external and internal threat. The final section examines violence devolution in post-Ba'th era, when the Iraqi state is struggling to regain its coercive capacity in the midst of a hostile regional environment and aggressive internal rivals for power.

## IMPERIALIST INCEPTION, 1914–1931

When the British entered Iraq in 1914, the region had been a backwater of the Ottoman Empire for nearly four centuries. In contrast to the imperial heartland, the Sublime Porte was content to deal with Mesopotamia's local notables as quasi-feudal local lords and tax farmers. The writ of the state was small and indirect in the cities and minimal at best in the countryside.[3] During the mid-1800s era of Ottoman reform, the army and the gendarmerie began to suppress some tribal raiders and pirates, foreign trade was expanded, and new agricultural and industrial techniques were introduced. The cornerstone of the reform agenda was the conversion of traditional collectively held tribal lands into small private plots, thereby providing incentive for nomads to adopt small-scale peasant proprietorship. Few tribesmen, though, would risk submitting their names to government registers that could someday become a conscription or tax roster, and registrars could be bribed to block rightful claimants for obtaining deeds. Either by choice, trickery, or duress, tribesmen forfeited their titles to tribal elders or urban notables in return for tenancy. Tribal sheikhs, in turn, moved from a position of paramounts in a relatively egalitarian nomadic community to semifeudal and often absentee landlords. Local foremen emerged to act in the sheikh's stead, taking a share of rural surplus and organizing village militias for self-defense.[4]

The Ottomans sowed competition among the various branches of tribal confederacy to weaken tribal cohesion. Encouraging factionalism within the leading families lessened the capacity of any single tribe to mount a challenge to the state. But in recognizing the tribes themselves, the Ottomans continued to empower individual tribal leaders to serve as mediators between the state and society and activators of broad retinues of private military retainers.[5] The limits of the Ottomans' penetration were obvious on the eve of the empire's disintegration. Even as major international threats loomed, the Ottomans could extract little in the way of services and support from the population of Iraq. Shi'i opposition remained strong, particularly over the issue of conscription. Tribal sheikhs typically obtained exemption for their kinsmen and, in lieu, provided ad hoc service as tribal levies like the Kurdish Hamidiya corps.[6] When British troops landed in Basra, Shi'i clerics echoed the Sultan's declaration of jihad, and 18,000 joined the Ottoman army. Still, many tribal leaders around Najaf and Karbala, as well as in the Kurdish regions, held out, intent to play off the Ottoman and British for as long as possible.[7]

At war's end, the League of Nations tasked Britain to build a nation-state in formerly Ottoman Mesopotamia, a region where there had been at best a vague sense of regional identity and limited preexisting state infrastructure. The mandate was premised on a chauvinistic but liberal desire to alleviate "Oriental despotism" and ready Iraq for independence. Britain's own imperial interests and limitations on their commitment of military and financial resources to Iraq further complicated the matter. The initial inclination of colonial officials was to follow the example of Raj, annexing the strategic position of Basra while ruling through local potentates in the rest of the country. Nationalist sentiment was dismissed as the work of agitators from the urban elite and unrepresentative of the poor rural majority.[8]

The massive uprising (*thawra*) of 1920, which claimed the lives of 500 British soldiers and at least 6,000 Iraqis, scuttled these hopes and forced a reexamination of Britain's role in establishing the infrastructure of the state.[9] The uprising prompted the British to turn to the technology of aerial bombardment as a tool of pacification. Reliance on airpower allowed a rapid drawdown of ground forces, a perfect solution for an occupation that sought to retain the mantle of a civilizing mission but avoid the cost and stigma of imperial suppression. The airplane represented a force multiplier of untold effect, enabling the occupying power to deploy violence across virtually of all Iraq's terrain. Merely the sight or sound of an approaching bomber could terrify a rebellious tribal band into submission. "Bombing for taxes"—punishing groups who collectively refused to pay taxes or other government-imposed fees—became progressively less costly and less risky. The utility of airpower became a tenet of faith.[10] The British paired this with a reversion to the well-proven technique of co-optation, subsidizing local leaders empowered by customary and tribal law as instruments of internal order. Sheikhs were now granted immunity from the civil code in managing their land and its inhabitants. The British were able to pry away enough tribal leaders and urban notables that the uprising eventually crumbled in on itself. As the last holdouts, the southern Shi'i tribes suffered the brunt of British pacification efforts.[11]

The events of 1920 confirmed for the British not only the immaturity of the Iraqi people but also that at least a façade of self-rule had to be introduced. The British sought the support of the Hashemite scion Faisal, recently

expelled from French-held Damascus. Though his Sunni clan had no historical connection to Iraq, Faisal's status as a descendant of the Prophet made
him at least palatable to the Shi'is, and his foreignness kept him aloof from the
traditional animosities between Iraq's great families. The British convened a
transitional governing council composed of local notables, which duly offered
Faisal the crown in 1921, then staged a plebiscite to accept the presumptive
nominee to the throne.[12]

From the outset, the new Kingdom of Iraq was beset by profound threats.
Internally, Mahmoud Barzinji declared himself the king of Kurdistan and led
numerous rebellions against Baghdad. The Shi'a were more amenable to the
idea of their incorporation into the Iraqi state, but after the disaster of 1920
they felt betrayed and hostile to the potential for continued Sunni rule. Externally, Iraq's borders were long, porous, and ill-defined. Britain suspected
both French and Italy of complicity in cross-border arms smuggling.[13] To the
north, Turkey asserted a claim to oil-rich Mosul. To the east, Iraq inherited
the long-standing dispute between the Ottoman and Iranian empires over
control of the Shatt al-Arab River. To the south, Ibn Saud's *Ikhwan* raiders
were a constant menace. To the west, French-mandated Syria was both the
object of Hashemite ambition to reunify the Arab kingdom and a potential
rival within the regional system.[14]

In such an environment, the construction of an army was a critical test
of the mandate's efficacy and a focal point of a competition between the imperial ruler, the monarchy, and Iraq's embedded social elite. Contrary to the
British estimation of his pliability, King Faisal and his ex-Ottoman courtiers
used whatever concessions Britain made to transform Iraq from a dependency
to a viable state. Many ex-Ottoman officials were already enamored of German *Volk* ideology and its stress on martial virtues and organic unity. Military conscription was seen as the furnace to forge the Iraqi nation. In the first
months of the mandate, 'Askari raised the issue of conscription as a means
of building Iraq's defense and readying it for sovereignty. By 1921 enlistment
bureaus were opened in sixteen cities and Ottoman veterans began to form
the kernel of Iraq's officer corps.[15]

Both Kurdish and Shi'i leaders, however, were suspicious of any move
that would bring them further under Sunni domination. The Kurds sought
an entirely separate political status in the country. The Shi'a refused to serve
as cannon fodder below Sunni officers. In fact, some Shi'i leaders responded
to attacks by renegade *Ikhwan* on the Shi'i holy cities in 1922 by demand-

ing the government reinstate the Ottoman practice of arming tribes for self-defense rather than rebuilding the army.[16] As the mandatory power, ultimate responsibility for maintaining Iraq's security fell to Britain, an imperial role that British colonial officers had come to see as a debilitating burden.[17] On one hand, Britain expected Iraq to pay for its occupation and required Iraq to commit nearly quarter of its budget to defense. Conscription was the only economically feasible way the Iraqi government could afford to raise a capable army.[18] On the other hand, until military self-sufficiency was obtained, the Iraqi state could not enforce conscription without provoking an uprising comparable to the *thawra* of 1920. British High Commissioner Sir Henry Dobbs used the threat of withholding military assistance to the Iraqi government as the sheet anchor of British domination.[19] Instead, the British offered Iraq the services of the RAF and a small contingent of British-commanded levies as the mainstay of its defenses.[20]

In 1927, the Iraqi government passed a new National Defense Act and introduced a conscription bill that threatened to upset the precarious balance between state, society, and imperial overlord. The bill specifically stated that "since our neighbors, Turkey and Persia, possess two powerful and well-equipped armies . . . it is essential for Iraq to raise an army capable—albeit for a short time—of facing either of those two armies."[21] Again, Shi'i and Kurdish leaders protested. The British warned that they would not be involved in suppressing disturbances that Baghdad itself had provoked. King Faisal responded that the measure could win support in Iraq if it was coupled with a British pledge to back Iraq's bid for admission to the League of Nations. Alternatively, he implied, Britain could continue paying for Iraqi security indefinitely.[22] The Shi'i political leadership made their support of the measure conditional on receiving greater representation in the cabinet and the officer corps. The threat of a general tribal revolt loomed. In this atmosphere of political tension, the government was forced to resign in January 1928, scuttling the bill.[23]

Instead of the broad national institution that Iraqi nationalists had envisioned or the glorified police force that the British had intended, the army that emerged from the mandate was in many ways a disappointment to both Iraqi and British plans.[24] By March 1922, the Iraqi army counted 1,200 men in the Mosul garrison, 1,600 in Baghdad, and 800 in Hillah. This would grow to 7,500 by 1925 and around 12,000 by 1930. Still, the fiscal constraints kept the volunteer force consistently below the 15,000 to 20,000 the Iraqis believed was necessary for dealing with its myriad internal and external enemies. The

quality of the enlisted troops was generally low, desertion common, and retention of enlistees a constant concern.[25] A handful of British advisors oversaw
nearly every facet of the army's growth, from its recruitment to its armaments
to its logistics. Only a third of the Ottoman officers who initially sought com-
missions were accepted into the new national army as the British sought to
mold Iraqi officers in their own image.[26] Hundreds of volumes of military
manuals on subjects from infantry tactics to military law were translated from
English into Arabic.[27] A military academy modeled on Sandhurst, a staff college, and a host of specialized programs in armor, small arms, and even veterinary medicine were established. Iraqi officers were seconded to India and
England for further training and even participated in the age-old rituals of
football (soccer).[28] Most importantly, Britain helped to found the Royal Iraqi
Air Force (RIAF) in 1926, giving the Iraqi state the ability to use the same
coercive measures as the British imperial forces. Five Iraqis a year were sent
to Britain for flight certification. By the conclusion of the mandate, Iraq had
purchased fourteen antiquated but still operable De Haviland DH.60 biplanes.
RIAF was considered an integral facet of Iraqi defenses.[29] In 1929, Iraq's first
combat exercise featured Iraqi troops practicing ground maneuvers with RAF
providing air support.[30]

British reports to the League of Nations lauded the steady improvement
of the Iraqi army, but candid confidential assessments were pessimistic. The
Secretary of State for Air wrote in 1925:

> Without a British commander and an infusion of British officers in its units,
> there is not in my view, the least chance of the [Iraqi] Arab Army becom-
> ing efficient or of the Imperial forces ever being able safely and honorably to
> evacuate the country.[31]

To compensate for the seeming weakness of Iraqi soldiers, the British focused
on setting up a separate corps of levies, drawing heavily from the Assyrian
Christian community. The Assyrians had come to northern Iraq fleeing Turkish atrocities. The Assyrians were eager and grateful to receive British military
training, which they believed necessary for their own protection from Iraq's
Muslims. The British, in turn, relied on the Assyrians as the backbone of their
ground forces. Between 1921 and 1932, RAF and the Levies were called on 130
times to assist Iraqi forces.[32]

The British interpreted the failures of the Iraqi army not as an indictment
of their own training program but as an indication of the weakness of Iraqis as

soldiers.[33] Yet Britain kept seeking ways to reduce its military commitments to Iraq. From a peak in 1921 of thirty-three battalions of the British and Indian armies, six cavalry regiments, sixteen batteries, four armored cars, and four RAF squadrons, by October 1930 there were only four RAF squadrons and a single armored car backed by just two Levy infantry battalions.[34] As a result of the British drawdown, the Iraqi army had to assume an ever-larger role in Iraq's defense.

Understandably, Iraqi officers had a radically different take on the dilemmas of Iraq's military development. Those who entered the military academies in the 1920s joined an upper echelon of ex-Ottoman officers already hostile to Britain's interventions in Iraqi affairs. They saw themselves as the vanguard of progressive Arab nationalism in a country divided by atavistic sectarian lines and resented the implication that they were somehow unfit for self-determination.[35] It was the British, after all, who blocked conscription. As early as 1928, Iraq's defense minister complained—albeit diplomatically—that Iraqi graduates of British staff colleges had "outgrown" the need to be advised by British subalterns.[36] Britain's own inspector general in Iraq worried about emasculating a key institution of Iraq's nascent nationalism. Still, Britain blithely dismissed Iraq's sense of regional insecurity and was utterly confident that the service of a few thousand Assyrians and a handful of bombers could protect Iraq completely while keeping it thoroughly under British domination.[37]

King Faisal also elevated the status of military as the sine qua non of Iraqi sovereignty, but he used it as a symbol of national victimization, thwarted ambition, and broken promises. Coercion was the very essence of statehood, yet it was denied the aspirant state makers. There could be no compromise with societal elites demanding a greater share of power in return for their community's service because the very contestation of the state's right to extract military service imperiled the claim to sovereignty. Control over violence was too precious to be alienated. From both Iraqi and British perspectives, the coercive institutions that emerged in Iraq were a disappointment. Yet, as detailed below, this malformed replica proved to hold unforeseen capacities.

## WAR MAKING AND STATE MAKING IN IRAQ, 1932–1958

In a confidential memorandum of March 1933, less than a year after Iraq had joined the League of Nations, King Faisal lamented (somewhat hyperbolically) that the Iraqi state was still "far and away weaker than the people . . . [the people had] more than 100,000 rifles whereas the government possesses only 15,000."[38]

This was the direct legacy of Britain's purposefully impeding the accumulation of coercive capacity. Although rejecting the British colonial military as inadequate, Iraqi leaders soon recognized latent potential to apply force in a manner and scope unanticipated or unintended by the British designers. Specifically, the Iraqi army proved a potent tool for state making and the deployment of violence against armed groups within Iraqi territory. Instead of co-optation or negotiation, obstructionist tribal leaders or religious figures could be met with repression. Success at domestic pacification accelerated the push for war making, the deployment of violence against neighboring states, as Iraq struggled to assert its sovereignty within the regional order and against its erstwhile colonial mentor. The emergence of a regional arms race in the 1940s ratcheted up the need for further military expansion, as those states that failed to match their neighbors' capacities would suffer military defeat and possibly dismemberment. Ultimately, the emergence of Iraq's highly militarized state came not as the result of a grand plan but through a series of steps that progressively foreclosed the chance for violence devolution and instead increased the state's reliance on centralized, mechanized coercive institutions.

### State Making: Suppressing Domestic Challengers

While the end of the mandate provided juridical recognition of Iraqi sovereignty, internally the state's authority remained highly contested. Nothing exemplified this as much as the issue of the Assyrians, who insisted on separation from the Iraqi state. As the British readied to withdraw from Iraq, the Assyrian patriarch tried first to press the case of Assyrian autonomy in the League of Nations, then traveled to Baghdad to demand that the community of 40,000—a quarter of whom were British-trained soldiers—be permitted to live under his discrete authority. On August 4, 1933, Assyrians crossing into Iraq from Syria exchanged fire with an Iraqi border patrol. In the Iraqi army's first attempt to disarm the Assyrians, it initially suffered its typical ignominious defeat. However, the Iraqis turned to the British script for suppression of internal revolts. Disregarding the handful of British officers still serving as advisors, the Iraqi army deployed independently for the first time, marching on the Assyrian strongholds. RIAF planes provided surveillance and bombing just as RAF had before. The instigation of tribal looting against Assyrian villages and property, which Ernest Main labeled an "old Turkish custom," was actually entirely consistent with the British colonial practices of countering tribal uprisings with locally raised auxiliaries. The result was the death of several hundred Assyrians and forcible disarmament of the Assyrian population.[39]

The Assyrians represented a meager military opponent, and the Iraqi army showed no particular acumen by massacring unarmed civilians. For his part, King Faisal was horrified by the uses found for the army's military prowess. While the king had done everything he could to strengthen the Iraqi army in order to promote Iraqi sovereignty and state building, he also sought to find nonviolent means to integrate Iraq's fissiparous ethnosectarian and tribal groups. Faisal's death two weeks after the massacres deprived Iraq of perhaps the only figure capable of withstanding the militaristic tide.

The British, too, were shocked and dismayed by the decimation of a Christian community that had so loyally served them, but they were also aware of their role in fomenting the crisis. The British were particularly perturbed to learn that they had supplied the bombs the RIAF dropped on the Assyrians. Beyond mere technology, though, Britain was responsible for recruiting and training the officers who had perpetrated the attack. The commander of the Mosul garrison, General Bakr Sidqi, had been considered by British intelligence as one of Iraq's best commanders. Born around 1890 in Kirkuk, Sidqi had attended the Ottoman Military College in Istanbul, obtaining the rank of colonel, and had served on the Ottoman General Staff. It was the British who recommended Sidqi's commission in the Iraqi army and who promoted him through a stint at the British staff college. While senior Iraqi officers had received their initial training under the Ottomans, the backbone of the Iraqi army—its organizational structure; its recruitment, retention, and retraining programs; and its provision of airpower and other advanced military technologies—were British built.[40]

In most of the Arab sections of Iraq, though, the campaign was greeted as a vital step toward national independence. By avenging itself on a community that represented the physical insinuation of British domination, the long-stigmatized Iraqi army proved it could operate independently. Tribal sheikhs who had just a few years earlier blocked the move for mass conscription began volunteering for service.

Yasin al-Hashemi, a leader of the pan-Arab Nationalist Brotherhood party, seized on popular enthusiasm to pass a new national defense act that included provisions for military expansion and conscription in the winter of 1933–1934. The progressive-oriented Popular Party, supported primarily by Shi'is of the rural south, moved to oppose the bill and demanded that greater funds be used to improve rural irrigation for the south. The debate led to yet another rupture in Iraq's notoriously unstable parliament. Throughout the mid-1930s, Baghdad politicians incited their tribal allies in the countryside to rise up in resistance to the state's encroachment. The crisis that ensued vividly illustrated two profoundly different strategies for national integration. On the one hand, the opposition favored continued reliance on co-optation and economic incentives. On the other hand, Hashemi offered a new strategy, premised on coercing nonstate actors until they submitted to the state. Between 1934 and 1936, Iraq saw several waves of rural violence, with tribes destroying railway and telegraph lines, harassing tax collectors and conscription officers, and sacking police stations. The Shi'i Grand Ayatollah Kashif al-Ghita, circumventing the existing political party structures, built direct alliances with the rebellious mid-Euphrates tribes. Far beyond what parliamentarians had articulated, Ghita demanded a complete change in Iraq's socioeconomic balance: equal representation for the Shi'a in parliament, the cabinet, and civil service; greater funding for Shi'i religious institutions; the establishment of an agricultural bank; the cancellation of land rents; the replacement of civil servants of dubious character and curtailment of their salaries and pensions; and more investment in health and education in the south. British observers echoed Ghita's complaints, recommending that the government take more steps to address rampant poverty in the south and equalize its distribution of social and economic resources.

The balance of power, however, had already tipped in favor of the state, making compromise unnecessary. Under Hashemi's tenure, the military doubled in size to 23,000 men, and RIAF expanded to three squadrons of seventy-two planes. Enhancements in transportation infrastructure allowed troops to penetrate the country's more remote regions. After early attempts to woo rebellious tribes failed, Sidqi launched a brutal campaign of aerial bombardment and ground pacification. Rebel leaders were detained and executed under martial law. Once the army had subdued the tribes, there was no longer a need to negotiate with the Shi'i leadership.[41] The mid-1930s proved a turning point in Iraqi history. As Hanna Batatu notes,

> The ease and grim rapidity with which Bakr Sidqi's soldiers and airplanes suppressed the tribal outbreaks of 1935 and 1936 presaged the end of the shaikh's era. Prior to this, Iraq's history was to a large extent the history of its shaikhs and their tribes. Its problems, its convulsions, its politics were essentially tribal. . . . After the thirties, the towns came conclusively into their own. The history of Iraq became henceforth largely the history of Baghdad.[42]

Instead of the tribes, the military was catapulted to the forefront of Iraqi politics. In October 1936, Sidqi launched the first military coup in modern Arab history, using RIAF aircraft to drop pamphlets and a handful of bombs over Baghdad. Military intervention would be a chronic feature of Iraqi politics for the next three decades.[43] But even more fundamentally, the period saw a magnification of the state's coercive power and attempts by military and civilian elites alike to assert the state's dominion.[44]

### War Making: Iraq in the Regional System

The success of the Iraqi army in asserting the integrity of the state against domestic challengers also empowered Iraqi leaders to engage in greater activity in the international arena against international rivals. Until the early 1930s, Iraq was an active but incipient player in regional politics. King Faisal's diplomatic efforts to regain the Syrian throne and create a unified Hashemite Arab kingdom were summarily rebuffed by both France and Britain.[45] The Saadabad Pact of 1937 helped secure Iraq's regional relations with Iran and Turkey and provided for mutual cooperation against Kurdish secessionism. From a British perspective, the pact helped to solidify a reliable block against possible Italian or Soviet encroachment into the Middle East.[46] Desperate to protect the passage to India, British strategists proposed that indigenous Middle Eastern armies be upgraded so that local forces could defend the lines until imperial assistance could arrive.[47]

For the newly installed King Ghazi and Iraq's military elite, Britain was an obstacle to Iraq's playing the role of an Arab Prussia. Still tethered by its military dependence, Iraq's leadership pointed out the country's external vulnerabilities in asking for larger transfers of modern arms and material. In 1937, Turkey used military threats to force the detachment of Alexandretta from Syria. With its large Turkomen population, Iraq was susceptible to similar irredentist claims. Iran, reinvigorated under Reza Khan, could easily block Iraq's narrow passage to the Persian Gulf. Whereas the shah could mobilize forty-four infantry battalions to its western border in five weeks, Iraq could at best muster fifteen battalions with an air force half as large.[48] Britain, though, continued to downplay Iraq's need for anything more than an effective organ of internal pacification and claimed that its own military supplies were in shortage, making it impossible to fulfill Iraq's request for weaponry. What high-quality military technology Iraq did receive, like Gladiator and Lysander planes, were in small quantities.

To Britain's chagrin, Sidqi arranged through the German representative in Baghdad to purchase fifteen Italian Breda fighters and five Savoia bombers, along with the provision of Italian advisors for RIAF. Given its failure to supply comparable products, Britain was unable to protest. This was just one of the attempts by the various Iraqi governments to break away from the British military monopoly and seeking out American, Danish, Czech, and Japanese suppliers for armaments ranging from light arms to antiaircraft artillery. Britain's refusal to convert Iraqi dinar into sterling, however, stymied many of these efforts. Still, by 1939, Iraq's air force counted nearly one hundred pilots and its army numbered some 26,000 men and 1,400 officers.[49]

These new weapons were soon put to new uses in a series of international gambits in the 1930s and 1940s. The first such incident occurred when King Ghazi launched efforts to annex Kuwait in 1938. Along with Iraq's obvious strategic interest in gaining access to the Persian Gulf, Ghazi claimed that Kuwait had been illegally dismembered from Ottoman Basra and needed to be "returned" to Iraqi control. Britain suspected that King Ghazi was working at the instigation of the Axis powers, particularly when the young king referred to Kuwait as Iraq's "Sudetenland." At the height of the crisis in March 1939, Iraq drew up plans for invasion and massed forces at the border. Britain was able to forestall the conflict only by orchestrating a Saudi mobilization to force Iraq to back down. A month later, King Ghazi died in a car crash, adding currency to rampant theories of British conspiracies against Iraq's national aspirations.[50]

Iraq's flirtation with the Axis continued through the brief Anglo–Iraqi war of 1941. The intrigues that brought about the deposition of the new regent and the establishment of a military government of national defense led by Rashid Ali al-Kailani in April 1941 have been well covered elsewhere.[51] When Kailani held out against British demands that Iraq contribute to the Allied war effort, he worked with the false confidence that German assistance would be forthcoming at the crucial moment. Britain invaded southern Iraq to forestall any Iraq–German conspiracy. The Iraq army managed to bottle up the initial landing force of 2,000 to 3,000 British troops at Basra. The RAF base at Habbaniyya was also surrounded by Iraqi troops. By May, however, Glubb Pasha's Transjordanian Arab Legion had lifted the siege at Habbaniyya and marched on Baghdad.[52]

Most British military observers attribute their victory over the larger Iraqi forces to the stereotypical irresoluteness and ineptitude of the Iraqi military. Others point to the unavailability of German air support.[53] Often overlooked, though, is the extent to which the Iraqi army had adopted—indeed mimicked—the techniques of British of conventional forces. Official British sources confirm that the Iraqi maneuvers were predictable because they were exactly what had been practiced in joint exercises.[54] Iraqi officers were tentative and unimaginative. Glubb himself puzzled over the lack of resistance put up by the tribes.[55] The British resident in Baghdad concluded that the small British column could "scarcely have reached here had the desert tribes thrown in their lot with Rashid Ali."[56] Kailani's military clique had set up nationalist youth groups in the cities but ignored the hinterland tribes, apparently forgetting the lessons of mass mobilization from the 1920 uprising.[57] Instead, the Iraqi army held fast to the adopted model of conventional, mechanized warfare and abandoned the repertoire of decentralized insurgency.

Britain took substantive steps to defang the Iraqi army immediately after 1941. Two thousand officers were sacked, conscription suspended, and budgets slashed.[58] Eager to purge Kailani supporters, Prime Minister Nuri as-Said sought to reduce the army to a 10,000-man, all-volunteer force, backed by part-time conscript militias in each province.[59] But Iraq remained a crucial strategic asset, an imperial transit hub, and the bulwark of Britain's control of the Persian Gulf.[60] By 1944, the British military advisor in Baghdad, General J. M. L. Renton, adopted less draconian methods of military reform. Renton believed that contempt for Iraqi officers and refusal to make good on the promises of military supply caused anti-British sentiment to fester. British forces could not remain in Iraq indefinitely, making it imperative for Iraq to regain its footing. Renton tried to make room for a new generation of younger, British-trained Iraqi officers. By the end of the war, military budgets and force strength increased substantially as Britain continued to rely on Iraq in its regional defense plans. This relationship was not easy, though. Even after the war, Britain could not meet Iraq's demands for fresh arms. Offers of reconditioned tanks and trucks were rejected. When Iraq did get newly made fighter planes, they were hardly state-of-the-art prewar models.[61]

Still, Iraqi politicians realized that British support was crucial for the stability of the monarchy. In January 1948, the Iraqi press leaked details of secret negotiations of a new Anglo–Iraqi agreement. Although Britain would technically withdraw its permanent forces from Iraq, it reserved the right to enter Iraq during times of war and to use Iraqi airbases and bound Iraq to a joint military commission with the British high command. Faced with public outcry, the regent was forced to repudiate the agreement and the prime minister to resign. Even after this public humiliation, though, Iraq's integration with Britain's regional defense strategy continued.[62]

Iraq's entry into the Arab–Israel conflict in 1948 must be considered both in light of its dependency on Britain and its position in the regional and global order. Successive Iraqi governments had tried to find ways to appear resolute on behalf of the Arabs of Palestine without compromising their relationships with Britain. Behind the fraternal pan-Arab rhetoric were profound strategic rivalries within the concerts of Arab states. Iraq jockeyed with Saudi Arabia and Egypt for leadership in the Arab world, the Hashemite houses of Iraq and Transjordan competed over possible unity with Syria, and nearly all the Arab states were hostile to Hajj Amin Husseini, who had returned to the Middle East from his exile in Germany to become the leading Palestinian nationalist.[63]

Iraq faced some severe strategic challenges in its support for the Palestinians. Most obviously, over 500 miles separated Baghdad from Palestine, a distance over which even the most advanced army would have difficulty establishing a supply line (assuming Transjordan even offered Iraq transit rights). Militarily, the Iraqi army had regrown to about 40,000 men, although almost half were designated specifically for mountain warfare against the Kurds. British evaluations of Iraqi force readiness were mixed. Iraq's army held the highest standard of formation training of all the Arab forces and was deemed capable of participating in defensive maneuvers in conjunction with the British. Still, the British were pessimistic about Iraq's offensive capacity. Britain had fallen short in meeting Iraqi orders for weaponry and, after March 1948, embargoed further exports. Resultantly, the Iraqi army had significant shortages in tanks, artillery, armored personnel carriers, and trucks, and all forms of munitions. In his memoirs, the Iraqi chief of staff Salih Sa'ib Juburi described the difficulties of readying the Iraqi army for its first true expeditionary mission. From 1945 to 1947, plans to add mechanized companies and air force squadrons had been postponed because of budget shortfalls. Merely massing the Iraqi army at the Jordanian border required the army to make emergency requisitions of vehicles.[64]

Given these limitations, Iraq's first reaction to the prospect of war was to mobilize nonstate proxies. Iraqis were urged to join the Arab Liberation Army (*Jaysh al-Inqadh al-Arabi*, ALA), an irregular force created by the Arab League in December 1947 and placed under the field command of Fawzi al-Quwaqji, a Beirut-born Ottoman officer who had resigned his Iraqi commission to join the 1936 Palestinian uprising. ALA purported to represent the unified actions of the Arab governments to defend Palestine, but the force remained an organizational shambles, beholden to the Syrian government, which controlled its supply lines. Iraq seconded Assistant Chief of Staff Ismail Saffwat and General Taha al-Hashemi to serve with ALA, but to little improvement.

In the first months of the Arab–Jewish civil war before the mandate's expiration, there was little coordination among ALA units.[65] ALA refused to cooperate with Husseini's hodgepodge of village militias, whom Hashimi dismissed as ruffians.[66] Better-trained, better-armed, and better-organized Jewish forces routed the irregular Arab militias in the spring of 1948. The prospect of a total collapse forced the Arab states to shift to direct military intervention by national armies.[67]

The Iraqi army's performance in the first Arab–Israel war was hardly outstanding. In his annual report, the British ambassador ridiculed the Iraqi campaign as "characteristically inept."[68] Jewish forces repulsed between 3,000 and 5,000 Iraqi troops at Gesher on May 15, 1948, taking control of the vital Kirkuk-Haifa pipeline. The Iraqis successfully defended Jenin from Israeli attack in early June but at considerable cost of men and material. Once entrenched in the West Bank, the Iraqi army missed the opportunity to split the Jewish forces and drive a wedge to the Mediterranean. It is a matter of historical conjecture whether this was due to the incompetence of Iraqi officers themselves or the disjointedness of the entire inter-Arab command system.[69]

The Iraqi army's shortcomings in 1948 must also be measured against its unexpected and unacknowledged successes, however. First, as Edgar O'Ballance notes, the Iraqi army fought considerably better than ALA or the Mufti's militias. In fact, during the truce of June 11, 1948, the Iraqi army essentially recalled its forces from ALA. Second, the fact that Iraqi forces even took the field at all was a notable feat. Assembling such a large expeditionary force was probably beyond the means of many armies of the developing world. After taking Jenin, Iraq committed another 10,000 reinforcements (including some units designated for Kurdistan), one hundred armored personnel carriers, and fifty artillery pieces to maintain Arab control over the Jenin-Tulkarem-Nablus triangle. Almost the entirety of RIAF was stationed in Jordan, providing air support for the defense of Jenin. While Iraqi forces failed to take the offensive, they did not lose territory either, more than can be said for their Arab peers.[70] Finally, Iraqi army units showed strong resolve and cohesion. The fact that Iraqi officers who spent seven years under the thumb of British military advisors failed to seize tactical advantage is hardly surprising. Despite poor leadership and severe casualties, Iraqi units held together in combat, belying assumptions that the ethnosectarian cleavages in Iraqi society would cripple its military.[71]

The first Arab–Israeli war represents a culmination in the metamorphosis of Iraq's army from a colonial institution oriented toward internal pacification into a conventional fighting force capable of both domestic suppression and international expedition. The adoption of such a centralized and bureaucratic military structure was propelled by a complex interaction of domestic, regional, and global forces. It was not just that a common resentment of imperialism strengthened the resolve of the Iraqi leaders to use force to dominate society and build a nation. The 1920 uprising demonstrated that tribal sheikhs, religious leaders, and local, nonstate violence wielders could mobilize against foreign occupation, too. By the 1940s, though, Iraqi state makers and military officers looked on tribal sheikhs and religious dignitaries not as potential subjects of co-optation but as obstacles that needed to be disarmed, overcome, and overwhelmed. The colonial military legacy endowed Iraq with the coercive technology and infrastructure necessary to accomplish just that.[72]

Regional competition drove Iraq to intensify its military buildup and to eschew nonstate forms of mobilization. Militias like ALA and the Mufti's forces proved calamitously ineffective against better-trained and better-armed armies. The outcome of the 1948 war did not diminish confidence in the army as an institution within the Arab world. Rather, after 1948, Iraq strove to match its neighbors' burgeoning arsenals by importing more and more advanced weaponry, first from Britain and latter from the United States and the Soviet Union.[73] The repertoire of conventional force mobilization steadily replaced the vestiges of militia-based techniques.

## STATE CONSOLIDATION AND THE FAILURES
## OF VIOLENCE DEVOLUTION, 1958–1991

From 1921 to 1958, a combination of culturally derived notions about the role and mission of the military and the functional need to protect the state from internal and external challengers drove Iraq to erect a large, conventional, and bureaucratic army. Yet the imposition of regional and geostrategic competition placed a debilitating burden on an already precarious balance of domestic forces. While Gemal Abd al-Nasser promised a new Arab order, the Iraqi monarchy limped along on the crutch of the mid-1950s oil boom.[74] Ultimately, it was a contingent conjunction of internal and external element that precipitated the monarchy's demise on July 14, 1958. With Syria's unification with Egypt in the United Arab Republic (UAR) and Lebanon facing a possible pro-Nasser coup, Jordan requested reinforcement from its Hashemite brethren. Normally, Iraqi army units were forbidden to carry ammunition in Baghdad in order to avert a military coup. In the emergency westward deployment, however, two brigade commanders, Abd as-Salam Arif and Karim Abd al-Qasim, seized the opportunity to march on the capital. Within hours they stormed the palace, killed the royal family, and declared an Iraqi republic.[75]

Enthusiastic for radical social transformation, successive republican regimes sought to empower militia forces as an alternative to the army. Leaders believed that nonstate militias could provide a counterweight to the potentially disloyal officer corps, a reserve force in times of crisis, and an instrument of regime indoctrination. First, during the period of inchoate military governments from 1958 to 1968, both the Iraqi Communist Party (ICP) and Ba'th party tried to build party militias. Second, various Iraqi governments raised tribal militias against the Kurdish nationalist insurgency from 1960 to 1991. Third, after Saddam Husayn had assumed total control of the state in the 1970s, the Ba'th party made another effort to establish its Popular Army (PA, *Al-Jaysh ash-Sha'bi*). Finally, "neotribal" militias emerged as Saddam groped to retain control after the 1991 Gulf War.

Ultimately each of these experiments in violence devolution in Iraq ended in failure. The idea of arming civilians incited the ire and resistance of the officer corps, who resented any challenger to their own positions as professional wielders of violence. Even after the officer corps was subdued under Saddam, however, militias proved too unstable to be relied on by the regime's leadership and too weak to stand up to conventional military force in Iraq's competitive regional environment. The decentralization that made paramilitaries and militias an attractive option also made them functionally ill suited to Iraq's threat environment and the inescapable necessities of state making and war making. Instead of relying on militias, Iraq's leaders found ways to balance between the military's reliability and efficacy by innovating within the framework of the established centralized military institutions. The creation of a fully armed and hardened praetorian guard—as opposed to a civilian-based part-time militia force—proved effective in the dual tasks of internal repression and external defense.

### Military Rule and Party Militias, 1958–1968

The 1958 revolution marked the first venture by military officers to formally assume the reigns of state. These officers seemed the prime agents for radical social change. On the day of the coup, the leadership of the Iraqi Communist Party (ICP) wrote to Qasim asking for the authority to organize popular defense militias. ICP was the most formidable political party of the era, with tens of thousands of supporters, mainly from the country's disaffected Shi'i majority. Qasim was a natural ally to ICP. He sympathized with the call for social redistribution, especially land reform. As the son of a Shi'i Kurdish mother, he did not share the enthusiasm of many of his military cohort for pan-Arab integration. The ICP leadership reminded Qasim of the ouster of Mohammad Mossadeq five years earlier and urged the new leader to

> grant the people the freedom to organize, publish, and assemble . . . [and] to encourage the formation of People's Committees for the Defense of the Republic and the People's Resistance Force (PRF, *al-Muqawama ash-Sha'biyya*) and arm this force without delay.[76]

Lacking a foothold in the Sunni Arab–dominated army, ICP was intent on exploiting whatever armament and training it could get outside the formal military structure. As rioting enveloped Baghdad, ICP had already mobilized its armed networks.

Qasim was initially hesitant to compromise the military's ability to control coercion. He banned PRF militia activities and imposed a curfew to curb lawlessness. Once Arif's alignment with Iraq's pan-Arab nationalist movement and his courtship of Nasser became apparent, however, Qasim reneged. On August 1, 1958, he authorized PRF to resume operations under the oversight his personal intelligence chief. Army officers and noncommissioned officers led local PRF militia units in one-month training programs, consisting mainly of two hours of basic small arms training. PRF units were required to return their weapons to the military garrisons at the end of the day. ICP, however, saw the new militia as part of its own design, seizing control of the force by organizing candidates for election as unit commanders. In just one month, PRF more than doubled to 25,000 members, alongside a proliferation of communist-fronted youth and women's leagues and trade and peasant unions.[77]

Throughout Iraq, individual PRF detachments freely roamed the streets, setting up people's courts, attacking nationalist sympathizers, and extorting local populations to give funds for the upkeep of the local detachment. Some of these activities were linked to the campaign to suppress pro-Arif elements, but PRF activities became so flagrant that they pushed Iraq to the brink of chaos. After Sunni Arab army officers backed by Nasser botched an attempt to foment a rebellion among the tribes around Mosul in March 1959, communist-backed Kurdish militias rampaged through the city, killing hundreds. The PRF was also involved in similar vigilante attacks against so-called reactionary elements in Basra throughout the spring of 1959.[78]

Qasim remained unwilling to allow parliamentary elections, fearing an ICP victory, and soon deployed the military to curb PRF's activities. In January 1959, he reiterated that PRF "shall not carry out any activities before receiving a clear order from the General Commander of the Armed Forces or the Military Governor-General." He further specified that only PRF units bearing special permits would be allowed to operate.[79] By March 1959 the army commander in Basra forbade further enrollment. The army seized PRF arms depots. The justice ministry instructed judges to inflict maximum penalties on disturbers of the peace.[80] For its part, ICP offered its forces to augment the army's efforts to combat smuggling and infiltration, but regular army and police commanders insisted that popular militias defer to state authorities at all times.[81] After clashes between ICP-affiliated Kurds and Turkomen in Kirkuk killed dozens in July 1959, Qasim used this example of "anarchist" excess as a pretext for halting all PRF training.[82]

The tables rapidly turned on ICP and by the middle of 1960 it was the leftists who suffered harassment and intimidation. May Day demonstrations in the conservative Shi'i cities of Najaf and Karbala were assaulted, as were Kurdish ICP rallies in Kirkuk.[83] The last gasp for PRF came on February 8, 1963, when nationalist officers began a final move against Qasim. ICP had warned Qasim that a coup was imminent and offered to mobilize the popular militia, but Qasim refused. ICP members took to the street independently and were cut down by the army's tanks and machine guns. Jets strafed the defense ministry where Qasim held out. When Qasim surrendered, the newly constituted Revolutionary Command Council sentenced him to death by firing squad, leaving his bullet-ridden body propped on a chair for broadcast on Iraqi television.

The Ba'th party's rise and its effort to build its own militia, the National Guard (NG, *Al-Hars al-Qawmi*), dovetailed with the fall of ICP and its PRF. In 1958, the Ba'th party had at most 300 active members and a few thousand supporters.[84] Ba'thism's core pan-Arab nationalist ideology drew the party into immediate alliance with Arif and opposition to Qasim. From 1958 to 1963, the Ba'th organized clandestinely, building ties with anti-Qasim elements in the military and recruiting underground civilian cadres. As nationalist army officers made their move in February 1963, some 5,000 Ba'thi civilian militiamen took to the street with them, engaging in open battles with ICP supporters in Baghdad's slums. An estimated eighty Ba'thists and between 300 and 5,000 communist sympathizers were killed in the two days of fighting to control Baghdad's streets.[85]

For the rest of 1963, while Arif held the ceremonial post of president, real power rested with the civilian Ba'thist Ali Salih as-Sa'di. Without a base of support in the army, the Ba'th, like the ICP, relied on its party militia. To circumvent potentially disloyal army officer corps, NG was placed under the command of twenty-eight-year-old Air Colonel Mundhir al-Wanadawi. The Revolutionary Command Council's proclamation on the day of the coup authorized NG "to annihilate anyone who disturbs the peace. The loyal sons of the people are called upon to cooperate with the authorities by informing against these criminals and exterminating them."[86]

For the next ten months, NG launched a reign of terror against suspected Qasim supporters, rounding up thousands in sports stadiums and makeshift prisons, where they faced torture and execution. Membership in NG expanded from its original hard core to include youths and workers of all stripes, and part-time volunteers clamored to obtain weapons and green armbands. From February to August 1963, NG grew nearly sevenfold to 34,000 members.[87] As Eliezer Be'eri describes succinctly, NG was a "military organization without military discipline." NG's excesses outraged the populace and, more importantly, alienated the military leaders—including the Ba'thists—who saw it as infringing on the army's domain.[88] In the spring and summer of 1963 NG units were "virtually out of control," according to British consular reports, attacking people in the streets and fighting among themselves. Deserters took their weapons with them, leading to a sense of lawlessness and anarchy surpassing that fomented by independent PRF activities.[89] In November, a rival Ba'th clique moved to depose Sa'di. NG loyalists rampaged through Baghdad but could not hold out long against the army's combined air, artillery, and armor assault. With his erstwhile allies hopelessly divided, Arif moved to consolidate his personal control, pushing out the Ba'thists. Communiqué Number One of the November coup ordered all NG members to hand in their weapons on pain of death.[90]

Both ICP's and the Ba'th's bids to create failed for similar reasons. A regime based on the singular domination of military officers could not easily share coercive power with civilian forces. No matter the ideological banner, arming the masses ran contrary to the deeply ingrained norms of military elitism. That the communist-dominated PRF would somehow replace or eclipse the nationalist army was particularly anathema.[91] Functionally, too, the militias were a disappointment. The desertions, defections, and criminality were emblematic of the regime's inability to control militia forces. A lightly armed part-time force like PRF and NG could not protect a regime from an assault by a determined conventional force. This realization came too late for Qasim. But Arif managed with little trouble to suppress the Ba'th militia and assume sole control for himself. Instead of employing a parallel paramilitary structure, Arif built a security force from within the military itself, converting his old 20th Brigade into the first Republican Guard (*Al-Hars al-Jumhurriyah*), a conventional military unit placed under the command of Arif's trusted kin.[92]

The Republican Guard's rise coincided with the fall of party militias, ending all pretenses of incorporating the masses in security matters. Rather than deliver on the promises of popular sovereignty, anti-imperialism, and democracy, the 1958 revolution brought to fruition the militarism incubated by the mandate and monarchy. Iraq's highly competitive regional environment reinforced the perception that a strong state—and a strong army—was essential. Iraq faced continual regional and geostrategic pressures in the post-1958 period. Iraq could not escape the web of external pressures that surrounded it, no matter the revolutionary inclinations of the regime. Rivalry with Nasser and the UAR went well beyond propaganda to outright military interventions in the late 1950s. In 1961, Qasim's withdrawal from the Baghdad Pact and reassertion of Iraq's claims to the Shatt al-Arab and Kuwait again nearly led to war. Arif was more cautious in his foreign involvements but was still dragged into the 1967 Arab–Israeli war, hastily dispatching a few units to the Jordanian front.[93]

Military rule also arrived nearly simultaneously with an exponential increase in the state's domestic resource base. Oil first became a major component of Iraq's national income in 1952, growing even more important with the nationalization of the Iraqi Petroleum Company in 1964.[94] Military budgets quadrupled from their 1958 base in just ten years, comprising nearly half the state budget by 1968. The newfound wealth allowed the state to expand and upgrade the technologies of coercion, including lavish spending on the officer corps. With the British monopoly on Iraq's arms purchases broken, Iraq now imported the most advanced Soviet and American jets and tanks.[95] In stark contrast to these early experiments with party militias, the Iraqi state continued to build on its initial organizational model of military centralization.

### Tribal Militias and the Kurds, 1960–1991

Even as Qasim began to disband and demobilize PRF, he simultaneously launched another experiment in violence devolution in Iraqi Kurdistan in an effort to counter Mustafa Barzani and the nationalist Kurdish Democratic Party (KDP). Officially called the National Defense Battalions (*Qiyadet Jahafel al-Difa' al-Watani*, NDB) but better known by their Kurdish moniker, *jahsh* (donkey foal), the progovernment militias were specifically design to incorporate Barzani's tribal rivals to fight in conjunction with the state. Although NDB was premised on fundamentally different ideology as PRF or NG, it confronted the same organizational challenges and limitations. As Martin Van Bruinessen writes, NDB fighters were consistently

> happy to accept the arms and pay that the government gave them, [but] their participation in the conflict continued to depend more on the dynamics of their own relations with the Barzanis . . . than on policy decisions by the central government.[96]

Not only did NDB leaders refuse orders from the central government, they also eventually came to challenge their state patron outright for control.

Despite Qasim's early displays of sympathy for the Kurdish cause, demands for substantive Kurdish regional autonomy were soon rebuffed. After returning from exile, Barzani quickly began reassembling his guerrilla forces.[97] Qasim turned to Barzani's traditional tribal rivals, the Herki and Surchi, to organize a counterforce.[98] In contrast to PRF, NDB offered no rhetoric of national or class liberation; instead it was anachronistic, reinforcing and reifying the hierarchies of clan social structure. Chieftains, landlords, and village heads were granted the title of the state's *mustashar* (consultant) in return for mobilizing their kith and kin into a paramilitary force. Funding, orders, and commands were mediated through these local notables.

From 1961 to 1970, northern Iraq was stuck in a standoff: A few thousand KDP guerrillas would cut off isolated mountain garrisons. The army responded by rushing to secure the cities of the northern plains, then mounting artillery and air barrages to push back up the mountains, where armor would bog down and become susceptible to ambushes. With supplies replenished by Iran and those abandoned or ceded by his opponent, Barzani's forces would then drive the army back to the plains, beginning the cycle anew.[99] NDB detachments numbered no more than 10,000 auxiliaries, most of whom could be relied on mainly to loot the villages of rival tribes. When faced with strong resistance, NDB militias were known simply to surrender their arms.[100]

Following the Ba'th coup of 1968, and especially after the failed peace accord of 1974, the fighting in the north intensified. Emboldened by his earlier successes and the support offered by Israel, the United States, and Iran, Barzani sought a decisive victory by reorganizing his forces into a conventional, centralized force. This strategy, however, played directly into the army's hands. Iraq's military commitment to the north expanded to some 100,000 men, including large detachments of armor and aircraft. Helped by the use of the new road network built under the auspices of the abortive peace, the army improved its ability to reinforce isolated strongholds. Rather than blindly charge a position, troops waited for massive armor, artillery, or aircraft support to obliterate the opposition. As Kenneth Pollack describes, Barzani's units "stood, fought, and were blown to bits."[101] Seeing its Kurdish proxy decimated, Iran redoubled its support, even going so far as to provide artillery cover from across the border and dispatching Iranian troops to serve with the Kurdish guerrillas. In March 1975 Iraq offered Iran concessions on the Shatt al-Arab in return for Iran's cessation of interferences in north. The shah accepted, gaining a considerable geostrategic victory.

Without Iranian support, Kurdish resistance quickly collapsed. Government forces mounted an aggressive pacification campaign, establishing a three-mile cordon sanitaire on the Iranian border and resettling some 200,000 Kurds to modern communes in the lowlands. Some Kurdish fighters were co-opted into NDB as border guards. Barzani's death in 1979 further splintered the Kurdish leadership, with Jalal Talabani launching the breakaway Patriotic Union of Kurdistan (PUK) and Barzani's son Masoud leading the rump KDP, in addition to various smaller Islamic and leftist factions.[102]

By the outbreak of the Iran–Iraq war in 1980, the Iraqi government was confident that it could divide and rule Kurdistan. The Ba'th cultivated ties with Barzani's rivals through a number of avenues, including the leadership of the various Sufi orders. Regular army garrisons were redeployed to the front, replaced by NDB forces that had grown to nearly 250,000 men.[103] The Kurdish factions tried to build alliances with the new regime in Tehran. KDP troops joined in the Iranian advance at Haj Omran in July 1983. The Ba'th sought to counterbalance by backing PUK and other smaller Kurdish factions. Yet by 1985 talks with PUK broke down, and soon both major Kurdish parties were in open alliance with Tehran. By the mid-1980s the Iraqi army controlled little beyond Kurdistan's cities.[104]

In 1987, Ali Hassan al-Majid, head of the Ba'th Party's northern bureau, began a series of operations called *al-Anfal* (Spoils of War) aimed to permanently depopulate eastern Kurdistan. Relying on seized state documents and witness interviews, researchers have produced detailed accounts this campaign. Each phase of the Anfal bore a similar tactical hallmark: First, the army conducted aerial or artillery bombardment of a village, sometimes with poison gas, to drive inhabitants to the hills. Regular infantrymen and NDB militiamen then swept the area, arresting the alleged saboteurs and sending them by lorry to detention centers. Secret police interrogated the detainees, executing those who themselves or whose families were suspected of having ties with the insurgent. The rest were deported to government concentration camps.[105]

Why did this escalation take place at such a moment and in such a form, particularly as it diverted resources from southern front? On the one hand, the ultimate motivation for violence was not the Ba'th's exclusionary, racist, or totalitarian nature. The Ba'th had previously accommodated the Kurdish presence inside Iraq, even going so far as to offer up the idea of federal status for Iraqi Kurdistan. Indicatively, Saddam did not use such heavy-handed techniques in the mid-1970s, when the Kurdish opposition was far weaker and the state far more powerful.[106] On the other hand, the meticulousness evident in the state's documentation, plus Saddam Husayn's own claim of authorship of such acts, belies the notion that the destruction was committed chaotically in the fog of war.[107] Rather, the Ba'th turned to intensive, state-centered violence because the initial reliance on clientage relationships through the *mustashar* proved insufficient to keep the northern region under the state's control in the midst of the war.

As seen in state documents, NDB was an organizational weak link, consigned to low-level responsibilities like manning roadblocks, searching for army deserters, and handing over suspected insurgents to the authorities. Militia units were rotated to prevent them from growing too close to the local community. Any sign of independence brought harsh recriminations. In Badinan, for instance, a militia leader who refused to move his forces from their home district was executed for insubordination, his body publicly mutilated, and his villages burned to the ground.[108]

The Ba'th also offered positive incentives for the *mustashar*'s participation. For each soldier enrolled in his militia, a commander was granted eighty-five *dinars* ($255) monthly to use for salary and upkeep. Because NDB service was accepted in lieu of regular enlistment, many flocked to the *mustashar* to avoid conscription. Local notables inflated their rosters to get larger government subsidies but then keep the money in return for protecting their clients from the draft. As a result, few NDB units could ever be counted on to stand at full strength or with strong motivation. The state also encouraged tribesmen to pillage the property of eliminated villages. This was typical in tribal warfare, but the Ba'th sought to imbue the custom with even more homicidal intention by denouncing PUK and KDP fighters as heretics (*kafir*) deserving annihilation.

The state's demands of its agents were often at odds with the traditions of local patronage in the Kurdish community. Cases in which individual *mustashar* colluded with the advancing KDP and PUK, or took bribes to spare specific villages were common. Some NDB battalions threatened to defect if their villages were targeted by the Iraqi army. Even a committed collaborator might balk at knowing the fate intended for many Kurdish detainees. In a 1988 meeting, Majid reportedly threatened to execute a powerful *mustashar* from Qader Karam after he questioned whether the state would uphold its offers of clemency and resettlement. The state maintained an ultimatum to Kurdish clans to "return to the national ranks" by serving in NDB units or suffer the consequences.[109]

As the Iraqi state brought to bear its bureaucracy and technology of coercion directly, the fickle NDB became dispensable. The use of chemical weapons in the 1980s had a similar effect as the airplane in the 1920s and 1930s. In the words of an Iraqi military intelligence report, gas "has caused casualties among the saboteurs, has terrified and panicked them, and has weakened their morale, forcing many to return to the national ranks."[110] An insurgency that had been growing ever stronger for three years suddenly disintegrated. Even the state's own agents could not escape the impact of this new technology. As Majid said at a Ba'th party meeting in 1988, "I told the *mustashars* that the *jahsh* might say that they liked their villages and would not leave. I said I cannot let your villages stay because I will attack them with chemical weapons. And then you and your family will die."[111] There were some nominal policies to show favor to those affiliated with the NDB, but they were limited and haphazardly enacted.[112] With such power to destroy in state hands there was no need to be discriminating. Militias became ancillary to Baghdad's goal of suppressing the Kurdish insurgency. Like NG and PRF, the agents of NDB proved erratic during crisis and were thus abandoned by their state sponsor.

Once they were created, however, NDB units could not be simply be disbanded. Rather, Kurdish leaders found ways to use their structures to their own advantage. An estimated 80,000 NDB defected to the nationalists after U.S. forces decimated the Iraqi army in 1991. In some cities, NDB commanders negotiated the surrender of militias in an effort to secure their position as local power brokers. In others, violence turned internecine, with loyalist NDB commanders holding out against advanced KDP and PUK forces. Tribal feuds and revenge killings were rampant as Saddam's army regrouped and retook much of southern Kurdistan.[113] This coda seemed to validate the predictions by Iraq's own chief of staff in the 1980s that arming Kurdish tribes would form the kernel of a new Kurdish army.[114]

### Army and Militia in the Era of High Ba'thism, 1968–1991

From its seizure of power in July 1968 until Iraq's defeat in the 1991 Gulf War, Ba'thism was at its apex. The era was characterized by two apparently contradictory trends. On one hand, there was an expansion of coercive forces, in the form of the army, the Republican Guard, and various overlapping intelligence services. On the other hand, control over these institutions came to rest in the hands of a regime composed nearly exclusively of Saddam Husayn and his kinsmen. Reliance on such a patrimonial core allowed the Ba'th power untold in Iraq's history. As Batatu observes, in Iraq Tikritis "rule through the Ba'th party, rather than the Ba'th party through the Tikritis."[115] The establishment of the Popular Army (*Al-Jaysh ash-Sha'bi*, PA) was the pinnacle of party domination and the seeming fulfillment of the espoused goal of societal transformation. PA offered the party access to the means of violence circumventing the state's bureaucratic infrastructure. From its inception of 75,000 people to its expansion during the Iran–Iraq war to nearly one million, PA promised to rival the regular army. Just like PRF, NG, and NDB, however, the militia's organizational structure and operational capacity misfit the tasks that state assigned to it. In an environment of high regional threat, this decentralized, lightly armed, and poorly trained force had to be replaced by a centralized force that could protect the rulers and the state alike.

After being outmaneuvered and overpowered by their military coconspirators in 1958 and 1963, the Ba'th clique was more determined than ever to hold on to power in 1968. Early ambitions for establishing an alternative armed force under the interior ministry or even replacing the army with a reconstituted party militia, were tabled for fear of weakening Iraq's defenses.

In addition to the customary purges of the top military echelon, the Ba'th instead installed some 3,000 political commissars to monitor military units. The commissariat was directly answerable to Saddam, then head of the party's internal security and a cousin of the leading coup-plotter, General Ahmed Hassan al-Bakr.[116]

External threats continued to bear down on the new regime. For instance, Iran—in de facto alliance with Israel—seized the opportunity of yet more mayhem in the Iraqi ranks to abrogate its concessions on the Shatt al-Arab in 1969. Iraq responded by moving troops toward Kuwait, ostensibly to defend it against Iranian aggression but practically to protect its vital access to the Gulf.[117] As Jordanian forces quelled the Palestinian uprising during the infamous "Black September" of 1970, Iraq threatened that it would use its 12,000-man contingent in Jordan—a vestige of the 1967 war—to support the Palestinian cause. Iraqi troops, however, failed to budge from the barracks. General Hardan at-Tikriti, who was made the scapegoat for failing to aid fellow Arab revolutionaries, claimed he had only acted prudently given Jordan's military superiority and the need to husband Iraq's military resources for the Kurdish and Iranian fronts.[118] At the surprise outbreak of the October 1973 Arab–Israeli war, Iraq rushed an expeditionary force to the Syrian front. Already suffering from a ten-day nonstop journey without adequate trucks and tank-transporters and hampered by a lack of coordination with Syrian forces, Iraq lost 480 men, 111 tanks, and twenty-six aircraft before withdrawing with equal haste.[119]

In response to the apparent shortcomings in the army's performance, the 1974 Ba'th Party congress announced a two-pronged reform strategy. Oil windfall was funneled into force modernization and expansion, particularly in critical areas of logistics, antiaircraft defense, and reconnaissance. Conscription was enforced with greater alacrity, doubling the army's size to 240,000 men. Iraq became one of the world's leading arms importers, acquiring 1,600 Soviet tanks (including advanced T-72s), Brazilian armored troop carriers, French Mirage fighters, Italian frigates, antiaircraft missiles and batteries, and a host of other advanced weaponry.[120] Iraq jump-started its nuclear weapons program with the purchase of a French-made nuclear reactor and expanded its chemical weapons capability with the help of West German firms.[121] At the same time, the Ba'th military commissariat strengthened its hold over the institutions of coercion. Careful recruitment through the Tikriti cabal ensured that only those from selected clans gained admission to the military academies or senior commands. All non-Ba'thi political activity was banned within the ranks.[122]

Alongside these efforts of political inoculation, by the mid-1970s the Ba'th had also created PA as a parallel force structure to serve as the party's counterweight to the army. This mobilization program was also deemed necessary to counter Iran and Turkey's larger population bases while avoiding a drain on the economy.[123] As new recruits flocked to the Ba'th party, full-party membership was removed as a requisite for joining PA. The ranks swelled from 75,000 to over 250,000 by 1980. As if to emphasize the significance of this new party organ, Saddam Husayn was named the PA's field marshal in 1976.[124]

Unlike PRF, the new militia functioned entirely outside the army's purview. The smallest PA unit consisted of fifteen armed members under the leadership of a trusted local Ba'th cadre. While nominally supposed to respect the orders of ranking army officers, the chain of command went through the political commissars up to the Ba'th party itself, not the army battalion or division levels.[125] PA used Cuban advisors to provide light arms training, coupled with heavy doses of political education. Members kept their personal weapons at home to be ready in case of emergency.[126]

Beside to its military mission, PA was an instrument of ideological conversion, building Iraqis into a "fighting people" (ash-sha'ab al-muqatila). The 1977 first edition of PA's glossy, full-color eponymous official magazine bears the striking image of a woman wearing the PA's uniform striding with the Iraqi flag, a rifle slung over her back, flanked by a handful of similarly armed men. Women's empowerment was a constant theme in the magazine.[127] Indeed, the first edition of al-Jaysh ash-Sha'bi in 1977 is replete with articles comparing PA to militia groups in China, Algeria, and Palestine; pieces on the Ba'th party's social reform and on inter-Arab cooperation; and an extended analysis of the SALT-II negotiations, indicating far more interest in ideological than military issues.[128]

As Taha Yasin Ramadan, the first PA commander, states, the Iran–Iraq War of 1980 was the great test of the militia-based model.[129] Some 70,000 Iraqi troops forded the Shatt al-Arab in September 1980, following an invasion plan based largely on a colonial British contingency to seize the Abadan oil fields. Saddam hoped to gain enough of a foothold in Iranian territory to force the beleaguered Iranian regime to relinquish its claims to the Shatt al-Arab and cease inciting Iraq's Shi'i population to rebellion. The offensive quickly bogged down in Iran's southern marshes. As early as November 1979, PA units had to be shifted from the rear to reinforce the front line.[130]

In combat with Iranian forces, Pollack describes, PA proved "incapable of standing up to the Iranians and were the favorite target of Iranian assaults. As a result, the Iranians usually were able to push through the gaps or around the flanks of Iraqi defensive lines."[131] When Saddam authorized his commanders to undertake a strategic withdrawal back to the border in spring 1982, the regular army was able to coordinate aircraft and artillery fire to cover its retreat, but the poorly trained and ill-equipped PA crumbled, with thousands simply surrendering. In Saddam's judgment, PA had become a "burden to the regular army because of the enemy's ability to appear in the rear." The army high command resented the PA as a bunch of unfit amateurs.[132]

The PA's separate command structure and lack of military training was an obstacle to coordination between it and the regular army. By 1980 PA began training with heavy weapons. By 1981 army officers had assumed command of PA units, and the entire brigade structure was subordinate within the army's divisional hierarchy.[133] PA publications no longer hosted theoretical discussions of Maoist doctrine or geopolitical affairs but instead offered crude anti-Persian and anti-Semitic propaganda interspersed with sections devoted to practical "military lessons" (*ad-dirasat al-'askariyya*) and "military culture" (*ath-thaqafa al-'askariyya*), including the various technical terms for armored vehicles, missiles, and other weapons, with a sidebar explicitly urging all PA members to observe military orders In the drive to emphasize the value of force integration, a technical piece discussed the theory of combined air and armor operations, unironically using Israel as an example.[134]

As the war dragged on, the state began to turn away from militia entirely. Inducting students, women, pensioners, and non-Ba'thists diluted PA's ideological commitment and esprit de corps. Whereas tens of thousands had flocked to join in the late 1970s, desertion from what was redubbed the "Un-Popular Army" became rampant, forcing PA to resort to raiding Baghdad's working-class districts for forced conscripts.[135] PA proved too great a military liability. Its forces had to be reequipped, reorganized, and subordinated within Iraq military command hierarchy. By the war's end in 1988, PA numbered nearly one million people but had become an essentially defunct apparatus, with no real responsibilities.[136]

Instead of the militias, the problems of military control and efficacy were solved by redoubling efforts to build up the Republican Guard. In 1979, the

Republican Guard was little but the rump of the 20th Brigade, placed under the command of trusted officers from Tikrit. By 1980, however, it had been expanded and dispatched to the brutal urban warfare in Khoramshahr. The Republican Guard grew to five full brigades, with Tikritis comprising the upper-level officers but drawing on the best fighters regardless of ethnicity or sectarian background to fill in the lower levels. As a result, the Republican Guard was transformed from a praetorian guard garrisoning Baghdad into the spearhead of Iraq's efforts at the front, beating back Iran's advances in the south and forcing Iran to accept a cease-fire in 1988. Rather than move to violence devolution, innovation within the repertoire of the centralized and conventional military allowed the Ba'th to solve the problem of controlling the army without risking state security.[137]

## Neotribalism and State Frailty, 1988–2003

By the end of the Iran–Iraq War it was apparent that the Ba'th's hold over Iraqi society was weakening, necessitating a turn to new institutions. In the midst of Iran's attempt to reach Basra, the capital of the south, Arab tribes spontaneously mobilized to protect the city, declaring their hostility to Persian invaders and loyalty to Iraq. These actions provided a glimpse of the untapped power held by tribal institutions.[138] After defeat at American hands in 1991 and the subsequent rebellions, Saddam began to tap into tribal networks to defend his hold on power in earnest. Of course, the nucleus of the Ba'th since the mid-1960s had always been patrimonial, but this remained sub rosa in the early decades of Ba'th rule. The first Ba'th communiqué of 1968 equated tribalism to feudalism, and in 1976 tribal and regional surnames were banned. In the 1990s, however, the state began to privilege of primordial tribal identity overtly instead of bureaucratic forms of allegiance. In place of totalitarian aspirations, Ba'thist Iraq degenerated to a patrimonial, quasi-sultanistic regime.[139]

Immediately after the failure of the March 1991 uprising in the south, delegations of tribal sheikhs were honored at the presidential palace. Tribal rituals once disparaged as atavistic—war dances, oaths (baya'), and eulogies—gained prominence in the official media. As with the Kurdish NDB, Saddam endeavored to elevate new and pliant sheikhs. Tribal leaders were obliged to be loyal to Saddam and encouraged to provide adjudication under tribal law (including the reinstatement of honor killings and collective responsibility), levy taxes, and ensure security in their territory. In return, the state granted the sheikhs land, rations, and even diplomatic passports. Saddam himself became the sheikh of sheikhs, and the Ba'th party the tribe of tribes. Where police protection had broken down along with other public services in the 1990s, the citizenry turned to tribal heads for protection.[140]

Tribal fealty became the primary basis for recruitment into Republican Guard and intelligence branches. It also provided the backbone for the newly established *Fedayee Saddam* (Militants of Saddam, FS), a militia force of 15,000 to 20,000 men under the command of Saddam's younger son, Qusay. Tribes received rifles, grenade launchers, mortars, and even howitzers from the state. When a second insurrection seemed imminent in August 1992, sheikhs cabled Saddam declaring that they would "remain his men in times and crisis . . . their guns were at the ready."[141] After American air strikes on southern Iraq in December 1998, armed tribesmen in civilian clothing were seen patrolling key installations around the capital.[142]

This violence devolution corroded whatever bureaucratic structures and power remained in Iraq. Police, judges, and other civil servants were subject to intimidation or threats as tribes attempted to expand their authority. In the fall of 1991, 266 people were killed in a tribal land dispute, prompting an official Ba'th newspaper to complain that "tribes were given weapons to fight the United States . . . not to fight among themselves." In western Iraq, tribes astride the Amman–Baghdad highway took to hijacking and smuggling.[143] In effort to curb the independent use of force and supplanting of the state's civil jurisdiction, in 1997 Ba'th Regional Command Council forbade the application of tribal legal principles against government officials.

Neotribalism was singularly deleterious to the Iraqi army, which saw rampant shortages in both men and material. Even Republican Guard units were forced to accept older equipment to replace what had been destroyed in 1991. As tension with the United States escalated after 2001, Saddam's hopes hinged on stymieing the American advance through asymmetric warfare. He secreted thousands of arms caches around the country in the belief that the Iraqi masses would rise up to defend him. In fact, only the Republican Guard, special Republican Guard, and a few thousand dedicated FS eventually took up arms.[144]

Though useful in defending the regime from coups, conspiracies, and popular uprisings, neotribalism ultimately added to Iraq's vulnerability by siphoning power from the centralized, formal institutions of coercion. Of course, in both 1991 and 2003, the United States held such dominance in men and material that chances of Iraq's victory were slim. But the Iraqi military performed even worse than anticipated due to the impact of neotribalism, leaving Iraq even more susceptible.

## CONCLUSION: VIOLENCE DEVOLUTION IN THE NEW IRAQ

The American invasion of Iraq in April 2003 precipitated no less than a revolutionary upheaval and breakdown of a state already gutted by decades of sanctions and neotribal policies. Even before American troops reached Baghdad, gangs loyal to the young Shi'i cleric Muqtada as-Sadr seized police stations and weapons, redubbing the Shi'i slum districts of eastern Baghdad as Sadr City. Abu Hatim's Iraqi Hizbollah militia gained control in Amara and the southern marshes, a traditional redoubt of anti-Ba'th insurgents.[145] Most of the major exile parties that returned with U.S. forces, including KDP, PUK, the Da'wa Party, the Supreme Council for Islamic Revolution in Iraq (SCIRI), the Iraqi National Congress, and the Iraqi National Accord, also brought their own party militia forces, totaling between 60,000 and 100,000 men.

The insufficient size of the initial American invasion force and the decision to disband the Iraqi army in May 2003 left the Iraqi state with only a tiny fraction of its previous coercive potential. In the absence of the army or police and with looting rampant, local elites commanding nonstate forces moved to fill the gaps. In July 2003, Sadr announced the formation of the Mahdi Army (*Jaysh al-Mahdi*, JAM), combining nationalist sentiments opposed to the U.S. occupation, a spiritual revival aimed to seize authority in the Shi'i clerical hierarchy, and a classic extortion racket that "taxed" neighborhoods in return for providing protection. Other clerics and notables maintained their own armed corteges, often recruited from tribal followers and funded through the distribution of tithe funds. When Sadr's forces surrounded the office of Grand Ayatollah Ali Sistani in Najaf demanding that he cede his authority or leave Iraq, the senior cleric called in 1,500 armed tribesmen from the rural hinterlands to repel the rabble and restore order.[146]

In the Sunni heartland west and north of Baghdad, a similar combination of political and religious grievances and economic opportunism spurred the emergence of a separate insurgent front. Armed groups took to kidnapping and property seizures. With the aid of foreign al-Qaeda infiltrators, militants launched a string of devastating suicide attacks against the new Iraqi leadership and American troops.[147] Fearful of being undermined by the burgeoning criminal-militant nexus, some local Sunni leaders approached American authority with an offer to support the occupation in return for guarantees of autonomy and immunity from what they perceived as a hostile Shi'i–Kurdish central government. American military commanders favored such an arrangement, but civilian officials vetoed the proposal for fear that authorizing armed nonstate actors would undercut the civil law.[148]

In April 2004, the coincidental uprisings by Sunni insurgents in Fallujah and JAM forces in the south suggested the emergence of the first truly cross-sectarian resistance movement.[149] The Americans responded with a strategy of divide-and-rule. In Fallujah, U.S. Marines struck a deal with insurgents to place the city under the control of a newly constituted brigade commanded by a former Republic Guard commander. Both the civilian Coalition Provisional Authority (CPA) and the Iraqi defense ministry denounced the creation of this so-called Fallujah Brigade as inimical to Iraqi sovereignty. Most elements of the brigade dissolved or defected after a few weeks, returning Fallujah to insurgent control and necessitating a second assault on the city in November. In the meantime, however, the cease-fire allowed the United States to concentrate on suppressing JAM in the south. Sadr held out in Najaf for two months until Sistani brokered a truce to bring the upstart JAM into the fold as a political party.[150]

As the British had in the 1920s, it was soon clear that U.S. officials badly underestimated the amount of blood and treasure required to rebuild Iraq. In February 2004, CPA began intensive efforts to demobilize militias, decreeing that all armed groups would have to submit to integration under the new Iraqi army. Still, only minimal funding was allocated to help pension off or transition these armed men to other forms of gainful employment. Iraq's interim defense minister refused to induct Shi'i militiamen who had fought for Iran and sought instead to reinstate Sunni ex-Ba'thists. Moreover, the newly empowered Iraqi political parties had little interest in surrendering their respective military forces given the worsening security situation.[151]

The formal resumption of Iraq sovereignty in June 2004 and installation of a Shi'i-led government in 2005 did not end the pathologies of the occupation or lead to any significant enhancement of state power. Ordinary citizens organized their own armed retinues or sought out the protection of existing militia groups. While the Iraqi army and defense ministry remained a stronghold of Sunni control, newly appointed Interior Minister Bayan Jabr of SCIRI quickly began to integrate his party's militia into the national police.[152] Iraq's security forces became what Ahmed Hashim called "official ethno-sectarian militias in uniform," cooperating with nonstate actors in the abduction, torture, and extrajudicial killings.[153] After Sadr joined the ruling coalition in December

2005, his independent JAM forces were essentially deputized by the state to become primary security providers in Sadr City and other areas of the south. By 2006, Baghdad's ethnically mixed neighborhoods had become battlegrounds in a Sunni–Shi'i civil war.

While U.S. officials deplored the proliferation of government-backed militias and vigilantes and actively tried to block the predominantly Shi'i Iraqi police and its militia adjuncts from entering Sunni neighborhoods, in western Iraq the United States actually encouraged the proliferation of armed nonstate actors in the form of the Sunni tribal Awakening (*Sahwa*) movement.[154] With the degradation of public security, many communities had established informal tribal and neighborhood guards, ostensibly for purposes of self-defense but often by accepting the "protection" of insurgents. American field commanders realized that buying the loyalty of these tribes was cheaper and more effective than fighting them, especially considering the still dysfunctional condition of the Iraqi police and army. Defense Minister Sa'adon ad-Dulaymi, himself the scion of one of Iraq's largest tribes, funneled weapons and money to help set up these tribal paramilitaries.[155]

Both American and Iraqi officials saw the arming of Sunni groups as providing a counterbalance to the Shi'i-dominated central government. Among the first Sunni leaders to make an alliance with the United States was Abd as-Sattar ar-Rishawi (Abu Risha), a sheikh of the Dulaymi tribe from Ramadi. He had helped al-Qaeda in the first years of the occupation but grew wary of the movement's puritanical ideology and attempts to displace tribal leadership. In return for setting up a tribal militia to suppress insurgent in his area, the United States offered increased reconstruction aid and permitted the reassertion of tribal law and dominion. Tribal leaders became mediators between state and the people.[156]

The decision to introduce a surge of 40,000 additional American troops in 2007 coupled with the expansion of the Awakening movement to Babil, Nineveh, Salah ad-Din, Tammim, Diyala, and Baghdad provinces brought dramatic improvements in stability to regions of Iraq that had been virtually lawless in 2006. By the end of 2007, an estimated 75,000 to 100,000 men—almost all Sunnis— had joined the militias. U.S. forces tried to maintain control by vetting and collecting biometric measures of all militia members. They set up a payment system of $300 per month, handing over control of numerous neighborhoods and towns to tribal sheikhs.[157]

Still, the gains in security and stability came, as Adeed Dawisha notes, "not because of the state, but in spite of it."[158] In Baghdad alone there were seventeen separate militia councils. In western Iraq, tribal authority splintered after Rishawi's assassination in September 2007, leading to renewed intertribal conflict among the militias. In Babil, many militia fighters were believed to be former members of al-Qaeda, leading to suspicions that the entire force had been infiltrated by insurgents. In Diyala, Sunni militias seemed to merge with local crime syndicates.[159] Similar to the *kamra* uprising in Indonesia, Sunni militiamen demanded to be incorporated into the security services. The SCIRI-dominated national police arrested various militia leaders, deepening the distrust between Sunni fighters and the government.[160]

Prime Minister Nouri al-Maliki was suspicious of the possibility that the United States would maintain bilateral relationships with armed Sunni factions. As an advisor to the prime minister presciently complained, "We have enough militias in Iraq that we are struggling to solve the problem. Why are we creating new ones?"[161] It was not just Sunni militias that resisted central authority. In the north, there was increasing tension as KDP and PUK *peshmerga* encroached on the so-called blue line in effort to gain control over the oil-rich areas around Kirkuk.[162] In the south, defectors from JAM continued their periodic bouts with American and Iraqi security forces.[163]

The Iraqi army and police remained too weak to confront these challenges unassisted, despite increased American effort on training. Iraqi forces crumbled in April 2008 in the fight with JAM splinter groups in Basra and had to be rescued by U.S. reinforcements and air support. American assessments the following year continued to report only slow progress in building up the Iraqi armed forces. Less than a quarter of Iraq's planned 200,000-man security forces were deemed capable of planning, executing, and sustaining operations without U.S. support in 2009. In another echo of the mandate era, Iraqis accused the United States of blocking access to advanced aircraft and other weaponry to hinder the reestablishment of a formidable Iraqi army and ensure Iraq's long-term dependency.[164]

Despite his espousal of political centralization and the rule of law, Maliki responded to the failings of the state security forces by setting up a parallel force, essentially buying the services of one militia to turn against another. During the suppression of the April 2008 JAM uprising, Maliki turned to southern tribes for help in combating the "criminal gangs." In summer and fall 2008, he backed the formation of tribal councils in the southern provinces of Basra,

Dhi Qar, Wassit, Maysan, and Muthana provinces, declaring his respect for tribal autonomy and offering privileged access to government positions and funds to some of the country's largest tribal confederations, like the Dulaymi and Aniyza. Maliki's erstwhile parliamentary allies became alarmed that the prime minister had found a counterweight to their own armed wings, especially after Maliki received strong support in the December 2008 provincial elections.[165] During the March 2010 parliamentary election, Maliki further benefitted from the fragmentation of the Sunni Awakening movement. Most observers deemed the March election as success because there were "merely" sixteen major bombings during that month (a low figure by the standards of the new Iraq) and only minor instances of fraud and other irregularities. The success of former Prime Minister Iyyad Allawi, who received considerable backing from Sunni Arabs and secularists, was seen as sign of Iraq's consolidating democracy. Still, with both incumbent and challenger maintaining access to armed militias and the results still in dispute, a resurgence of internecine violence remains a distinct possibility.

The use of tribes and other militias in Iraq is in many ways reminiscent of the Ottoman technique of violence devolution, recruiting and isolating non-state actors to serve as the ruler's proxies. Such a turn represents a marked departure from the Iraqi state's continuous effort since the 1920s to amass control over the use of force. This trajectory was launched as postcolonial elites used a British legacy army to dominate Iraqi territory and wrest power from both the colonial overlords and embedded social actors like the tribal and religious leadership. Norms of military elitism and the necessities of external defense locked in this highly centralized, bureaucratic, and technology-intensive military model. Even when the Ba'th sought to devolve violence, the pressures of regional competition forced a return to the path of monopolizing violence.

The danger of Iraq's internal disintegration may have lessened since 2005 and 2006 (much less 1933) but remain considerable. Iraq today is not the artifice that it was when the British created it. As Sami Zubaida points out,

> In Iraq (as in many other countries) it is the state that made the nation. . . . Economic and fiscal administration, education, employment, military conscription, the media and social and cultural organization—all make the nation a fact or "facticity" compelling on the cognition and imagination of its members.[166]

These institutions have bound Iraq's polity together by collective interest if not by collective identity. The bid to carve out a separate "Shia-stan" in southern

Iraq has proven moribund. While the Kurds seek extensive autonomy, the potentially independent state of Kurdistan would be unviable economically and strategically. Political competition revolves around control over the state, not its negation.[167]

With the withdrawal of most U.S. forces in 2010, however, external threats loom largely unnoticed—at least by the Americans. Despite the crucial role in national defense, Iraq's navy and air force are basically afterthoughts in the U.S. plan for military reform.[168] While Iraq's neighbors may not have expressed an interest in dismembering the country, they still resort to military means as Iraq's turmoil continues to spill over their border. Turkey has launched incursions into northern Iraq in pursuit of Kurdish separatists and continues to lend support for Iraq's Turkomen minority. Iraqi leaders of all stripes deplored these violations of Iraqi sovereignty, but only U.S. intervention prevented escalation that could lead to a Turkish invasion of northern Iraq.[169]

Maliki has drawn noticeably closer to Tehran, but even here relations are volatile. In December 2009, for instance, Iranian troops seized a portion of the disputed Fakka oil field.[170] While the incident was resolved peacefully, it demonstrated that international borders remain contentious and that coercion is still an integral element to interstate relations. According to the U.S. military, Iran continued to support JAM breakaway factions involved in attacks on rival Shi'is.[171] Moreover, rapprochement with Iran complicated Iraq's domestic politics and jeopardizes its position in the Arab world. Many Sunnis saw Tehran as Iraq's mortal enemy and accused Shi'i politicians of betraying Iraq's Arab heritage in favor of their sectarian brotherhood with the Islamic Republic. In the wider Arab world, Saudi Arabia, Jordan, and Egypt, among others, expressed concern about the nefarious expansion of an Iranian-backed "Shi'i Crescent." Unsurprisingly, many of Iraq's neighbors have been accused of supporting Sunni militants to counter the presumed Shi'i ascendance.

As currently envisioned, the Iraqi army is unsuited to fulfill its historical mission of deterring Iraq's neighbors and preserving the state's domestic supremacy. Warned one senior Iraqi army officer, the collection of gendarmerie and militias in the new Iraqi army may be successful at counterinsurgency, but it is "a lame horse in the competition with neighboring states."[172] Additionally, Iraq's military culture militates against simply granting military rank and insignias to undisciplined, militia-based forces. Defense ministry officials, often holdovers from the old regime, question the loyalty of those who sided with

Iran in the 1980s and refuse to treat Shi'i and Kurdish irregulars as comparable to professional soldiers.

Iraq today has in many ways reverted to its origins, struggling to construct a military force merely adequate for domestic suppression. The presence of U.S. forces temporarily suspended the need for an externally oriented army. Still, the Middle East remains a region of fierce competition, where the militarily strong dominate the militarily weak and states exploit the distress of their neighbors. If Iraq does not regain its military stature, it may well endure a fate similar to Lebanon, where a precarious intercommunal peace is enforced under foreign hegemony. In this scenario, Iraq's diminished sovereignty will rest at the mercy of its meddling neighbors and the machinations of geopolitics. Alternatively, Iraq might resume its course of military development, attempting to reconstruct the immensely powerful coercive apparatus that held domestic opposition in check and foreign enemies at bay. Such a process will probably entail yet more flagrant violence of the type that has typified Iraq's earlier history. In any future scenario, the same historical and international forces that have defined Iraq's trajectory of state formation and military development since the 1920s will continue to impinge as leaders try to reshape state institutions in the twenty-first century.

# 4 IRAN

DESPITE A HISTORICAL LINEAGE dating back two and half millennia, similar challenges of consolidating state power prevailed in Iran as in Iraq and Indonesia's colonially constructed edifices. Persian-speaking Shi'is made up a slim majority, while Kurds, Turks, Arabs, Baluchs, and other ethno-sectarian groups had long historical roots within the imperial domain of the shahs.[1] Stability and control demanded continuous efforts to recruit, restrain, and negotiate with tributaries and satraps. Beginning as early as the 1730s, Iranian leaders sought to import Western military technologies and organizational techniques, replacing this feudal patronage system with a more centralized state apparatus.[2] The efforts continued under the Qajars in the nineteenth century and the Pahlavis in the twentieth century, with the aim both to suppress domestic opposition and to improve Iran's standing in a hostile and predatory international environment.

Ayatollah Ruhollah Khomeini and the new revolutionary regime came to power in 1979 with dramatically different notions about the nature of state–society relations and how to organize coercion. Just as in Indonesia, a revolution premised on harnessing mass protests envisioned a devolved, militia-based military. Yet attempting to change the trajectory of military development left Iran profoundly vulnerable to its neighbors. Within two years, in the midst of the Iraqi invasion and ongoing struggle with the leftist guerrilla and ethnic separatists, Khomeini and the Islamic Republic had begun to return to the model of a centralized, professional army.

Iran is therefore a crucial case for demonstrating the determinative impact of colonial legacies and external threat on choices about military centralization or decentralization.[3] This chapter traces the way successive Iranian regimes have sought or abjured the monopoly over the use of force. The first section examines the monarchical period, when Iran undertook protracted efforts to adopt Western military technology and organizational forms. As in similar periods of Chinese, Ottoman, and Japanese imperial history, what was initially conceived as a purely military reform had larger economic, political, and cultural ramifications.[4] The second section examines the revolutionary period and the struggle to shift toward a decentralized militia model. The emergence of the Iranian Revolutionary Guard Corps (*Sepah-e Pasdaran-e Enqelab-e Eslami*, IRGC), the various local revolutionary *komitehs* (committees), and the Basij forces embodied the new regime's confidence in popular mobilization strategies and its eschewal of conventional military structures. Still, like most postrevolutionary states, Iran was paradoxically both extremely threatening to its neighbors, because of its announced goal of exporting the revolution, and extremely vulnerable due to the fragmentation of its military forces.[5] Iraq's invasion in September 1980 and the cataclysmic eight-year Iran–Iraq War precipitated a return to military centralization, as the former imperial forces (*Artesh*) were rehabilitated and IRGC reconstituted to mirror Artesh's organizational format. The third section examines the ongoing process of military reform in the 1990s and 2000s, particularly the ascent of IRGC as the premier military branch. Even as it retained links to its revolutionary heritage of popular mobilization, the Islamic Republic has adopted a conventional force structure that circumscribes the role of nonstate violence wielders.

## DEFENSIVE MODERNIZATION, 1804–1978

Iran entered the twentieth century with a basically feudal system of rule. Tribal leaders and landed nobles supplied the shah with levies in return for maintaining hereditary rights of tax collection and rudimentary supervision of law and order.[6] Large tribal confederations like the Bakhtiari, Khamseh, and Boir Ahmad had been encouraged by the state in the previous centuries to consolidate; their leaders held aristocratic titles and served as mediators of royal authority. In the Zagros Mountains, for instance, the Qashqai confederation functioned as a state within a state, with 5,000 tribesmen under the command of an *ilkhan* (chieftain) who claimed royal appointment and noble lineage. A British observer remarked that the government

> either acknowledges or is unable to oppose [the *ilkhan*'s] appointment and sometimes face-savingly grants them a mandate to keep the peace in their ter-

ritory, a responsibility it cannot itself undertake. . . . Taxes are not paid to the government but tribute is rendered to the khans. Tribesmen signify their support of the *ilkhani* by the offering of "presents" which are really in the nature of a voluntary tax.[7]

In the cities, *lutis*—armed young hooligans—served as shock troops for local political and clerical elites in controlling neighborhoods. Like the *jago* in Indonesia, connotations of virility and social banditry surround the mythology of the *luti*. In practice, however, they were as likely to be predatory thugs, mere club wielders (*chomaqdars*), than champions of the poor.[8]

The need to confront Russia, Britain, and the Ottomans spurred continual interest in importing Western military and administrative models. Fatih Ali Shah (1797–1834) sought to mimic the Ottoman's military reforms, bringing British and French military advisors to reorganize and train the army in the vain hope of exploiting Russia's weakness during the Napoleonic war. The reign of Nasser al-Din Shah (1848–1896) saw more attempts to emulate the Ottomans. Again, foreign experts were summoned, conscription reformed, and new logistical systems implemented to guarantee troops sufficient rations and wages. Accompanying these military changes, new administrative offices and bureaucracies were established. The first modern schools opened, teaching science, mathematics, and foreign language. By the 1870s, an indigenous arms industry, military hospitals, and staff colleges were formed, and a police force was introduced in Tehran. The shah even approached the United States about purchasing a naval fleet to contest British hegemony in the Persian Gulf, albeit unsuccessfully. As Defense Minister Mirza Husayn explained, the program aimed for

> an army, which by virtue not only of its bravery, its endurance both physical and spiritual, its obedience, but also by virtue of its new science and new invented arms could be considered one of the greatest armies in the world.[9]

The results of these reforms were consistently disappointing, however. Iran succumbed in consecutive wars with Russia in the Caucasus (1804–1813 and 1826–1828) and the British in Afghanistan (1856–1857), each time losing territory and falling further behind its international rivals.

The dictates of state-led modernization clashed with the Qajar dynasty's tendencies toward patrimonialism. On one hand, the old Qajar nobility serving as provincial governors, ministers of court, or military officers treated their posts as prebendal appointments. They resisted efforts to raise revenue or field an army that might shift the internal balance of power. Embezzlement remained endemic, leading soldiers to mutiny, desertion, and banditry. In the continuing absence of an effective army, the government was forced to rely on provincial governors to maintain an increasingly precarious domestic security using village guards, urban gangs, or tribal militias. Tribal leaders resented impingements on their prerogative to extort from the local population and allied with noble courtiers to limit the expansion of the central government. In 1877, the shah acceded to the nobles' demands that local military commanders serve under provincial control, effectively undercutting the entire logic of military centralization.

On the other hand, reform threatened not only the privileges of the old aristocracy but also the autocratic prerogatives of Nasser al-Din himself. Several of the most prominent reformist ministers were suspected of having designs on the throne and eventually were deposed in palace conspiracies.[10] To finance his notoriously profligate spending, the shah turned increasingly to concessionary agreements with European powers, alienating the right to collect duties and taxes on tobacco, postage, and (most importantly for the future) oil.[11] This corrosion of Iranian sovereignty became most blatant in 1870, when Nasser al-Din invited Russian officers to set up a special Cossack cavalry brigade to serve as his personal bodyguard.[12]

During the Constitutional Revolution of 1905 to 1911, the newly established Iranian parliament (*majles*) again tried to confront the power of embedded nonstate actors and build the state's core coercive and administrative capabilities. A coalition of liberal merchants and clerics led the movement to place constitutional checks on royal power. Still, the new constitutional government remained hostage to the intermittent loyalties of its own military arm. In Tehran, Bakhtiari tribesmen allied with the constitutionalists seized the capital to block a Cossack-led countercoup. Bakhtiari tribal leaders were indeed prominent ministers in the new government's cabinet. In the provinces, however, these same tribal leaders embedded themselves as warlords, taxing the population at will and receiving subsidies from the British for protecting the Anglo-Persian Oil Company's installations in the southwest.[13] In Tabriz, revolutionary leaders appealed to the *luti* ideals of honor and masculinity to draw these urban toughs into a communard-style defense against counterrevolutionary forces. The *luti*, however, refused to disarm following the battle and continued to run rampant through the city.[14]

In 1910 the second parliament launched reform of the interior ministry and invited Swedish officers to help train a new gendarmerie corps. This domestic security service quickly proved the most reliable and effective unit in the government's arsenal for collecting taxes and combating brigandage. Some merchants even began volunteering funds to pay for its upkeep. By 1913 the gendarmes numbered 6,000 troops, with three regiments in Tehran and one in Shiraz.[15]

Still, with the constitutionalists themselves badly divided, hopes for a significant enhancement in state coercive capacity remained largely unfulfilled. The old Qajar elite and conservative clerics saw the reform movement as undermining traditional values and their status within Iranian society. Figures like Qavam al-Mulk, the chief of the Khamseh tribal confederation and sometime governor of Fars, continued to resist government troops that threatened his lucrative role providing night watchmen on provincial roads.[16] Russia and Britain took advantage of Iran's weakness to extend their respective spheres of influence over the north and south of the country. Britain deepened its alliance with the Arab tribes in Khuzestan, supporting Sheikh Khazal's claim to local suzerainty and subsidized him directly from the oil concession. Russian forces took control of Azerbaijan. During World War I, despite Iran's declaration of neutrality, Russia took control of the Cossack brigades and seized the capital itself, while Britain entered the crucial ports on the Persian Gulf. For their part, Ottoman and German agents sought to incite the Qashqai and Kurds to revolt. Following the war, Britain tried to reestablish a functioning central authority by offering aid and assistance to expand the gendarmerie and reform the ministries, but at the cost of sacrificing any semblance of Iranian sovereignty.[17]

When Reza Khan emerged, first as a military dictator in 1921 and then as shah in 1926, he took command of what Ervand Abrahamian dubs "a classic 'failed state.'" The regime was paralyzed by internal fissures, the government ministries had scant presence beyond the capital, and Iranian territory was divided between various foreign occupiers, warlords, and rebels.[18] Yet, in a matter of two decades, Reza was able to realize many of the goals set by the nineteenth century reformists, most importantly, establishing a centralized military force. Certainly, part of this success was due to Reza's shrewdness, disdain for dissent, and willingness to use violence. Yet earlier shahs had many of the same qualities. What allowed Reza to succeed was the dramatic transformation of the global system following World War I, which provided a unique opportunity to expand state power.

Nearly exhausted by the burdens of upholding its empire, Britain initially encouraged Reza's rise from an ambitious Cossack colonel to commander in chief of the armed forces in 1921. Reza appeared to the British sufficiently anticommunist to hold the country together in face of continued Soviet occupation in Azerbaijan, a self-proclaimed socialist republic in Gilan, and ubiquitous tribal unrest.[19] On his promotion, however, Reza surprised his erstwhile backer by signing a treaty of friendship with the Soviets, gaining back Azerbaijan and undercutting the Gilan uprising. This proved to be the first of his major successes in asserting central authority.[20]

In his early years in power, Reza engaged in the divide-and-rule strategies typical of his predecessors. The tribes had more manpower and better armaments than the government's meager 8,000 gendarmes and 8,000 Cossack troops. Prominent tribal leaders who supported Reza, such as Dust Mohammed of the Baluch and Sardar Asad of the Bakhtiari, were rewarded with appointments as provincial governors or parliamentary deputies. Reza recruited Kurdish tribesmen in Mashhad to block a coup attempt by rival army officers. While Britain relinquished its sponsorship of the tribes in favor of a direct alliance with Tehran, Reza merely waited for an opportunity to destroy each of those tribes one by one. Government troops moved to subdue restive groups in the south and west. Chiefs were held captive in Tehran to ensure the compliance of their followers. By the decade's end, even the Bakhtiari saw their leaders arrested or executed, their militias disarmed, and their traditional concessionary rights to land and oil revenue appropriated by the central government.[21]

Gradually, Reza transcended the need to co-opt nonstate actors by centralizing coercive power in state hands, dissolving independent military units, and creating a unified standing army. In part, Reza was concerned about the emergence of rivals from within the officer corps. Positions of high command were restricted to colleagues from the Cossack brigades. The gendarmerie were transferred to the war ministry and merged with the Cossack brigade, creating a unified five-division army, totaling 40,000 to 50,000 men. A new national police force was established to take over many of the functions of the gendarmerie, pairing a Tehran-based regular officer with locally based troops to serve as village or road guards.[22]

In a larger sense, though, Reza concurred with Iranian nationalist sentiment in seeing tribal leaders, *lutis*, and other nonstate actors as social vestiges as threats to the state and obstacles to modernization.[23] In 1925, a new conscription system was adopted, requiring two years in active duty and four in the reserves. Military training was viewed as an instrument for dissolving allegiances to clans or ethnic groups and fashioning a new Iranian citizen. Though initially limited to Tehran and its neighboring provinces, conscription rosters had been expanded to cover the entire country by 1929. The military reached 80,000 men by 1930 (plus 12,000 in the national police), 105,000 by 1937, and 126,000 by 1941.

More than mere manpower, the armed forces also acquired new force-multiplying technologies. In 1928, Iranian officers were dispatched to the Soviet Union for flight training. Within six years Iran had over 145 British-, French-, German-, and Soviet-built planes. Following the example of the British in Iraq, planes were critical in the suppression of tribal revolts in the southwest. New gunboats, purchased from Italy in 1932, attacked smugglers and rebels along the Shatt al-Arab frontier. Emphasis on the improving officer training followed this advanced technology, as new schools and military academies were founded and junior officers sent to France for training. The 1930s saw further efforts to revise the conscription, pension, and promotion systems, placing a new premium on modern educational attainment.[24]

By the end of the 1920s, for the first time the Iranian state seemed capable of unadulterated coercion against nonstate actors, a policy that a British consul dubbed "massacre, then embrace." The initiation of land registries and prohibition on pastoralism represented even further state penetration into everyday life. Once defeated militarily, nomadic tribesmen were forcibly conscripted and settled in model villages. Peasants were reduced to tenants in the estates of large landholders, accelerating migration to the cities. Following the example of Kemalist Turkey, citizens were mandated to wear Western clothing (including abandonment of the veil and tribal costumes) and adopt Persian as a national language. Protests continued, but on an increasingly localized scale. Peasants and tribesmen attacked the very tribal leaders who had failed in their obligation to mediate and protect their followers from the state.[25] As Stephanie Cronin notes, by the late 1920s, the great khans "had lost all of their power, most of their influence and a considerable portion of their wealth."[26] They no longer held the lucrative provincial governorships, were barred from collecting road tolls, and were obliged to pay tribute to the new shah to retain their now meager posts. The balance of domestic power had shifted decisively in favor of the state.

By pacifying nonstate actors, Reza asserted not only the state's monopoly over violence within Iranian territory but also the state's authority to extract economic resources from within it. With the regional warlords eliminated, Reza was able to ensure that oil rents went directly to the state treasury. Customs duties more than doubled. New taxes were imposed on personal income and consumer goods. Scofflaws risked imprisonment or asset seizures. Overall, government revenues increased more than tenfold from 1925 to 1941, and spending rose at an even greater rate. The war, finance, and education ministries were expanded, and new bureaucracies were established to oversee industrial and agricultural policy. Road, railway, and telegraph networks improved Iran's commerce and facilitated governmental control over the width and breadth of Iranian territory.[27]

The Iranian state's ability to exert influence in the regional environment grew in proportion to its disarmament of internal rivals. By the 1930s, Iran's army rivaled Turkey's and dwarfed neighboring Iraq's. A burgeoning domestic arms industry included foundries for rifles, machine guns, artillery, and aircraft assemblies.[28] The Iranian navy asserted Iran's claims over several islands in the Persian Gulf. In 1937, Iran successfully forced Iraq to concede territory on the Shatt al-Arab waterway near Abadan.[29] In that same year, the creation of the Saadabad Pact among Iran, Iraq, Turkey, and Afghanistan helped further solidify the principles of mutual noninterference and cooperation by collaborating in repressing the ongoing transnational Kurdish uprising.[30]

Still, Iran's sovereignty remained ultimately dependent on the vagaries of great power geopolitics. Indeed, much of Reza's foreign policy in the 1920s and 1930s amounted to a determined effort to navigate between the Soviet Union and Britain and gain support from a "disinterested" Western power. As in Iraq in the 1930s, Nazi Germany offered a nationalist role model and, more importantly, a counterweight to British imperialist hegemony. Despite Reza's declaration of neutrality in the run up to World War II, Iran appeared to tilt toward the Axis. Once the Soviets joined the Allies in 1941, the pincer was set, with Soviet troops moving from the north and British forces from the south. The Iranian military was not trained or equipped to withstand such formidable enemies. The air force was crippled, the navy badly outgunned, and the infantry and mechanized forces quickly overwhelmed. Iran was placed under joint Soviet-British military occupation for the duration of the war, and Reza was forced to abdicate in favor of his minor son, Mohammed Reza Pahlavi.[31]

With the collapse of state authority in 1941, tribesmen throughout the country retrieved old weapons caches, absorbed deserting conscripts, and sacked police stations. Banditry and raiding returned to the countryside as tribes sought to regain their former pasturages. In the southeast, German agents instigated an uprising by the Qashqai, Arab, and Lur. British occupation forces tried to suppress the insurgency, but ultimately the government had to concede to demands for tribal autonomy, returning responsibility for local security to the *ilkhans* again. In the northeast, the Soviets backed Kurdish and Azeri secessionist bids.[32]

Such rural rebellions against the state, however, never achieved the scale or impact that they had in previous generations. This became evident during oil nationalization crisis of 1951 to 1953 under Prime Minister Mohammed Mossadeq. Britain and the United States feared Mossadeq's alliance with the Communist Tudeh party as a bridgehead for a Soviet-backed takeover. The Qashqai tribes supported the prime minister's government but failed to provide him military backing for fear of inciting the army's repression. Ultimately, U.S. and British intelligence agents conspired with royalist army officers to bribe the notorious Tehran gangster Shaban Jafari to organize hired thugs (*chomaqdars*) into street mobs, forcing Mossadeq's ouster.[33]

The 1953 coup represented to the combustion of the two elements that would define the trajectory of Iranian state formation over the next three decades. The first element was Iran's entanglement in the Cold War and its strategic alliance with the United States. A small American advisory mission first came to Iran during the Allied occupation. The U.S. role was initially limited to reforming the interior ministry and gendarmerie to guarantee the overland supply routes to the Soviet Union and the security of oil through the Persian Gulf. Iranian leaders recognized the United States as the long-sought counterweight to Britain and the Soviet Union and did their best to deepen and expand this relationship from the outset. As global conflict with the Soviet Union began to take form in the postwar era, Iran's strategic value became more apparent.[34] In one of the first superpower confrontations of the Cold War, the United States backed Iran's diplomatic efforts to force the Soviets to finally quite Iran's northeastern Azerbaijan province in 1946. The shah was able to claim this as a major victory in preserving the territorial integrity of the state. By 1953, the Eisenhower administration designated Iran a state "of critical importance" to American national security and dedicated more resources to arms and advise Iran, including aid to establish the shah's new intelligence service, SAVAK. The Baghdad Pact (1955) solidified Iran's position as part of the northern tier strategy, a bulwark against a Soviet thrust toward the Persian Gulf. By the mid-1950s, U.S. strategic planners anticipated that

Iranian forces could delay an advancing Soviet army until U.S. and British forces could arrive. This role became doubly important after the deposition of the Iraqi monarchy in 1958.[35]

The second element was Iran's oil resources, which was the immediate concern of the U.S. and British attack on Mossadeq. From the mid-1950s to the mid-1970s, Iran's oil rents increased more than twentyfold, permitting Mohammed Reza Shah to spend virtually limitlessly on one of the largest and most technologically advanced armies in the developing world. Accompanying this military modernization program was the launching of the White Revolution in 1963, a plan to use oil rents to foster complete societal transformation, through land redistribution, state-sponsored industrialization, and educational and religious reform.[36]

The combined impact of American military support and nearly boundless oil wealth was clearly visible in the Iranian countryside in the 1950s and 1960s. In the words of a U.S. military journal, the American-trained Imperial Gendarmerie corps was "the manifestation of the central government authority" for much of the rural population. Troops served government notices, settled disputes, and hunted down smugglers, looters, and draft dodgers with increasing alacrity thanks to improvements in radio communication, jeeps, and helicopters.[37] Aerial strafing easily quashed the last remnants of tribal resistance in 1963. Legions of civilian government agents fanned out to implement land registration, to set up mobile schools, to introduce modern agricultural and veterinary techniques, to organize women's associations, to provide medical and family planning advice, and, of course, to collect taxes. By the late 1960s, the power of the chiefs had been definitively replaced by a central bureaucracy, backed by the ubiquitous military.[38]

The stronghold of resistance to the state shifted to the cities, but even there the SAVAK and other security agencies appeared to be well in control. The shah permitted—and possibly encouraged—some clerics to retain to organize private militias through the *hojjatiyyah* movement. Mainly, this was a sop to the anti-Bahai and anticommunist inclinations of the more conservative religious factions, for whom the monarchy's legitimacy rested on its stance against such heresies. Still, this armed nonstate force was miniscule compared to those seen just a few decades earlier, totaling about 12,000 in 1977.[39] More radical clerics like the young firebrand Ayatollah Khomeini refused to accede to the shah's rule, accusing him of undermining Iran's traditional Islamic values by allying with the United States. In 1963, Khomeini publically denounced the White Revolution, sparking a major conflagration between government troops and seminarians in Qom. When sympathetic protests erupted in Tehran and other cities, the shah not only deployed the army to the street but again called in *chomaqdars* to break up the disturbances. Khomeini was forced into exile, and many of his followers were imprisoned or worse. After quelling the riots, however, many of Tehran's underworld leaders themselves were arrested or sent into internal exile. The responsibility to suppress or intimidate the opposition now rested squarely with the SAVAK, the bureaucracy, and the army, not the "professional" mob or tribal warlord.[40]

Force centralization at home went hand-in-hand with Iran's enhanced international position. On one hand, Iran saw threats stemming from Soviet-backed Arab regimes like Egypt, South Yemen, and Iraq. In 1964, Nasser and the Arab League revived a claim on Iran's southwestern province of Khuzestan, claiming it as part of historical "Arabistan." Additionally, periodic unrest among the ethnic minorities or leftist insurgents in Iraq, Oman, Pakistan, or Turkey could also spill across Iran's borders. On the other hand, Iran saw a chance to regain what it considered to be its legitimate status as a global power. With Britain planning to evacuate the Persian Gulf, the Nixon administration gave Iran permission to purchase any and all (nonnuclear) weapons, sanctioning Iran's role as the region's new policeman.[41]

In technology, organization, and orientation, the Iranian military began more and more to resemble a scaled-down replica of its American counterpart. Iran's commander structure featured chiefs of staff for each service branch, although the shah purposefully ensured that each chief reported directly to him in order to prevent a possible military conspiracy.[42] Following the suppression of the 1963 revolt, the imperial army was retasked to prioritize external defense, shunting responsibility for internal security to the national police and gendarmerie.[43] Iran expanded its ground forces to three armored divisions, three infantry divisions, and four brigades. Iran had 800 armored personal carriers and 800 American-made M-47 and M-60 tanks, plus an assortment of antitank and antiaircraft weapons. When Iraq acquired advanced Soviet T-72s tanks, Iran countered by ordering nearly 2,000 British-made Chieftains, an arsenal equal to that fielded by Egypt and Israel combined in the 1973 October War (though less than half were actually delivered). The Imperial Air Force, long favored by the shah because of its technological mystique, acquired advanced American F-14 fighters as well as an assortment of air-to-ground and air-to-air missiles. The imperial navy began to look beyond the Gulf and reached the Indian Ocean, adding bases in Mauritius and purchasing American Spruance-class destroyers.[44] The shah even investigated ways to use U.S.–supplied nuclear facilities to develop a covert nuclear weapons program.[45]

Some American officials doubted the wisdom of Iran's military build-up. A special advisor in the Kennedy administration griped that the shah insisted on "an expensive army too large for border incidents and internal security and of no use in an all-out war" and counseled instead to prioritize spending on social services.[46] The admonition to attend to economic and social problems in part spurred the launching of the White Revolution in 1963. American military observers found Iran's army heavily dependent on foreign advisors and unable to integrate advanced technology into its arsenal. Still, assessments held that the Iranian military was powerful enough to handle internal unrest and engage a regional adversary like Iraq.[47]

Indeed, Iran's new found military might was put to significant use abroad. In the 1960s and 1970s, Iran established de facto alliances with Israel and Pakistan aimed at countering the power of the Arab core. In the midst of Britain's withdrawal from the Gulf in 1972, Iran seized Abu Musa and the Tunbs islands, which the emirate of Sharjah claimed as successor to the British-held Trucial Coast. Three years later, Iran forced Iraq to make further concessions on the Shatt al-Arab waterway by supporting Kurdish insurgents with heavy weapons and artillery.[48] In 1973, the sultan of Oman invited Iranian help in suppressing the ongoing communist-backed insurgency in Dhofar. A 4,000-man Iranian expeditionary force backed up a small contingent of British commandoes in the counterinsurgency operation. The imperial air force took over operations of Oman's airbases, using them as forward positions against the People's Democratic Republic of Yemen, the revolt's foreign sponsor.[49]

By the mid-1970s, thanks to the combination of a propitious geostrategic environment and increasing global demand for oil, Iranian state power appeared at its pinnacle. Mohammed Reza was finally able to adopt a Western-military format, centralizing coercive control and eliminating domestic competitors. This success at state making was again connected to success at waging (or at least threatening) war against other states. While the shah's boasts that Iran was a global power could be dismissed as delusions of grandeur, Iran was clearly becoming a dominant regional power. With the consolidation of state control, outside forces could no longer subvert Iran's sovereignty by recruiting nobles and warlords to serve as proxies. Still, as discussed in the following pages, the drive for coercive centralization and its concomitant transformation of everyday life spurred new forms of resistance that neither the shah nor his U.S. backers fully appreciated. This resistance would culminate in the revolution of 1979, whose leaders sought to replace the model of coercive centralization with one based on devolving coercive-initiative to popular militias.

## REVOLUTION, DEVOLUTION, AND WAR, 1978–1988

Iran's efforts at defensive modernization through most of the nineteenth and early twentieth centuries were caught between a conservative aristocracy opposed to measures that might diminish its independent power and a rising middle class demanding an ever more rapid pace of change.[50] With seemingly unassailable economic and military power, Muhammed Reza Shah wagered that he could obtain societal transformation and state centralization without concession to popular representation or significant checks on his authority. In fact, his efforts engendered new forms of opposition that the shah was ill prepared to confront. Led by Ayatollah Khomeini, an urban counterelite systematically broke down the state's control by using guerrilla violence and mass public protests. Following the revolution of 1979, Khomeini tried to convert the institutions of revolutionary insurrection—popular committees, urban militias, and village guards—into institutes of rule. In the face of profound international threat and continued challenges from within, however, the revolutionary regime eventually had to return to the model of centralization bequeathed during the imperial era.

By the 1960s, the shah faced his most significant resistance in the cities, not the countryside. The rural magnates and tribal leaders who had held the fate of the state in their hands in the first half of the century were in terminal decline even by the 1950s. The White Revolution further undermined the standing of the landed elite and added impetus to rural flight. Tehran alone grew from 400,000 people in 1940 to 1,500,000 by the mid-1950s and over 2,500,000 by the mid-1960s. Its population would double again within the next decade.[51] The economy was booming, but the benefits were skewed toward a slim sector of state-allied bourgeois, government bureaucrats, and, of course, the security sector. Recent urban migrants confronted inadequate wages, housing shortages, and widening income inequality, all of which compounded the popular perception that the government was indifferent or incompetent to address the needs of everyday citizens.[52]

In February 1971, *Fedayeen-e Khalq* (FEK, People's Insurgents), a Maoist guerrilla group, killed three gendarmes in Gilan province. Shortly thereafter,

*Mojahideen-e Khalq* (MEK, People's Holy Warriors), adherents to a syncretistic Islamo-Marxism ideology, began a string of robberies, bombings, and assassinations, aimed at both Iranian and Western targets. Although these attacks provoked brutal government reprisals, they demonstrated the resurgence of armed opposition.[53] Beginning in 1977, the slums of Tehran saw increasing agitation over rent hikes and evictions. Professionals and even some former officials openly aired their complaints. Long-banned opposition parties began to reconstitute. The situation intensified by 1978. While the familiar enemy of left-wing factions in factories and student unions could be easily crushed by the SAVAK, Khomeini and the radical clerics had built an even more formidable base of support among the clerics and the traditional bazaar merchant class. Responding to increasing government repression, Khomeini orchestrated larger and larger protests, calling on the people to overthrow the shah's dictatorship in the name of Islam. The shah hesitated to commit the full force of the military to counter the revolutionary forces. The United States pressured the Iranian regime to improve its embarrassing record of human rights abuses and avoid a bloody crackdown. The shah himself instinctively feared that empowering his own generals would lead to a palace conspiracy against him.[54]

The result of this vacillation was a steady bleeding of central authority. Senior officers remained steadfast, but conscripts and noncommissioned officers began to defect or desert en masse. Demonstrators fought on the streets with club-wielding toughs paid by the shah's official political party. By autumn 1978, students were organizing neighborhood defense units, many centered in mosques and guided by local clerics. *Komitehs*—derived from the French revolutionary *comité*—provided security for communities and ensured supplies of food, heating oil, and other staples. Laborers seized control of factories and established their own consultative (*shura*) councils. When the shah left Iran on January 16, 1979, many smaller cities and provincial capitals were already in rebel hands.[55]

With Khomeini's return from exile on February 1, Islamist and leftist factions began to compete to incorporate local uprisings into their national organization. FEK, MEK, and the Tudeh stepped up their assaults on Imperial Guard outposts, gaining both arms and membership as defections accelerated. By February, these parties had an estimated 15,000 to 20,000 fighters and many more members and sympathizers. Led by Massoud Rajavi, the Islamo-Marxist MEK was particularly aggressive in transitioning its underground force into a full-on political party, with youth, women, and workers' leagues.

Rajavi also reached out to the Kurdish leaders and other national minorities to create a cross-ethnic alliance.[56]

Relying on the hierarchical network of Shi'i mosques, Khomeini deepened his ties with the *komitehs*. Clerical authority, however, remained fragmented. Beside Khomeini, Ayatollah Mahmud Taleqani maintained strong support with the workers' councils and the Kurdish opposition, Ayatollah Mohammed Kazem Shariatmadari was the most respected cleric among Iran's estimated 14,000,000 Azeris, and Ayatollah Mohammed Taher Shubayr-Khaqani held his own base of support within Iranian's Arab community.[57] Militias were proliferating in both cities and countryside, with an estimated 1,500 in Tehran alone. Revolutionary vigor was becoming increasingly indistinguishable from common criminality, as *komitehs* extorted "revolutionary taxes" and launched brazen attacks on military officers, police, bureaucrats, landlords, informants, or other so-called "royalists."[58]

In late February 1979, Khomeini declared that the army and police were now "in the service of Islam and the nation" and that the government needed these forces intact to safeguard the country. Citizens were asked to refrain from attacking the army and police or seizing property. Khomeini appointed Mehdi Bazargan as provisional prime minister, charged with preparing the country to transition to a new government. But even as Bazargan expressed alarm about the chaos in the streets and tried to shore up the state's weakened infrastructure, Khomeini systematically undercut these efforts in favor of carrying the revolution further. A revolutionary court system, headed by the notorious "hanging judge" Sadeq Khalkhali, was created to try the enemies of Islam. When Bazargan sought to minimize the disruption of the still-fragile state institutions by taking these cases into the civil courts, Khomeini decreed Islamic law to be ultimately superseding, essentially authorizing militias to ignore civil rulings. Bazargan offered to induct 4,000 *komiteh* militiamen into the national police in an effort to encourage some revolutionary forces to disarm or stand down. Khomeini responded that although some *komitehs* had succumbed to irresponsible leadership, "The committees need purging, [but] not disbanding . . . as long as corrupt individuals exist, there is need for committees."[59] The result, as Bazargan aptly summarized, was that Khomeini "put a knife in my hands, but it's a knife with only a handle. Others are holding the blade."[60] This situation continued through the dismissal of the provisional government and the election of Abolhassan Bani Sadr as the first president of the republic in early 1980.

Instead of absorbing the militias into the state security service, Khomeini circumvented the state through the Revolutionary Central Committee. The Central Committee was dominated by clerics loyal to Khomeini and extended his personal patronage through upper- and middle-ranking clerics down to the neighborhood preachers and mullahs who guided the militias. In some sense, this was a contemporary elaboration of the classic relationship between clerical sponsors and *luti* agents. As Guillain Deneoux describes, the bands of militiamen

> reflected a great degree of grassroots initiative and relied heavily on personal ties between cleric and followers . . . [M]any revolutionary groups were at first often no more than patron–client clusters that bound lower middle class and lower class militant youth to radical clerics. The latter used these networks to implement decisions and eliminate their rivals. In exchange, upwardly mobile youth staffing the revolutionary bodies were given access to the privileges and benefits controlled by leading clerics.[61]

Darius Rejali points out that the *komitehs* were fast becoming at once "police agencies, welfare services, and societies for moral guidance." Those young men who might have gravitated to the conservative *hojjatiyah* gangs a few years earlier were now joining the revolutionary militias.[62] Mid-ranking clerics in Isfahan, Mashhad, and other provincial cities submitted themselves, their lower-ranking clerics, attendees, and local agents to Khomeini. Ali Khamenei, one of Khomeini's closest aides, reportedly distributed over a million dollars in cash to win the allegiance of clerics in the Sistan-Baluchistan province. The *komitehs* also provided the backbone of the Islamic Republic Party (IRP) and its shadowy network of armed supporters known as the *hezbollah-e* (faction of God). During referendum on the establishment of a new Islamic republic in March 1979, these armed militants attacked the leftist and liberal political factions and suppressed uprisings by the peripheral minorities. While some IRP leaders decried these actions as overzealous, they blamed MEK or the leftists for instigating the violence. These militias were also involved in subduing followers of Khomeini's clerical rivals, like Ayatollah Taleqani and Ayatollah Shariatmadari. Indicatively, the militias were increasingly referred to as *chomaqdar*, the same derogation as had been applied to the shah's hired thugs.[63]

Just as Khomeini fostered the creation of parallel Islamic institutions to the police and judiciary, in May 1979 he launched a parallel army in the form of the

Islamic Revolutionary Guard Corps (IRGC). Unlike Artesh, this new force was explicitly oriented to be part of Khomeini's declared "army of twenty million" citizens, standing against counterrevolutionary forces at home and abroad.[64] At IRGC's core were some 6,000 former guerrillas. Many had been university educated, were familiar with Marxist ideology, and had trained with Palestinian or Lebanese Shi'i militias before joining Khomeini's Islamic faction. Some had even defected from MEK. The ranks were fleshed out by militants from the *komitehs*, often less-educated, lower-class young men looking for avenues of advancement. By autumn, IRGC numbered 25,000 to 30,000 men.[65]

IRGC fighters considered themselves to be a vanguard under Khomeini's guidance and resisted submitting to civil authority. IRGC retained its amorphous organization structure, a conglomeration of independent urban guerrillas, clerical militias, and army defectors, each associated with individual leaders but professing personal loyalty to Khomeini alone. The corps' leaders rejected Abbas Zamani and Morteza Rezai, Bani Sadr's first two appointments for IRGC commander (despite their personal credentials as revolutionary guerrillas) and refused to integrate under the reconstituted defense ministry. Instead, IRGC leaders successfully demanded that one of their own, Mohsen Rezai (no relation to Morteza), be named the corps' commander. Khomeini dispatched clerical emissaries as political commissars to individual units through the Political-Ideological Directorate. IRGC was financed through its close relationship with clerically controlled foundations and charitable endowments (*bonyad*), which had appropriated assets of the shah and other royalists. Drawing on its guerrilla experience, IRGC emphasized volunteerism, individual initiative, and a mass base of popular support for the creation of a grassroots people's army.[66]

The ascent of IRGC paralleled the degradation of Artesh. The new regime doubted the loyalty of the shah's former military forces. In the first half of 1979, six alleged military plots against Khomeini were uncovered within Artesh. Despite an offer of amnesty, 40 percent of the officers, including 80 percent of the flag officers, were purged, arrested, or went into exile. The shah's elite Imperial and Immortal Guards were disbanded, as was SAVAK. The rank and file began to disintegrate as well. Conscription had virtually ceased, as had most provisions of military wage and ration. Foreign military advisors left the country, and military sales were embargoed, rendering much of Iran's most advanced technology unusable.[67] Some revolutionary leaders advocated breaking up the old army entirely by establishing "soldiers' councils"—analogs of the workers' councils—to assume command responsibility. IRGC even set up checkpoints to prevent unauthorized movement to and from Artesh barracks.[68]

IRGC, meanwhile, played a prominent role in Khomeini's bid to consolidate his personal power. Along with its *hezbollah-e* auxiliaries, IRGC was instrumental in suppressing MEK, which opposed the Islamic Constitution and launched a protracted guerrilla campaign against the regime through the early 1980s. IRGC soldiers forcibly removed belligerent workers' councils and replaced them with reliable pro-Islamic leadership.[69] A similar combination of repression and cooptation was applied to the myriad ethnic and tribal uprisings seen in Azerbaijan, Fars, Khuzestan, Khurasan, and elsewhere, with IRGC seeking to replace rebellious leadership with a pro-Islamic local *komiteh*.[70] IRGC and Artesh units worked together for the first time to suppress the Kurdish Democratic Party-Iran and its MEK allies in Kurdistan.[71]

But the inchoate makeup of the republic's coercive institutions contributed to the regime's underlying instability. Khomeini spoke of the need to curb vigilantism and restore law and order repeatedly in 1980 and 1981. It was not just the wildcat strikes that were troublesome. The continued proliferation of armed young men prowling the street enforcing Islamic dress codes and confiscating property in the name of the revolution disturbed even Khomeini's allies. With the oil industry virtually paralyzed by strikes and deserted by international investors, economic disaster loomed. Moreover, intraregime competition became more violent. Rival clerical entourages brawled in the street for control over mosques, tithes, and authority. As Bani Sadr clashed with Khomeini over the extent of clerical political oversight, the beleaguered president began to rely on MEK militias for protection and support. Iran's political infighting verged on civil war.[72]

Despite the fragility of Iran's coercive institutions, Khomeini remained intent on exporting his revolutionary message. Indeed, as in many revolutionary moments, Iran became more aggressive in the international arena when its military capacity was weakest. The student takeover of the American embassy in November 1979 poisoned Tehran's already deteriorating relationship with Washington. While initially more promising, ties with the Moscow also quickly soured.[73] Khomeini sought to incite the Shi'i populations in Lebanon and the Persian Gulf. He even reasserted the long-standing imperial claim to Bahrain.[74] Relations with Iraq were especially fraught. Saddam Husayn soon began to advocate reclaiming Iraqi rights to the Shatt al-Arab and offered support to Iran's restive Arab minority. Khomeini, in turn, lent support to Iraq's Shi'i opposition parties. In response to escalating border skirmishes, in September 1980 Iran announced its unilateral abrogation of the 1975 Algiers Accord.

With the crisis deepening, Iranian leaders revisited their military policy. The more doctrinaire held that a religiously devout (*maktabi*) army like IRGC was "preferable to a victorious army." Khomeini, however, disagreed. He explained that, unlike in the imperial era, military service was now a "divine matter . . . the defense of the Islamic realm" and hence obligatory. He soon authorized the reinstatement of conscription and called up the reserves.[75] Ultimately, however, this did little to dissuade Saddam that Iraq could finally take advantage of Iran's military weakness and international isolation.

On September 22, 1980, Iraq launched a massive air and ground assault from Kurdistan to Persian Gulf, catching Iranian forces badly unprepared. Some of the most able Artesh units had been diverted north for the campaign against the Kurds, and many others remained well below full strength. Shahram Chubin and Charles Tripp estimate that against Iraq's ten divisions, at most Iran was able to muster two divisions, with barely over 120 tanks.[76] Iraqi forces took Qasr-e Shirin and Mehran within the first day. In oil-rich Khuzestan, Iran's 92nd Armored Division had been decimated by purges and was unable to field even company-sized formations. IRGC militias flocked to the front, setting up haphazard defenses using light or improvised weaponry, often material recovered from fallen comrades or looted from government caches during the revolution.

The invasion brought the domestic rivalry between IRGC and Artesh into even sharper focus. IRGC enjoyed Khomeini's favor and trust and was able to claim credit for successes and blame Artesh for failures. IRGC's guerrilla tactics helped to blunt the Iraqi advance on Abadan. Militia forces took advantage of Iraq's tactical mistakes and hesitation, causing Iraqi armor to bog down in the city streets and the southern marshes. By December 7, 1980, Saddam announced a halt to the offensive. Iraq would adopt a defensive stance until Iran conceded to adjustments on the Shatt al-Arab.[77]

Despite the somewhat pyrrhic nature of its victory, the ability to stall the Iraqi army further emboldened IRGC's vision of itself as popular ideologically based force with no need for specialization or technical expertise. IRGC's unconventional tactics tended to impress with sheer bravery and devotion more than to seize positions. The prime example of this was the use of "human wave" attacks—frontal assaults charging directly into the line of fire until Iraqi positions were overrun. Similarly, IRGC believed it could undermine enemy morale and spur defection among Iraq's mostly Shi'i conscript army. By 1982 Iraqi forces had indeed retreated back to the border, and Saddam began to sue for peace. Artesh officers counseled that once the Iraqi advances were reversed, Iran could dictate peace terms. IRGC commanders, however, received Khomeini's backing to continue the war in the confidence that Saddam's regime would soon collapse entirely.[78] Mohsen Rezai stated that "only an ideologically-motivated army like ours, like the ones which liberated Vietnam and Algeria, is capable of mobilizing the people for the long war of attrition which we plan to wage until the Iraqi regime falls."[79]

As Iranian forces tried to turn the tables and advance into Iraq in 1983 and 1984, this approach proved to have enormous liabilities. The Artesh leadership, trained specifically to confront the Iraqi army, pointed out that IRGC tactics proved less effective as Iraqi soldiers became stouter in defending their own homeland and took a needless toll in Iranian lives. Lack of coordination, poor discipline, and inexperience cost Iranian forces the element of surprise and inhibited their ability seize strategic superiority. Without sufficient training or expertise, IRGC offenses turned into fiascos, like the disastrous series of operations through the Hawizeh marshes between 1983 and 1985.[80] As Dilip Hiro summarizes,

> the problem was that [IRGC] commanders had not yet mastered the professional army technique of maintaining sufficient resupplies of men and weapons. Enthusiastic advance units forged ahead without proper plan for succeeding waves to replace them as they reached the point of collapse out of sheer physical and mental exhaustion. . . . In a sense, the revolutionary guard behaved like a large-scale guerrilla force, adept at harassing and exhausting enemy troops rather than overrunning and securing territory.[81]

Though kept out of setting larger strategic objectives, Artesh was gradually able to prove its mettle and took on a larger tactical role coordinating joint operations with IRGC.

IRGC commanders, too, began to develop ways of reshaping their force into a conventional structure comparable to Artesh. Often using captured Iraqi equipment, IRGC set up separate armor and artillery units to support their infantry assaults. Specialized naval and air detachment also emerged.

In 1986, each of the IRGC land, air, and naval branches were placed under a unified joint staff.[82] Belying its initial confidence in an amateur army, by the summer of 1981 IRGC instituted a mandatory basic training regiment under the joint supervision of Artesh and IRGC instructors. IRGC recruits were required to have at least a sixth-grade education. The following year, IRGC established the first specialized military academies, combining general education, theology, and military training under the guidance of veteran fighters. By 1986, a full IRGC university was founded, offering training in military science, engineering, and medicine; it was later expanded to a faculty in basic sciences and strategic studies.[83] In a clear reversal of previous policy, a revolutionary prosecutor declared that

> those who wrongly interpret the Koran as saying our armed forces do not need modern weapons are either ignorant or traitorous. If we want to survive in this part of the world and protect and expand our revolution, our armed forces should be equipped with most advanced weapons.[84]

Operational collaboration between IRGC and Artesh were crucial to improving Iran's military performance, particularly in the initial capture of the Fao peninsula in 1986.[85]

Expansion of bureaucratic infrastructure accompanied the pursuit of greater specialization and differentiation within IRGC's ranks. In 1982, a new ministry of the IRGC was created.[86] Its head, Mohsen Rafiqdust, was well aware of the limitations of IRGC's militia-based model. He noted that "when we wanted to send the IRGC to the battlefield, this force did not have the necessary military formation or organization."[87] IRGC and Artesh were placed under a unified Soviet-style logistical network system, although this did little to dampen interservice competition for access to scarce resources. Most significantly, IRGC grew closer still to the Artesh model in 1985 when it began accepting conscripts, a conclusive departure from its early ethos as a strictly voluntary force.[88]

Still, as the IRGC leadership began to mimic the organizational patterns of Artesh, they were careful to preserve the corps' institutional autonomy and independence. IRGC veterans continued to develop their own specialized programs for training and weapons production. As IRGC officers gained more battle experience, they improvised novel uses for weapons and armament to add to conventional approaches.[89] The IRGC naval detachment, for instance, becoming adept at asymmetrical naval warfare using Zodiac, small boats, and even Jet Skis to compensate for Iran's aging fleet of frigates and destroyers.[90]

Unlike Artesh, IRGC remained responsible for domestic suppression, even as more units were devoted to the front. In the first years of the war, each IRGC unit worked in conjunction with clerically-controlled endowments in its home province to recruit fighters and obtain weapons and material. This ad hoc system added to IRGC's autonomy but also contributed to units of uneven sizes, levels of training, and armaments.[91] In 1984 the process was systematized when ten IRGC regional councils were established under to IRGC Commander Mohsen Rezai. Beneath the regional command were the district-level commanders, who were responsible for maintaining order at home, working in conjunction with the *komitehs*, and finding recruits through mosques, schools, and factories. IRGC district headquarters were deliberately situated in the center of cities and towns to facilitate contact with the general population. This system provided further incentive for IRGC commanders to maintain strong local ties while simultaneously helping to regularize logistics.[92]

As IRGC grew became more centralized, specialized, and professionalized, it found ways to retain contact with the masses through the *Basij* (Mobilization) corps. The Basij originated as an informal auxiliary volunteer force that flocked to serve in Khomeini's vision of a people's army, mirroring in many respects IRGC's initial organizational structure. Rezai appointed Basij commanders to recruit volunteers for three-month tours of duty, taking students, pensioners, illiterate peasants, and others considered ineligible by IRGC's standards. Their training was rudimentary: just two weeks of weapons and tactics mixed with heavy religious indoctrination. By 1985, an estimated 600,000 Basijis had served in some capacity. The Basij formed the fodder for many of IRGC's human wave attacks, often taking the brunt of Iraqi minefields, artillery, and machine guns.[93] Eventually, however, the more experienced and skillful IRGC commanders began to see the folly of such suicidal missions. By the end of the war, the notion of fording the Shatt al-Arab with a mass of some 500 Basij battalions was abandoned as futile.[94]

After two years of fighting to recover its own territory and six years trying to bring the war to Iraq, Iran's seemingly indefatigable fervor was fading by 1987. Around 200,000 men were lost on the battlefield, nearly 40 percent of whom were Basijis. Many more civilians had been killed or displaced, and the pool of enthusiastic recruits was beginning to dry up. The oil industry, by far the most important sector of the economy, was in tatters. Desperate to defend their own territory, Iraqi forces began using poison gas and attacking Iranian cities with ballistic missiles. Iran's efforts to replenish material were blocked by the Western arms embargo. The commencement of U.S. naval operations in the Persian Gulf spelled the definitive turn of the international community against Iran. Ali Khamenei, then Khomeini's designee as president of the republic, and Ayatollah Husayn Ali Montazeri, Khomeini's presumed clerical heir, spoke out about the weaknesses inherent in Iran's decentralized and fragmented command structure. IRGC Commander Rezai counseled that victory could come only through protracted and more intense mobilization coupled with the introduction of nuclear weaponry. In June 1988, Khomeini made the dramatic move of appointing Akbar Hashemi Rafsanjani as acting commander in chief of the armed forces, tasking him both with restructuring Iranian forces and with finding a way to end the war. This presaged Khomeini's final decision to accept the U.N.–brokered peace proposal on July 20, 1988.[95]

Violence devolution during the Islamic Revolution left Iran profoundly vulnerable to its neighbors, a weakness that Iraq exploited. The eight years of war proved a crucible, testing the resilience, flexibility and efficacy of Iran's coercive institutions. As Shaul Bakash summarizes, the war

> permitted the armed forces [Artesh] to regain credibility and standing in the eyes of the Iranian public, to rebuild the shattered command structure, and to revitalize such neglected areas as logistics, [and] maintenance. . . . the war also accelerated the rise of the Revolutionary Guard. Numbers were expanded, recruitment regularized, training improved, command structure strengthened, war experience acquired.[96]

The scale of these changes was enormous. IRGC grew more than tenfold over eight years, reaching 250,000 men by war's end, not counting the additional 350,000 active in the Basij. Artesh's ranks doubled in size from 1980 to 1988, reaching slightly over 300,000. Still, there could be little doubt about IRGC's ascendance, as it developed its own independent air and naval forces essentially from scratch. In contrast, the regular air force and navy branches shrank.[97] This reckoning did not come easily. IRGC commanders learned on the battlefield about the benefits of military centralization and adopted a more integrated system for technology, training, and operations. They began to meld Artesh's organizational format into the repertoire of popular mobilization acquired during the revolution. Ultimately, in salvaging Artesh and reforming IRGC, Iran returned to the path that the old regime had blazed, developing a centralized coercive apparatus designed both to suppress domestic opposition and to confront external foes.

## THE CONFLICTING LEGACIES
## OF REVOLUTION AND WAR, 1988–PRESENT

If the shahs faced a dilemma typical of modernizing autocrats, then the revolutionary regime faced a common challenge of incorporating the techniques of mass mobilization that had been part of the revolutionary legacy into a stable state structure. Since 1988, struggles in Iranian politics have revolved around the question of when and how to transition from emphasizing revolutionary mobilization and to building stable institutions of state power.[98] Despite his appointment to the post of supreme leader (*rahbar*) following Khomeini's death, Khamenei lacked the clerical credentials and personal charisma that Khomeini used to control the fractious revolutionary coalition. In the absence of a singular authority, the political arena was open for organized political factions to vie for power and position by claiming to be the rightful heirs to Khomeini's legacy.[99] On one hand, hardliners drew on Khomeini's early career in power to argue for a permanent Islamic revolution instigated through mass mobilization. Continued reliance on the popular revolutionary forces—militias, vigilantes, and other nonstate actors—was a crucial tool in carrying on Khomeini's banner. On the other hand, pragmatists and reformers pointed to Khomeini's latter years and his seeming postponement of revolutionary expansion in favor of consolidating the institutions of the Islamic Republic. They used this example to justify policies that maintained the rule of law and opposed any measure that would undercut civil authority.

The domestic contestation about when to achieve "Thermidor" in Iran was crucially informed by the strategic imperatives of state making and war making. The catastrophe of the Iran–Iraq war demonstrated that revolutionary popular militias were no substitute for a centralized, professional, and technologically advanced military. The continued threat posed by the United States and its regional allies, combined with the danger of internal subversion (which many Iranians also attributed to American authorship), seemed to necessitate strong state institutions to defend Iran. Rather than abandon the technique of revolutionary armed mobilization outright in the face of such challenges, though, Iran found ways to augment its centralized, conventional military force structure while subordinating the independent Basij and the other state-sponsored militias.

Rafsanjani's ascent in 1988 as Khomeini's appointee as acting commander in chief, followed by his election as president the following year, seemed to give new momentum for pragmatism. Rafsanjani immediately set out to rationalize the military's chain of command and force structure, declaring that Iran must rely "on regular and organized forces," not volunteers.[100] Tied-in with this effort, he also sought to change IRGC's mission and its organizational culture, making it part of a more conventional strategy of deterrence. While Iran "had to fight with Molotov cocktails, with sticks and stones, with RPGs, and whatever else," in 1980, today

> the IRGC must not think that when it is attacked it can fight with Molotov cocktails. An armed force must be so prepared that others will not dare attack. It is the guardian of borders and territory.[101]

Rafsanjani seconded Rezai's claim that Iran's very survival depended on acquiring the most advanced armaments, including chemical, biological, and nuclear weapons.[102] Once elected president in 1989, he placed both IRGC and Artesh under the purview of the Defense and Armed Forces Logistics Ministry, headed by an independent technocrat. IRGC was reorganized with formal divisions and brigades and a standardized system of military ranks and uniforms paralleling that of Artesh. The *komitehs*, which had served in ancillary support for IRGC, were merged with the municipal police and rural gendarmerie into the Law Enforcement Forces (LEF). The Basij militiamen were reoriented to serve in a postwar "construction *jihad*."[103]

Rafsanjani was also far more cautious about exerting Iranian military strength abroad. He pursued rapprochement with Iran's Arab neighbors in the Persian Gulf and with the newly independent states of Central Asia and the Caucasus. In Lebanon, Tehran encouraged the Shi'i Hizbollah militia to join the 1989 Taif peace process.[104] While asserting Iranian claims to Abu Musa and Tunbs islands in response to continuing U.S. presence in the Persian Gulf, Rafsanjani also warned that only a rational and logical policy could achieve revolutionary aims. Most significantly, Iran remained neutral during the 1991 Gulf War between Iraq and the United States, allowing the United States to decimate Iran's long-standing foe.[105]

Rafsanjani's meddling with IRGC's internal structures, however, met with considerable resistance. Many IRGC commanders had militated against settlement of the Iran–Iraq war and saw their mission as the continual expansion of the revolution. They blocked measures that might lead to their merger with Artesh and quibbled over the assignment of ranks to an organization that was famous for its egalitarianism. With Khomeini gone, IRGC became even more assertive of its own institutional interests, working in alliance with regime hardliners. In 1988, IRGC Minister Rafiqdust, who had always been considered an outsider interfering in the corps' affairs, was ousted on dubious grounds of having tampered with the IRGC logistical system. In November 1992, hardliners in the Majles passed a law that empowered the Basij by making it equivalent to LEF. Khamenei instructed the Basij "to protect revolutionary-Islamic values" throughout the public sphere.[106] With veterans returning to civilian life, Basij units expanded across all sectors of Iranian society, helped by generous government stipends and subsidies. By 2004, Basij volunteers were exempted from conscription.[107]

While Iran's official military budget dropped dramatically following the war, IRGC augmented its long-standing ties with clerically controlled religious foundations whose ostensive purpose was to aid war veterans and other dispossessed elements of Iranian society. The largest of these foundations employed an estimated 50,000 workers across a myriad of sectors.[108] Complementing its already established military industries, IRGC's engineering brigade won no-bid government contracts in the civilian sphere as well. Military vehicles were put to use for commercial transportation. Saïd Arjomand estimates that some 45,000 people were involved in this burgeoning military-industrial-commercial complex by 1992. This rent seeking even led IRGC officers to become involved in illicit activities like smuggling government-subsidized gasoline, contraband, and narcotics.[109]

Still, only a relatively narrow clique of insiders reaped the direct benefits of military off-budgeting. Iran was buffeted by significant signs of social unrest in the early 1990s, with riots in the capital and several small cities in 1991 and 1992. In Mashhad, at least 300 people were arrested, and several police officers were killed or injured. While the government dismissed the instigators as mere ruffians or hoodlums, the protests underlined the continued discontent over economic mismanagement, particularly the lack of employment and housing for veterans. When riots erupted in Qazvin in August 1994, IRGC units reportedly refused to fire on civilian demonstrators. Special units of the Basij had to be airlifted to the scene to suppress the uprising. The incident indicated that the regime could not presume IRGC units to be reliable, especially as the corps' ranks were no longer drawn exclusively from highly motivated volunteers.[110]

The IRGC high command's response to the continued danger of internal unrest was twofold. On the one hand, they returned to the revolutionary model of mass mobilization by expanding the Basij. Augmenting the core constituency of the rural and newly urbanized poor, new Basij cells were organized in universities, schools, factories, and among the tribes, enabling the organization to become an instrument of ideological propagation and monitoring. On the other hand, as the Basij ranks swelled, measures were taken to counteract the dilution of military capacity by creating a separate and more specialized force. Full-time paramilitary units—the Ashura battalion for men and Zahra battalion for women—were broken out, trained, and equipped specifically for riot control under IRGC supervision. These specialized units saw active service in the restive areas like Azerbaijan, Ardabil, and Khuzestan. In the more volatile regions of Kurdistan and Baluchistan, they were backed by LEF and IRGC forces.[111]

With the election of the reformist President Mohammed Khatami in 1997, hard-liners became even more reliant on networks of nonstate actors to intimidate their domestic opponents. As Michael Rubin notes, these vigilantes enjoyed support from certain government officials, including Khamenei, but did not formally belong to the state structures or even the parastatal Basij or religious foundations. *Ansar-e Hezbollah* (Supporters of the Faction of God) and other obscure groups with close ties to the clerics were implicated in attacks on reformist politicians, student protesters, and journalists, often using equipment or weapons allegedly stolen from IRGC or Basij units.[112] While some individuals in the security establishment took the initiative to clamp down on what was clearly detrimental to the state's bid to maintain law and order, the IRGC high command was generally complicit in covering up or protecting the attackers.[113]

This vigilantism became fully evident with the suppression of the student protests of July 1999. The protests began with picketing at Tehran University over the closure of a reformist newspaper but soon escalated with calls for an end to censorship and the implementation of democracy and spread to other cities. Police and IRGC forces were seen standing aside while Basij militias and common criminals broke up the demonstrations using clubs, knives, and other weapons. Hundreds were injured and thousands arrested.

Both the reformists and the hard-liners recognized the ramifications of this use of nonstate actors. As protests proliferated following the initial violent confrontation in Tehran, the government initiated a halfhearted investigation into the attacks, implicating a handful of rogue agents in an effort to mollify the demonstrators and distance the government from the crackdown. Khamenei himself claimed to regret the incident but then implicitly licensed the Islamic vigilantes, saying that "the greatest dream and honor for me is that I give my life in this noble, glorious, magnificent path." He pointed to the revolution's enemies, including the United States, as the fount of instability.[114] The IRGC high command followed suit. The protesters, in turn, alleged that government moles instigated the violence to provide a pretext for the assaults. They chanted slogans such as "Either Islam and the law, or another revolution!" and "Ansar commits crimes, and the Leader supports them . . . Shame on you, Great Leader!," essentially calling on the government to enforce its own laws against armed nonstate actors.[115]

Yet when faced with more direct regional challenges, Iran could not deny the logic of force centralization. In September 1998, following a crisis that nearly brought Iran to war with Afghanistan's Taliban regime, Khamenei appointed the first supreme commander for Artesh forces. For the first time in the history of the Islamic Republic, the shah's former military force was effectively elevated to a bureaucratic stature equal with IRGC. Despite IRGC's primacy as the protector of the revolution, the move signaled the general recognition that national security required an equally strong commitment to conventional deterrence and force projection. When the United States invaded Afghanistan in 2001, Tehran tacitly supported the move to depose a regime that it considered a mortal enemy.[116]

The suppression of the student protests in summer of 1999 saw the crest of the pragmatic reformist movement. Though Khatami was reelected in 2001, the reform agenda was permanently obstructed by Khamenei, IRGC, and the clerical establishment. The 2005 election of President Mahmoud Ahmedinejad, an IRGC veteran, marked the definitive ascent of hard-liners who pointed to what they saw as a new crisis in revolutionary practice and ideology. With the U.S. invasion of Iraq in 2003 and the U.S. threat to carry out regime change in Tehran as well, Iran found itself surrounded by the forces of a belligerent superpower. Hard-liners also blamed insidious Western cultural encroachment for undermining popular commitment to Islam. Declining electoral turnout seemed just one symptom of the popular apathy—if not antipathy— toward the regime.

In response, Ahmedinejad and the IRGC leadership announced their intention to reemphasize the principles of revolutionary mobilization using the Basij militias. In an apparent bid to mimic the success of Iraqi insurgents,

IRGC sought to stress guerrilla warfare training, integrating the population into its operations through the Basij.[117] Record high oil prices gave IRGC and the Basij unprecedented economic resources. Billions of dollars in contracts went to IRGC-fronted companies for projects ranging from building a new subway system to constructing oil pipelines. The Basij became a kind of job corps, receiving specially earmarked funds for construction projects as well. Over 8,000,000 people were involved in the Basij's extensive network for distributing patronage and subsidies. As part of the drive to maintain this culture, Basijis played a prominent role as morality police, entrapping suspected prostitutes, homosexuals, and drug users.[118]

From a military perspective, however, this attempt at force restructuring drew more lessons from the viscera of war in the mid-1980s than it did from the mass mobilization of the revolutionary heyday in 1978 and 1979. Iran's periodic threats to undermine American naval supremacy by blocking the Straits of Hormouz, for instance, rests on the expert use of antishipping missiles, nautical mines, and other advanced weapons. Such a tactics demand military expertise, not amateur enthusiasm.[119] Similarly belying populist rhetoric, Iran's displays of ballistic missile technology and its opaque nuclear posturing indicate a fairly conventional strategic approach aimed primarily at deterring Israel and the United States.[120]

In fact, even with Ahmedinejad and his hard-line allies in power, there remained significant tension between the goals of popular mobilization through institutions like the Basij and the necessities of preserving a strong and militarily effective state. This contradiction was most visible in the changing relationship between IRGC and the Basij following Khamenei's appointment of Major General Mohammed Ali Jafari as IRGC commander in 2007. Jafari, the first IRGC commander to have graduated from IRGC's War College, declared that, in the past,

> too much emphasis was put on the military nature of [IRGC] while its revolutionary and popular nature was not given well-deserved attention. Defending the achievements of the revolution is not restricted to hard military struggle . . . the main mission of the Basij and the IRGC is to fight internal enemies.[121]

Though calling for closer cooperation between the Basij and IRGC, Jafari did not envision such cooperation to be amongst equals. Rather, by reassigning the head of the Basij as a deputy IRGC commander, the Basij was placed in a subsidiary role under IRGC's umbrella. IRGC's thirty-one provincial commands were also reorganized, with at least six former Basij battalion commanders reappointed as IRGC provincial commanders and thirteen reappointed as deputy commanders. The move was carefully calibrated to allow each Basij commander to remain in his original province so as to retain his local contacts and networks of supporters. In essence, IRGC was beginning to appropriate some of Basij's independent functions of mass mobilization back into state hands.[122]

Ahmedinejad's bid for reelection in the summer of 2009 saw considerable reliance on networks of armed nonstate actors. Because IRGC was precluded by law from involvement in the election, it was left to Basij civilians to loiter at polling stations and intimidate voters. Despite the advantages of this incumbency, Ahmedinejad still faced a strong field of challengers. Mir-Husayn Mousavi, a veteran of the revolution and former prime minister, led the resurgent reformist movement. Former IRGC commander Mohsen Rezai also entered the race as a hard-line candidate, criticizing Ahmedinejad for mismanagement and rash policies that endangered the regime.

When official spokesmen declared Ahmedinejad the victor just a few hours after polls closed on June 12, 2009, supporters of Mousavi and the other candidates took to the streets en masse declaiming the apparent fraud. In a larger-scale replay of the suppression of the student protests a decade earlier, the regime confronted this growing "Green Movement" by turning loose the Basij and its auxiliaries on the demonstrators. Thousands were beaten and arrested and possibly hundreds killed. Armed not only with clubs and knives, but also with firearms and live ammunition, the militias appeared to be animated by a mixture of Islamic conservatism and class hatred for what appeared to be a largely middle- and upper-class protest. By some reports, militiamen were recruited from outside the capital by offers of stipends, room, and board.[123]

Opposition leaders tried to win the backing of these so-called popular forces away from their state sponsor. On June 20, 2009, in the midst of the some of the largest and bloodiest demonstrations, Mousavi appealed directly to the Basij and IRGC to defect:

> We are not up against the Basij, they are our brothers. We are not up against the IRGC, they protect our revolution and our political system. We are not up against the army, the army protects the security of our borders. We are not up against our holy political system and its legal structure, it protects our freedom, independence and the Islamic Revolution. We are up against lies and deviations, and we wish to reform it [the system] by returning to the pure principles of the Islamic Revolution.[124]

Mousavi went even further in a statement marking the anniversary of the establishment of the Basij in November 2009:

> Imam [Khomeini] did not want the Basij as a tool of authority, but a place for people to project their own power, a place that would allow them to have a part in their own future. It was supposed to be that the actions and behavior of the Basij would be an example to the people, not to have the power of the Basij crush the people. The Basij was not supposed to be on the government payroll and was not supposed to receive bonuses for arresting people for participating in demonstrations. It is a sad day if the Basij becomes just another political party. This is not what the Imam wanted for the Basijis. The Basij was not supposed to be an instrument to take away people's freedom in their votes.[125]

Ayatollah Montazeri, Khomeini's former protégé turned opposition religious leader, questioned the religious legitimacy of the Basij's vigilante action, saying "those who beat up the people have done something which is against religious laws. . . . It would be a misfortune to go to hell for the sake of the worldly desires of others."[126] It is difficult to gauge how successful these opposition efforts were at undermining the connection between the state and the militias. Certainly, Rezai's opposition to Ahmedinejad indicates at least some fractures within the regime's core.

Even hard-liners, though, recognized that discipline was an inherent problem among the militias. In response to public outcry over the violence, officials claimed that a handful of impostors, foreign agitators, and overzealous agents had instigated the attacks. As in 1999, some arrests were made. Still, the notion that the militias had acted illegally or without due authorization in using force against the protesters was difficult to refute. In October 2009, IRGC Commander Jafari made the surprising announcement that IRGC ground forces would absorb the Basij's military wing, signaling a further diminishment in the militia's autonomy.[127] Some observers see this move as the logical continuation of the filial relationship between IRGC and the militias dating from the revolutionary era and step toward empowering the Basij.[128] However, incorporating the Basij as a state organ also reinforced the distinction between legal use of force by IRGC as a military organization and the presumably illegal activities of the civilian Basij. General Masud Jazayri, the deputy commander of Iran's joint staff, explained that Khomeini "never said that the Basij was a military force . . . one cannot regard the Basijis as military personnel per se," but rather as members of a cultural organization with independent ties with

IRGC.[129] Because it was not a legal military entity, it would follow that Basij's use of force could also be questioned. General Mohammed Reza Naqdi, Jazari's newly appointed head of the Basij, offered a blunter and more practical explanation: "After identifying the vulnerabilities of Basij [in military operations], a change in the structure of Basij was needed." Clearly, IRGC commanders felt that better military performance could be obtained by eliminating the Basij's coercive prerogative and assuming that role directly.[130]

Understandably, some Basij veterans—including strong supporters of Ahmedinejad—responded critically. They claimed that the new emphasis on military professionalism neglected the lessons of popular mobilization and zeal that the Basij had helped to cultivate among the masses.[131] Still, when Khamenei addressed the Basij in November 2009 at the anniversary commemoration, he chose to focus on the organization's role as a vanguard in the "soft" cultural war and hardly mentioned its military activities. This omission seemed to further support the move to take coercive power out of the militia's hands.[132] In January 2010, as tensions between government and opposition continued to simmer, Khamenei again made an oblique criticism of the Basij: "Those without any legal duty and obligations should not meddle with these affairs . . . Everyone should hold back from arbitrary acts [and instead] go through the framework of the law."[133] This effort to disarm the Basij was another step away from IRGC's original revolutionary model of popular mobilization and toward centralizing coercive control within the formal state structure. Systematizing and formalizing the ambiguous relationship between IRGC and Basij militias further undermined the autonomy of nonstate actors and consolidated violence under unmediated state control.

## CONCLUSION: THE REVOLUTIONARY
## INSTITUTIONALIZATION OF VIOLENCE IN IRAN

Iran presents a crucial case for understanding the process of Third World military development and the factors that contribute to military centralization or devolution. Iran's path of military reform in the imperial era was comparable to that of other empires seeking to stave off foreign encroachment and foster societal modernization by adopting Western models of military and administrative centralization. A concatenation of geopolitical and economic factors allowed Mohammed Reza Shah to move the furthest in this direction in the 1960s and 1970s. The gains made in enhancing the state's military and economic hold over society, however, ultimately deepened Iran's dependence on Western power and undermined the shah's base of support.

Khomeini and the revolutionary leadership sought to sweep away the imperial legacy by emasculating Artesh and relying instead on popular mobilization through IRGC, the *komitehs*, and the Basij. This was not merely a tactical move to ensure a more trustworthy army. Rather, it epitomized the disdain for the Western institutional models that the shah had imported. Khomeini and his followers harbored an alternative vision of an Islamic social and political order in which everyday people imbued with revolutionary Islamic principles could use violence effectively and legitimately. The revolutionary leadership emulated contemporary revolutionaries as role models and drew on the indigenous repertoire of neighborhood strongmen acting in alliance with local religious magnates, a script that had been activated in response to the breakdown of the state in 1978 and 1979. Knitting together these local forces was crucial to building the revolutionary army.

Just as geopolitical and economic conditions had permitted the Pahlavis' drive for military centralization, these same factors precluded Iran from switching paths and devolving violence after the revolution. Post-revolutionary international isolation and the weaknesses inherent in the militia-based model rendered Iran incapable of defending its own territorial boundaries. Iraq's invasion in 1980 exploited this largely self-inflicted vulnerability. Strong external threats forced Iranian leaders to retain Artesh and to professionalize and centralize IRGC, essentially returning to the previous era's model of a large, conventional fighting force.[134]

But Iran's leaders did not abandon the idea of revolutionary mass mobilization entirely. Rather, emblematic of what Dan Brumberg calls the institutionalization of Iran's dissonant political legacies, various factions within the political elite drove multiple currents of military innovation and reform.[135] IRGC borrowed selectively from the repertoire of Artesh, standardizing its command structure, specializing its training, adopting larger unit structures, and integrating more advanced weaponry into its arsenal. In sum, IRGC became a fully formed parallel army, comparable in many ways to Iraq's Republican Guard. At the same time, IRGC retained contact with the masses and its popular revolutionary roots through the informal networks of the Basij and its shadowy adjuncts, similar to the way the Indonesian military continued to rely on nonstate actors for domestic suppression. This combined commitment to maintaining revolutionary institutions while improving state cohesion contributed to IRGC's ascendance as a major force in Iran's domestic political arena.

To confront external challenges, Iran now relies on the bifurcated military structure of its two professional standing armies, IRGC and Artesh. In moments of domestic crisis, such as the Green Movement protests of 2009 and 2010, the regime deployed state forces directly through IRGC and LEF and orchestrated the mobilization of the parainstitutional Basij and other vigilante militias. Still, the independence of these nonstate militias remains circumscribed by IRGC's military, economic, and administrative power. As both internal and external threats continue to loom, IRGC commanders and Khamenei himself appear dissatisfied with the reliability and efficacy of these nonstate actors. Disarming the Basij and absorbing its military components into IRGC represents a significant move toward force centralization, subordinating an independent institution of the revolution to state control. Whatever ideological predilections are expressed in favor of popular mobilization and revolutionary zeal, war making and state making necessitate that Iran seeks to maximize state control over violence and avoid compromising its monopoly over force.

# 5 LEARNING TO LIVE WITH MILITIAS

THIS BOOK EXPLORES HOW late-developing states (LDSs) organize violence, particularly in their utilization of militias and other nonstate actors as agents of internal control. Traditional assumptions hold that states strive to maintain control over "standing armies and police forces while eliminating militias and gangs." Only impotent, failed, or otherwise deficient states would permit such nonstate actors to exist.[1] Some contend that militias are used as a subterfuge to avoid blame for violence commissioned by the state.[2] However, learning to live with militias is a more complex historical process. The roots of violence devolution often emerge during periods of revolution and decolonization. LDSs permit and employ armed nonstate actors not just as a last resort or to deflect responsibility but in response to the specific set of opportunities and incentives that history and the international environment affords them.

Understanding how LDSs have come to embrace militias has significant implications for policy makers tasked with countering the presumed scourge of state frailty. On one hand, recognizing the systemic factors that make state-sponsored militias ubiquitous in many parts of the developing world calls into question the international community's policies aimed at fostering state building. The current tool kit of aid, assistance, and intervention does little to alter the conditions that ultimately lead states to devolve violence. On the other hand, these findings suggest that the axiom that states are indispensable for viable political order is also faulty.[3] The international community, too, must learn to live with militias if it is to cope with the complex problems of ensuring international and human security.

## HOW LATE-DEVELOPING STATES
## LEARNED TO LIVE WITH MILITIAS

By conceptualizing violence devolution as a mode of military development rather than as a defective mode of state formation, this book offers an empirically grounded view of the contingent and varied pathways that lead some LDSs to militias and others to conventional, centralized, and bureaucratic armies. The crucial elements of this theory are critical junctures, path dependence, and bounded innovation. The case studies of Indonesia, Iraq, and Iran demonstrate these in detail. In each of these countries, the establishment of modern and unmediated state institutions was just beginning in the early twentieth century. Nonstate actors—tribal leaders, village strongmen, local notables—maintained independent access to violence alongside the state's still incipient centralized coercive institutions. The legacies of decolonization endowed these states with military institutions of varying organizational forms. Indigenous state elites had the opportunity to make choices about how to reorganize and reform these institutions. They borrowed, transposed, and transplanted institutional repertoires from one setting to another, applying lessons learned in the early experience of decolonization to later challenges. They used the military training, equipment, and protection provided by outside powers to achieve their own ulterior ends.

The demands of war making—regional rivalry and external threat—constrain the menu of military reform. In Iraq, the combination of an initial endowment of colonial military forms and the persistent challenge posed by regional states forced the abandonment of plans to entrust violence to party or tribal militias. By contrast, Indonesia's revolutionary legacy provided experience in organizing and mobilizing nonstate actors, a repertoire perfected in the absence of a strong external threat that would necessitate a stronger and more centralized national army. Iran is a crucial case because it illustrates the cost of adopting a military format unsuited to the particular regional subsystem. Under the Pahlavis, Iran followed a path of defensive modernization parallel to Iraq's, attempting to adopt a Western military model by hiring military advisors and spending enormous sums to purchase military technology. Khomeini sought to reverse this trend in 1979, encouraging the devolution of violence to nonstate actors who formed the vanguard of the popular revolutionary movement. Iraq's invasion the following year, however, demonstrated the vulnerabilities of a people's army in the face of a conventional, professional, and centralized adversary. Ultimately, Iran has been forced to return substantially to the model of military centralization set by the previous regime.

In all three cases, leaders have been instrumental and innovative in response to military necessities. In Indonesia, Sukarno found ways to domesticate nonstate actors, controlling their access to money and weapons while still leaving them in place to guarantee local security in the far-flung outer islands and Java's urban underbellies. Saddam Husayn, by contrast, carved out the Republican Guard from within his own army to be a specialized and hardened fighting force that could protect the regime and fight at the front. Since 2003, though, the Iraqi state—denuded of its accumulated coercive capacity—has been forced to rely on nonstate actors once again. This has resulted in some measure of internal stability but leaves Iraq profoundly vulnerable to outside pressures and meddling. Iran represents an ongoing and uneasy attempt to synthesize both the decentralized and centralized models but with the latter becoming progressively more prominent. Iran's Islamic Revolutionary Guard Corps, once the vanguard of popular mobilization, has been reorganized and reoriented as a conventional and centralized force, coming to dominate the vestigial institutions of revolutionary militias. In each of these cases, the bequeathal of colonial models, geopolitical threats, and subsidiary positions within the hierarchical international system conditioned the choices of institutional innovation.

Overall, Indonesia's path is most typical and seen throughout the Third World.[4] The legacy of the Japanese withdrawal and colonial collapse following World War II similarly led to the embedding of localized militia-based forces among many of Indonesia's regional neighbors, including Burma, the Philippines, Malaysia, and Vietnam.[5] With most of Southeast Asia inhabited by militarily devolved states, there was little external threat compelling individual states to centralize their armies. Excluding Vietnam, where French and American invasions eventually forced Ho Chi Minh to transition from a militia-based force to a centralized and professional army, Southeast Asian states survived intact heavily reliant on militias and with relatively meager coercive resources under direct government control.[6] This roughly parallels the path seen in Latin America. Miguel Centeno shows how the collapse of colonial order in the mid-nineteenth century left regional states dependent on various forms of militia-based armies, rendering them incapable of waging war on their neighbors. Again, the result was the emergence of a region of impotent peace. States could continue to deputize nonstate actors to combat internal challenges while remaining heedless of interstate threats.[7] In Africa, as Jeffrey Herbst describes,

states emerged under slightly different conditions in the mid-twentieth century but reached the same self-reinforcing equilibrium: Limited warfare conducted by militia armies contributed to the maintenance of states with limited
capacities to control their own territories. The regional environment gave no
incentive to further build state capacity.[8] The latest wave of decolonization in
post-Soviet Eurasia in the 1990s repeated this pattern. Successor states inherited a bevy of militias, self-defense units, part-time fighters, and mercenaries,
rather than conventional armies.[9] The difference between nominal states like
Georgia and Moldova and state-pretenders like Abhazia and Transnistria is
not their respective abilities to establish monopolies over the use of force (none
come close) but the international recognition accorded to each.[10]

The Middle East stands out as the regional exception that proves the rule.
The direct inheritance of European military technology contributed to a
uniquely bellicose regional order. The threat of external predation necessi-
tated that states take measures to monopolize violence. Besides Iraq and Iran,
Israel, Jordan, Syria, and Egypt all faced similar challenges of subordinating
violence under state control in the midst of a severely hostile international environment.[11] Those that failed to establish central control over violence—such
as the Palestinians in 1948 or Lebanon in the 1970s—suffered subjugation or
elimination from the regional subsystem.[12] When viewed in global perspective, the Middle East has followed closer to the path of European state formation than any other developing region.[13]

A theory linking the manner in which states gain sovereignty and the impact of the international environment on larger trajectories of military development invites a more critical approach to the international community's role
in state building. Given the unlikelihood of strong, centralized states emerging in the developing world, the international community could do well to
integrate domains of limited state control into the international system. This
means dealing directly with the nonstate actors who are the actual providers
of security instead of continually trying to prop up defunct nominal states, an
approach that current policies seldom consider.

## WHY THE INTERNATIONAL COMMUNITY
## MUST LEARN TO LIVE WITH MILITIAS

The argument that deep-seated historical factors propel violence devolution
casts state-sponsored militias in a dramatically different light than is common
in policy-making circles. Contrary to Robert Rotberg's contention that the

failure of states to control violence within their territory is fundamentally the result of poor leadership decisions that erode state institutions, this book points out that Third World leaders are uniquely constrained by distant historical junctures and the structure of the international system.[14] Such a focus on path dependence is often cold comfort to policy makers. Understanding these limitations, however, is essential for evaluating the feasibility and desirability of measures aimed at ameliorating the dangers emanating from frail and failed states.[15]

The international community faces two crucial choices: First is whether to intervene in conditions of state weakness; second is whether to reinforce the prevailing norms of sovereignty.[16] The most common response to the challenge of state frailty today is to help incumbent states realize their claim to sovereignty—essentially making states more "statelike"—through peace building. Such exercises are often spearheaded by the dispatch of military advisors to train and equip security forces, followed by other specialists in the legal, economic, and other sectors. The global war on terror brought even more commitment to reinforcing a state-based order.[17] It is presumed that strengthening and professionalizing security forces eliminates zones of lawlessness where terrorists can find succor and diminishes the need for "dirty tricks" like the mobilization of nonstate actors to attack opposition. Security sector reform helps to reinforce the rule of law and guarantees protection to all citizens, reducing the uncertainty that leads groups to mobilize in self-defense.[18]

When states fall too far short of the goal of protecting their citizens and providing order, the international community has also resorted to more invasive measures, revoking sovereignty and replacing it with a form of international trusteeship. Foreign troops, typically under U.N. aegis, supersede the state's security organs while international experts assume oversight for other state functions.[19] International trusteeships and occupations of Bosnia Herzegovina, Kosovo, Sierra Leone, Haiti, Somalia, Iraq, and Afghanistan, among others, represent this more intensive attempt to excise defective state institutions by replacing them with a better functioning international regime.

Both peace building and international trusteeship, though, have inherent moral hazards and adverse selection risks.[20] Peace building cannot work without the consent of the host state, many of which harbor ulterior motives and designs for the use of increased coercive power. Australian Prime Minister Gareth Evans reflected that long-standing Western military aid to Indonesia had "helped only to produce more professional human rights abusers."[21]

This concern goes beyond human rights to the value of strategic engagement with regional allies. After decades of American military assistance, Pakistan remains incapable of repelling Taliban and al-Qaeda infiltrators. In fact, elements within the Pakistan's military and intelligence services are known to share equipment, intelligence, and funding with militants, undercutting the very notion of security sector reform and Pakistan's alliance with the United States.[22] Even seemingly innocuous—and badly needed—humanitarian aid becomes a dangerous weapon in a repressive state's hands, often funneled to armed nonstate actors as reward for doing the state's bidding.[23]

Efforts to promote stability by the United States or other outside powers, as Stephen David notes, are especially difficult when the problem lies with the existing regime.[24] Merely revising a ministry's policies and procedures does not displace a well-established repertoire of repression. The lines between state and nonstate actors remain hazy, allowing security services to continue to outsource violence deployment. Colombian and Mexican police and army officers, the very actors the United States seeks to treat as partners in upholding state authority, are known to collude with the kingpins of the drug cartels. Entire villages and towns are essentially ceded to these modern day *caciques* and *caudillos*.[25] International legal cannons are just beginning to impose penalties on states for violence commissioned through state-sponsored militias, but there remains significant leeway for states to continue practicing violence devolution while avoiding penalties or sanctions.[26] For its part, the international community tends to turn a blind eye or even promote such state-organized crime as long as it seems to enhance short-term stability, regardless of its long-term impact on the development of an efficient and effective state.[27]

International trusteeship removes obstructive incumbents from power but ultimately runs into similar dilemmas. If it is difficult to get domestic parties to accept security sector reforms when offered as advice and counsel, then resistance is almost inevitable when such reforms are imposed by foreign mandate.[28] Multiple interventions in Somalia and Haiti have ended ignominiously, undermined by both popular and elite resistance. In the Balkans, an ostensibly limited NATO-led mission has proven interminable and yielded little real political reconstruction. Moreover, such direct interventions run the risk of emboldening opposition groups to continue their violent struggles rather than to seek a negotiated solution. Rebels in Darfur, the Balkans, and Rwanda have all counted on the international community to protect them when they knew their actions were likely to provoke violent retaliation by the state. No matter how well intended, interventions often provide a safety net to warring factions and diminish the incentive to peaceful conflict resolution.[29]

Not surprisingly, many LDSs see the new norm of humanitarian intervention as a ruse to reestablish neoimperial dominions.[30] These fears are not unfounded. Interventions too easily degenerate into all of the trappings of dependence, domination, and defiance typical of the age of liberal imperialism, when developing states submitted to the "tutelage" of the great powers. Intervening powers are liable to shirk the necessary investment of time, money, and personnel to make reform sustainable. More damning, they may then use the stalled reconstruction as a pretext to continue insinuating their control over the target state, provoking an inevitable nationalist backlash.[31] The U.S. experience in trying to rebuild the Iraqi army since 2003 parallels Britain's experience in the 1920s, in which the intervening power failed to provide adequate attention to raising and training an Iraqi army that could stand on its own and then criticized the Iraqis for the lack of substantive reform. Like the British before them, U.S. forces have been disappointed and dismayed when Iraqi troops refused to serve under foreign command or to fight against their own kin. In both cases, the seemingly interminable presence of foreign troops inspired mass hostility toward the occupation and a popular revolt that took a costly and unexpected toll on the intervening power.[32]

This book shows how the dynamics of competition between various domestic and international forces provides an incentive for states to rely on nonstate actors instead of maximizing control over violence. State weakness and the emergence of militias do not constitute an aberration, dysfunction, or result of a failure of will.[33] Contrary to David Klare's contention that militias "usually seek to eliminate all the vestiges of central government within their area of operations," the case studies show how militias and state officials routinely cooperate with and mutually reinforce one another.[34]

Given the resilience of armed nonstate actors as elements within the domestic political arena of developing states, it is hardly surprising that the international community often retreats from the ideals of state building (though it seldom acknowledges it as such).[35] When an American was taken hostage by Somali pirates in April 2009, U.S. authorities did not reach out to the nominally sovereign transitional government in Mogadishu but to the tribal leaders controlling the quasi-autonomous region of Puntland.[36] In the global war on terror, Western powers are seen to rely on nonstate actors where states have proven incapable. This technique has proven so successful in Iraq that it is being duplicated in Afghanistan.[37] As Amin Saikal notes, after the pro forma gesture toward the need for a strong and legitimate central government in Kabul, the goal is to

> allow the functionary micro-societies sufficient internal autonomy ... [to] enable influential powerbrokers and actors to remain content, with incentives not to mount serious challenges to the central authority either individually or in alliance with one another.[38]

Whispers that the government in Kabul is negotiating a truce with at least some elements of the Taliban continue, and the United States itself appears to be backtracking in its commitment to eradicating the lucrative opium cultivation that funds many local warlords for fear of alienating crucial local power brokers.[39]

Still, the devolution of violence to nonstate actors in Iraq and Afghanistan has come only belatedly, after the exhaustion of all other options. Formal doctrine remains wedded to the notion that the state is the sole enactor of violence. Even the vaunted 2006 *U.S. Army & Marine Corp Counterinsurgency Field Manual*, credited with transforming American military tactics, warns that militias "constitute a long-term threat to law and order" and must be disarmed.[40] Maintaining the autonomy and authority of village headmen and tribal leaders and minimizing the intrusion of the central government can ease conflict and yield greater stability. Such mediated governance, however, runs exactly contrary to the ideals of equal protection for all citizens under the rule of law. Building states from the bottom up ultimately promotes and maintains the kinds of unequal relationships that modern states are supposed to displace.[41]

For proponents of territorial restructuring, the solution is clear but brutal: The international community should refrain from intervening in conflicts in the developing world until a clear winner has emerged and reserve the bestowal of sovereignty until a political entity proves successful in claiming control over violence in its territories. In Edward Luttwak's pithy but chilling phrase, "Give war a chance." Rather than a policy of benign neglect, this would be a manifestly perverse path to peace.[42] There is no reason to believe that states with centralized armies will do less harm to civilians than those with decentralized, militia-based ones. In fact, highly militarized states endanger both their neighbors and their own citizens.[43] Iraq's ability to project violence abroad was directly related to the coercion of its own citizens. Similarly, in Rwanda, the mobilization of the Hutu-supremacist *interahamwe* militia and the subsequent mass killing of the Tutsis was the last gasp of a state that had suddenly lost its superpower sponsor and been stripped of external defenses. Even as these Hutu militias ravaged defenseless civilians, the invading Tutsi exile army easily overran the country.[44] Heightened external threat increases the chances that a state will lash out at potentially hostile segments of its own population.[45] In a sense, this cure for state weakness is worse than the disease itself. Even more unconventional options must be explored.

## HOW THE INTERNATIONAL COMMUNITY
## CAN LEARN TO LIVE WITH MILITIAS

"Everybody agrees," *The Economist* magazine recently noted, "that more effective government around the world is desirable."[46] The problem is that so many efforts to strengthen states and eliminate militias have proven quixotic if not counterproductive. Existing policy options do little to alter the fundamental incentive structure that allows leaders in most developing countries to continue to rely on localized, informal militia forces. Peace building and international trusteeships are susceptible to subversion both by their sponsors and their recipient or target states. Reenacting Europe's blood-drenched history by allowing strong states to weed out the weak is dubious on both practical and moral grounds.

Critical engagement breaks this intellectual logjam by inviting the relegation of states to mere minority providers of security and jettisoning the trappings of statehood altogether. Not surprisingly, this view is frequently championed by specialists in Africa, such as Chris Clapham, Jeffrey Herbst, Ken Menkhaus, and Will Reno, who see the costs of artificial statehood most vividly. Where formal states are mere shadows and distant patrons, neighborhoods, villages, and clans rely on indigenous elites and networks of violence wielders to enforce order. Trying to build states on such a foundation is folly. Instead, the critical perspective seeks novel ways to integrate *terra nullius* into the international system.[47]

Abandoning the aspiration for hegemonic states comes with considerable costs. For those living without the protection of a state and its enforcement of property rights, economic progress will certainly be stunted. Power will likely revert to patrimonial networks based on clan or tribal solidarity, thwarting ambitions for social development and equality.[48] Even James C. Scott, a trenchant skeptic of state power, concedes that state-created order is essential for "our ideas about citizenship, public-health programs, social security, transportation, communication, universal public education, and equality before the law."[49] These sacrifices in public goods, however, must be weighed against the potential gain from acknowledging the power that nonstate actors already wield and working with them to protect ordinary people. The essence of human security remains basic human survival, the ultimate end toward which international policies must strive.[50]

Translating this critical perspective into substantive policy means rejecting orthodox assumptions about the necessity of states to provide a livable order and expanding the international community's toolkit for responding to state crises. Such a policy entails the deployment of local security solutions for local security problems. David Kilcullen argues that effective counterinsurgency requires an "indirect approach that appli[es] local solutions to local problems whenever possible."[51] Nearly all states dealing with guerrilla warfare have, eventually, sought ways to establish ties with local power brokers, to identify informants, and to raise a parainstitutional force. Yet for a professional and bureaucratic army whose main mission is to prevail in large-scale conventional combat, this knowledge is quickly and often deliberately ignored. As John Nagl notes, when the United States undertook the occupation of Iraq in 2003, its institutional knowledge about insurgency had so atrophied that most officers were better acquainted with the strategies of the American civil war than a century of American counterinsurgency engagements.[52] Commitments to uphold the state monopoly on violence and operational training that emphasizes force centralization make it anathema—in a sense unthinkable—to rely on militias.[53]

The first step in enacting the critical policy, then, is to make violence devolution the primary option instead of the last resort when dealing with frail and weak states. Rather than trying to displace militias by rehabilitating and augmenting state security services, the international community must focus on recruiting the services of tribes, ethnic groups, and village strongmen to serve as what Mancur Olson calls "stationary bandits."[54] If nonstate actors have already replaced state agents as the providers of protection in the local communities, then trying to remove them will only add to the impetus for short-term predation and further endanger human lives. On the other hand, defending the position of militia leaders and solidifying their ties in a local community encourages them to form a vested interest in the community's sustainability and productivity. The examples of the *sungusungu* militias that protected villages in east Africa during decades of civil war or the tribal reconciliation councils that achieved a measure of peace and stability in unrecognized Somaliland are indicative of the potential for nonstate actors to provide local security.[55]

The second step is to protect weak states from external rivals. Contrary to the rationales for peace building, territorial restructuring, and neotrusteeship, the critical approach is more concerned with the dangers stemming from state strength than from state weakness. As Kal Holsti observes, most of the mass killings of the twentieth century were organized by states against their own citizens.[56] To make violence devolution work, weak states must be confident that no external rivals can exploit their vulnerabilities. Otherwise, threatened states will be forced onto the path of military centralization, disarming nonstate actors and subjecting the population to general conscription. These steps in turn trigger international arms races that lead to far more disastrous interstate wars. The international community must stem the flow of weapons to LDSs to guarantee security to devolving states and forestall the emergence of regional competition. Additionally, such an effort would help diffuse the security dilemma between states and potential rebels groups and prevent the leakage of arms into the black market, factors that exacerbate the risk of internal conflicts.[57] Only the deliberate maintenance of state impotence can deliver the promise of peace.

The third step is to delay democracy in favor of stability. Democratic elections are often assumed to be the solution for endemic social strife and the key to bolstering the legitimacy of a regime. Legitimacy, however, is meaningless when the state ranks as but one of a number of sources of coercion citizens may rely on for their security. Notwithstanding deductive propositions about the emergence of "warlord democracy," electoral competition between candidates who have recourse to their private armed forces has repeatedly proven to intensify conflict. To paraphrase Sukarno, mixing militias and democracy is the height of living dangerously. Elections themselves become venues where political factions vie to gain control over the state's organs of violence and in turn use them against domestic opponents. The ability to impose the rule of law equally on all citizens remains a prerequisite for democratic consolidation, but it is clearly outside the grasp of failing or frail states.[58] At best, such arrangements approximate Colombia's oligopolistic democracy, where each faction is permitted to maintain its own private militia in the manner of a feudal baron. At worst, they lead to civil war, as in Lebanon's abortive attempt to maintain a consociational sectarian balance.

Ultimately, the decision to engage nonstate actors must be based on a realistic assessment of the context in which state building is to occur. Simply stated, robust and responsive states are unlikely to emerge any time soon in much of the Third World. State institutions remain captive to ethnic cliques, making a mockery of assertions that the state might be more egalitarian and progressive in its provision of public goods. The loss of the presumed state-held monopoly on violence is commonly identified as a harbinger of anarchy. But the monopoly over the use of force is an abstract ideal, not an empirical property, of existing states. Learning to accommodate those nonstate actors who are actually providing security to local communities is a better alternative than waiting in vain for strong states to replace them.

**REFERENCE MATTER**

# NOTES

Introduction

1. Report of the International Commission of Inquiry on Darfur to the United Nations Secretary-General, Geneva, January 25, 2005; retrieved on March 19, 2007, from: www.un.org/News/dh/sudan/com_inq_darfur.pdf; Usman A. Tar, "The Perverse Manifestations of Civil Militias in Africa: Evidence from Western Sudan," *Peace, Conflict, and Development*, 7 (2005).

2. Mary Kaldor, *New and Old Wars: Organizing Violence in a Global Era*, 2nd ed, (Stanford, CA: Stanford University Press, 2007), 9.

3. John Mueller, *The Remnants of War* (Ithaca, NY: Cornell University Press, 2004); Martin Van Creveld, *The Rise and Decline of the State* (New York: Cambridge University Press, 1999).

4. Stanley Hoffman, *Chaos and Violence: What Globalization, Failed States, and Terrorism Mean for U.S. Foreign Policy* (New York: Rowman & Littlefield, 2006), 9; Francis Fukuyama, *State-Building: Governance and World Order in the 21st Century* (Ithaca, NY: Cornell University Press, 2004); Robert Kaplan, *The Coming Anarchy: Shattering the Dreams of the Post Cold War* (New York: Random House, 2000).

5. U.N. Report on Protection of Civilians, 9/1999/957; see also Michael Ignatieff, "Intervention and State Failure," in Nicolaus Mills and Kira Brunner, eds., *The New Killing Fields: Massacre and the Politics of Intervention* (New York: Basic Books, 2002), 236.

6. The National Security Strategy of the United States, September 2002; retrieved on March 3, 2009, from: www.globalsecurity.org/military/library/policy/national/nss-020920.pdf.

7. Robert M. Gates, "The Future of U.S. Security Assistance," *Foreign Affairs* (May/June 2010).

8. This idea is fundamental to some of the most important recent works on state development and failure. Robert Bates uses the presence of militias as the sole indicator in his categorical measure of state failure. See Robert Bates, *When Things Fell Apart: State Failure in Late-Century Africa* (New York: Cambridge University Press, 2008), 147–148. Robert Rotberg argues that "failed states are unable to provide security—the most central and foremost political good—across the whole of their domains." See Robert Rotberg, "The New Nature of Nation-State Failure," *Washington Quarterly*, 25 (2002): 87.

9. Edward Newman, "The 'New Wars' Debate: A Historical Perspective Is Needed," *Security Dialogue*, 35 (2004); Bradford Booth, Meyer Kestnbaum, and David R. Segal, "Are Post–Cold War Militaries Postmodern?" *Armed Forces & Society*, 27 (2001); Errol Henderson and J. David Singer, "'New Wars' and Rumors of 'New Wars'" *International Interaction*, 28 (2002).

10. Michael Mann, *The Sources of Social Power, Volume 1: A History of Power from the Beginning to A.D. 1760* (New York: Cambridge University Press, 1986), 11.

11. J. P. Nettl, "The State as Conceptual Variable," *World Politics*, 20 (1968).

12. The concept of military development is derived from Jeremy Black, "Military Organization and Military Change in Historical Perspective," *Journal of Military History*, 62 (1998); Keith Krause, "Insecurity and State Formation in the Global Military Order: The Middle East Case," *European Journal of International Relations*, 2 (1996).

13. For a survey of the state of research, see David Laitin, "Comparative Politics: The State of the Subdiscipline," in Ira Katznelson and Helen V. Milner, eds., *Political Science: The State of the Discipline* (New York: Norton, 2002); Joel Migdal, "Studying the State," in Mark Lichbach and Alan Zuckerman, eds., *Comparative Politics: Rationality, Culture, and Structure* (New York: Cambridge University Press, 1997).

14. William H. McNeill, *The Pursuit of Power: Technology, Armed Forces, and Society since A.D. 1000* (Chicago: University of Chicago Press, 1982).

15. Charles Tilly, *Coercion, Capital, and European States* (Cambridge, MA: Blackwell, 1992); William R. Thompson and Karen Rasler, "War, the Military Revolution(s) Controversy, and Army Expansion," *Comparative Political Studies*, 32 (1999); Otto Hintze, *The Historical Essays of Otto Hintze*, ed. Felix Gilbert (New York: Oxford University Press, 1975).

16. Tuong Vu, "Studying the State through State Formation," *World Politics*, 62 (2010). For a few tentative attempts to examine the non-Western world, see Georg Sorensen, "War and State-Making: Why Doesn't It Work in the Third World?" *Security Dialogue*, 32 (2001); Brian D. Taylor and Roxana Botea, "Tilly Tally: War-Making and State-Making in the Contemporary Third World," *International Studies Review*, 10 (2008); Anthony W. Pereira, "Armed Forces, Coercive Monopolies, and Changing Patterns of State Formation and Violence," in Diane Davis and Anthony W. Pereira, eds.,

*Armed Forces and Their Role in Politics and State Formation* (New York: Cambridge University Press, 2003).

17. Youssef Cohen, Brian R. Brown, and A. F. K. Organski, "The Paradoxical Nature of State Making: The Violent Creation of Order," *American Political Science Review*, 75 (1981).

18. Miguel A. Centeno, *Blood and Debt: War and the Nation State in Latin America* (State College: Penn State Press, 2002).

19. Robert Jackson and Carl Rosberg, "Why Africa's Weak States Persist: The Empirical and the Juridical in Statehood," *World Politics*, 35 (1982).

20. Raju G. C. Thomas, "What Is Third World Security?" *Annual Review of Political Science*, 6 (2003); Mohammed Ayoob, *The Third World Security Predicament: State Making, Regional Conflict, and the International System* (Boulder, CO: Lynne Rienner, 1995); Robert E. Harkavy and Stephanie G. Neuman, *Warfare and the Third World* (New York: Palgrave, 2001).

21. Robert Holden, *Armies without Nations: Public Violence and State Formation in Central America, 1821–1960* (New York: Oxford University Press, 2004).

22. Nazih Ayubi, *Over-Stating the Arab State: Politics and Society in the Middle East* (New York: I. B. Tauris, 1995).

23. Eliot Cohen, "Distant Battles: Modern War in the Third World," *International Security*, 10 (1986).

24. Renate Mayntz, "Mechanisms in the Analysis of Social Macro-Phenomena," *Philosophy of Social Sciences*, 34 (2004): 254.

25. Francis Fukuyama, *State-Building: Governance and World Order in the 21st Century* (Ithaca, NY: Cornell University Press, 2004).

26. Peter Hall and Rosemary Taylor, "Political Science and the Three New Institutionalisms," *Political Studies*, 44 (1996); André Lecours, "New Institutionalism: Issues and Questions," in André Lecours, ed., *New Institutionalism: Theory and Analysism* (Buffalo, NY: University of Toronto Press, 2005).

27. Theda Skocpol and Margaret Somers, "The Use of Comparative History in Macrosocial Inquiry," *Comparative Studies in Society and History*, 22 (1980).

28. John Gerring, *Case Study Research: Principles and Practices* (New York: Cambridge University Press, 2007), Chapter 6; Charles Ragin, *The Comparative Method: Moving beyond Qualitative and Quantitative Strategies* (Berkeley: University of California Press, 1987).

29. Craig Calhoun, "Explanation in Historical Sociology: Narrative, General Theory, and Historically Specific Theory," *American Journal of Sociology*, 104 (1998).

30. Cameron Thies, "A Pragmatic Guide to Qualitative Historical Analysis in the Study of International Relations," *International Studies Quarterly*, 3 (2002); Joseph M. Bryant, "On Sources and Narratives in Historical Social Science: A Realist Critique of Positivist and Postmodernist Epistemologies," *British Journal of Sociology*, 51

(2000); Ian Lustick, "History, Historiography, and Political Science: Multiple Historical Records and the Problems of Selection Bias," *American Political Science Review*, 90 (1996).

## Chapter 1:  The Origins and Persistence of State-Sponsored Militias

1. Max Weber, "Politics as Vocation," in H. H. Gerth and C. Wright Mills, eds., *From Max Weber: Essays in Sociology* (New York: Oxford University Press, 1958), 78 (italics in original).

2. For a recent example of a definition of stateness very much dependent on Weber, see Margaret Levi, "The State of the Study of the State," in Ira Katznelson and Helen V. Milner, eds., *Political Science: The State of the Discipline* (New York: W. W. Norton & Company, 2002), 40; and Joel Migdal, *State in Society: Studying How States and Societies Transform One Another* (New York: Cambridge University Press, 2001), 14–15.

3. Douglass North, *Structure and Change in Economic History* (New York: W. W. Norton, 1981), 21.

4. The premier example of the statist literature is Peter Evans, Dietrich Rueschmeyer, and Theda Skocpol, eds., *Bringing the State Back In* (New York: Cambridge University Press, 1983). For a summary of the critiques, see Karen Barkey and Sunita Parikh, "Comparative Perspectives on the State," *Annual Review of Sociology* 17 (1991).

5. A. D. Smith, "State-Making and Nation-Building," in John A. Hall, ed., *States in History* (London: Basil Blackwell, 1986). For historical studies of the state and its rivals, see David Robinson, *Bandits, Eunuchs, and the Son of Heaven: Rebellion and the Economy of Violence in Mid-Ming China* (Honolulu: University of Hawaii Press, 2001); Karen Barkey, *Bandits and Bureaucrats: The Ottoman Route to State Centralization* (Ithaca, NY: Cornell University Press, 1994); and Janice E. Thomson, *Mercenaries, Pirates, and Sovereigns: State-Building and Extraterritorial Violence in Early Modern Europe* (Princeton, NJ: Princeton University Press, 1994).

6. Michael Mann, *The Sources of Social Power, Volume 1: A History of Power from the Beginning to A.D. 1760* (New York: Cambridge University Press, 1986), 7–8. For a further discussion of the evolution of feudal into modern state armies, see Azar Gat, *War in Human Civilization* (New York: Oxford University Press, 2006).

7. Brian Downing, *The Military Revolution and Political Change: Origins of Democracy and Autocracy in Early Modern Europe* (Princeton, NJ: Princeton University Press, 1992), 10; William H. McNeill, *The Pursuit of Power: Technology, Armed Forces, and Society since A.D. 1000* (Chicago: University of Chicago Press, 1982), 142.

8. Charles Tilly, *Coercion, Capital and European States, A.D. 990–1992* (Malden, MA: Blackwell, 1992).

9. Jeff Goodwin, *No Other Way Out: States and Revolutionary Movements, 1945–1991* (New York: Cambridge University Press, 2001), 60–61; and Raju G. C. Thomas, "What Is Third World Security?" *Annual Review of Political Science*, 6 (2003).

10. For instance, see James Fearon, "Why Do Some Civil Wars Last So Much Longer than Others?" *Journal of Peace Research*, 41 (2004).

11. Stathis Kalyvas, *The Logic of Violence in Civil War* (New York: Cambridge University Press, 2006).

12. The term *parainstitutional* is meant to incorporate paramilitaries and militia groups together. See Carlos Medina Gallego and Mireya Tellez Adila, *La violencia parainstitucional: paramilitary y parapolitical en Colombia* (Bogota: Rodrigez Quito, 1994); Robert Holden, *Armies without Nations: Public Violence and State Formation in Central America, 1821–1960* (New York: Oxford University Press, 2004); and Julie Mazzei, *Death Squads of Self-Defense Forces? How Paramilitary Groups Emerge and Challenge Democracy in Latin America* (Chapel Hill: University of North Carolina Press, 2009).

13. Cited in William Aviles, *Global Capitalism, Democracy, and Civil–Military Relations in Colombia* (Albany: SUNY Press, 2006), 110–111.

14. Russell Crandall, *Driving by Drugs: U.S. Policy Toward Colombia*, 2nd edition (Boulder, CO: Lynne Rienner, 2008); Frank Stafford and Marco Palacios, *Colombia: Fragmented Land, Divided Society* (New York: Oxford University Press, 2002); and Max G. Manwaring, *Non-State Actors in Colombia: Threat and Response* (Carlisle, PA: U.S. Army War College Strategic Studies Monograph, 2002).

15. This is closely related to both Mann and Theda Skocpol's minimalist definition of the state as constituting a specific set of elites inhabiting an executive authority. See Michael Mann, "The Autonomous Power of the States: Its Origins, Mechanisms, and Results," in John A. Hall, ed., *States in History*, (New York: Basil Blackwell, 1986), 125; and Theda Skocpol, *States and Social Revolutions: A Comparative Analysis of France, Russia, and China* (New York: Cambridge University Press, 1979), 29.

16. George M. Thomas and John W. Meyer, "The Expansion of the State," *Annual Review of Sociology*, 10 (1984); Theo Farrell, "World Culture and Military Power," *Security Studies* 14 (2005): 455; and Emily O. Goldman, "The Cultural Foundations of Military Diffusion," *Review of International Studies*, 32 (2006): 72.

17. Öyvind Öserud, "The Narrow Gate: Entry to the Club of Sovereign States," *Review of International Studies*, 23 (1997).

18. The idea of "mirroring" comes from John J. McCuen, *The Art of Counter-Revolutionary War: The Strategy of Counter-Insurgency* (London: Faber & Faber, 1966), 50. On the cellular organizational of insurgent groups, see Sun-Ki Chai, "An Organizational Economics Theory of Antigovernment Violence," *Comparative Politics*, 26 (1993).

19. William Chambliss, "State-Organized Crime," *Criminology*, 27 (1989).

20. Quoted in Robert Joe Stout, "Letter from Oaxaca: No End in Sight," *American Scholar*, 77 (2008): 8.

21. See Alice Hills, "Warlords, Militia and Conflict in Contemporary Africa: A Re-Examination of Terms," *Small Wars & Insurgencies*, 8 (1997); Kimberly Marten, "Warlordism in Comparative Perspective," *International Security*, 31 (2006/07).

22. Robert Bates, *When Things Fell Apart: State Failure in Late-Century Africa* (New York: Cambridge University Press, 2008), 29.

23. Eric Hobsbawm, *Bandits* (New York: New Press, 2000), 61.

24. On private military contractors, see Deborah Avant, *The Market for Force: The Consequences of Privatizing Security* (New York: Cambridge University Press, 2005); and P. W. Singer, *Corporate Warriors: The Rise of Privatized Military Industry* (Ithaca, NY: Cornell University Press, 2003).

25. Abdulkader Sinno, *Organizations at War in Afghanistan and Beyond* (Ithaca, NY: Cornell University Press, 2008), 47, 87–89.

26. Jeremy Weinstein, *Inside Rebellion: The Politics of Insurgent Violence* (New York: Cambridge University Press, 2007).

27. Oliver E. Williamson, *Markets and Hierarchies, Analysis, and Antitrust Implications: A Study of Economies of Internal Organization* (New York: Free Press, 1975); see also Patrick Bolton and John Farrell, "Decentralization, Duplicity and Delay," *Journal of Political Economy*, 98 (1990); and Oliver Hart and John Moore, "On the Design of Hierarchies: Coordination versus Specialization," *Journal of Political Economy*, 115 (2005).

28. Kalyvas, 175; Robert E. Harkavy and Stephanie G. Neuman, *Warfare and the Third World* (New York: Palgrave, 2001), 198; and Sunil Dasgupta, "Understanding Paramilitary Growth: Agency Relations in Military Organization," Paper presented at the Centre for International Relations, Liu Institute for Global Issues, University of British Columbia, Vancouver, November 13–15, 2003.

29. Usman A. Tar, "The Perverse Manifestations of Civil Militias in Africa: Evidence from Western Sudan," *Peace, Conflict, and Development*, 7 (2005); Jason Lyall, "Are Coethnics More Effective Counterinsurgents? Evidence from the Second Chechen War," *American Political Science Review*, 104 (2010); Kalyvas, 107.

30. Adam Roberts, *Nations in Arms: The Theory and Practice of Territorial Defense* (New York: International Institute for Strategic Studies, 1976); and John Ellis, *Armies in Revolution* (New York: Oxford University Press, 1974), 238.

31. Bruce B. Campbell, "Death Squads: Definition, Problems, and Historical Context," in Bruce B. Campbell and Arthur D. Brenner, eds., *Death Squads in Global Perspective: Murder with Deniability* (New York: Palgrave Macmillan, 2002); Stanley Cohen, *States of Denial: Knowing about Atrocities and Suffering* (Malden, MA: Polity Press, 2001), 108–109; Neil J. Mitchell, *Agents of Atrocity: Leaders, Followers, and the Violation of Human Rights in Civil War* (New York: Palgrave Macmillan, 2004); and Phillip G. Roessler, "Donor-Induced Democratization and Privatization of State Violence in Kenya and Rwanda," *Comparative Politics*, 27 (2005).

32. Kalyvas, 107–109.

33. See William Reno, *Warlord Politics and the African States* (Boulder, CO: Lynne Rienner, 1998).

34. Joel Migdal, *Strong Societies and Weak States: State–Society Relations and Capabilities in the Third World* (Princeton, NJ: Princeton University Press, 1988), 214–222.

35. Joseph Kostiner and Philip Khoury, eds., *Tribes and State Formation in the Middle East* (Berkeley: University of California Press, 1990); and Richard Tapper, *Frontier Nomads of Iran: A Political and Social History of the Shahsevan* (New York: Cambridge University Press, 1997).

36. Sharon Kettering, "The Historical Development of Political Clientelism," *Journal of Interdisciplinary History*, 18 (1988): 425–426; and Barkey, 10–14.

37. Stephen Biddle, *Military Power: Explaining Victory and Defeat in Modern Battle* (Princeton, NJ: Princeton University Press, 2004); and Martin Van Creveld, *Supplying War: Logistics from Wallenstein to Patton* (New York: Cambridge University Press, 2004).

38. Hillel Frisch, "Explaining Third World Security Structures," *Journal of Strategic Studies*, 25 (2002); James T. Quinlivian, "Coup-Proofing: Its Practice and Consequences in the Middle East," *International Security*, 24 (1999); and John Mackinlay, *Globalisation and Insurgency* (New York: Oxford University Press, 2002), 44–54.

39. Steven David, *Choosing Sides: Alignment and Realignment in the Third World* (Baltimore: Johns Hopkins University Press, 1991); and Mohammed Ayoob, *The Third World Security Predicament: State Making, Regional Conflict, and the International System* (Boulder, CO: Lynne Rienner, 1995).

40. Brian D. Taylor and Roxana Botea, "Tilly Tally: War-Making and State-Making in the Contemporary Third World," *International Studies Review*, 10 (2008); and Georg Sorensen, "War and State-Making: Why Doesn't It Work in the Third World?" *Security Dialogue*, 32 (2001).

41. See David.

42. Arie M. Kacowicz, *Zones of Peace in the Third World: South America and West Africa in Comparative Perspective* (Albany: State University of New York Press, 1998), 38–39, 194.

43. See H. E. Chehabi and Juan J. Linz, "A Theory of Sultanism 1: A Type of Non-Democratic Rule," in H. E. Chehabi and Juan J. Linz, eds., *Sultanistic Regimes* (Baltimore: Johns Hopkins University Press, 1998), 12.

44. Gregory Sanjian, "Promoting Stability or Instability: Arms Transfers and Regional Rivalries, 1950–1991," *International Studies Quarterly*, 43:3 (1999); "Cold War Imperatives and Quarrelsome Clients," *Journal of Conflict Resolution*, 42:1 (1998).

45. Bruce Bueno de Mesquita, Randolph Siverson, and Gary Woller, "War and the Fate of Regimes: A Comparative Analysis," *American Political Science Review*, 86 (1992): 641–643; and H. E. Goemans, "Fighting for Survival: The Fate of Leaders and the Duration of War," *Journal of Conflict Resolution*, 44 (2000).

46. Robert M. Rosh, "Third World Militarization: Security Webs and the States They Ensnare," *Journal of Conflict Resolution*, 32 (1988); and A. F. Mullins Jr., *Born*

*Arming: Development and Military Power in News States* (Stanford, CA: Stanford University Press, 1987). Even Wendt and Barnett, who emphasize cultural diffusion of military norms, detect an "action–reaction dynamic" among competing states. See Alexander Wendt and Michael Barnett, "Dependent State Formation and Third World Militarization," *Review of International Studies*, 19 (1994).

47. Renate Mayntz, "Mechanisms in the Analysis of Social Macro-Phenomena," *Philosophy of Social Sciences*, 34 (2004): 254; and Jack Goldstone, "Initial Conditions, General Laws, and Path Dependence in Historical Sociology," *American Journal of Sociology*, 104 (1998).

48. James Mahoney, "Path Dependence in Historical Sociology," *Theory and Society*, 29 (2000); and Paul Pierson, "Increasing Returns, Path Dependence, and the Study of Politics," *American Political Science Review*, 94 (2000).

49. Eliot Cohen, "Distant Battles: Modern War in the Third World," *International Security*, 10:4 (1986); Jeremy Black, "Military Organization and Military Change in Historical Perspective," *Journal of Military History*, 62 (1998); and Hendrik Spruyt, *The Sovereign State and Its Competitors* (Princeton, NJ: Princeton University Press, 1994), 18.

50. On the importance of bottom-up processes, see Charles King, "The Micropolitics of Social Violence," *World Politics*, 56:3 (2004); and Douglas McAdams, Sidney Tarrow, and Charles Tilly, *Dynamics of Contention* (New York: Cambridge University Press, 2001), 333. On the distinctive features of revolutionary armies, see Katherine Chorley, *Armies and the Art of Revolution* (Boston: Beacon Press, 1973).

51. This pathway corresponds to what Jonathan Adelman calls "secular military modernization," as opposed to revolutionary transformation. This is part and parcel of a more general trend of "defensive" modernization of the state apparatus. See Jonathan Adelman, *Revolutions, Armies, and War: A Political History* (Boulder, CO: Lynne Rienner, 1985), 206–207; and Hans Joas, "The Modernity of War," *International Sociology*, 14 (1999).

52. Cynthia Enloe, *Ethnic Soldiers: State Security in Divided Societies* (Athens: University of Georgia Press, 1980).

53. Claude Welch, "Continuity and Discontinuity in African Military Organisations," *Journal of Modern African Studies* 13 (1975); and David Killingray, "Guardians of Empire," in David Killingray and David Omissi, eds., *Guardians of Empire: The Armed Forces of the Colonial Powers, c. 1700–1964* (New York: St. Martin's Press, 1999).

54. Elisabeth Jean Wood, "The Social Processes of Civil War: The Wartime Transformation of Social Networks," *Annual Review of Political Science*, 11 (2008): 541.

55. Risa Brooks, "The Impact of Culture, Society, Institutions, and International Forces on Military Effectiveness," in Risa Brooks and Elizabeth Stanley, eds., *Creating Military Power: The Sources of Military Effectiveness* (Stanford, CA: Stanford University Press, 2007), 10.

56. Bertrand M. Roehner and Tony Syme, *Pattern and Repertoire in History* (Cambridge, MA: Harvard University Press, 2002), 22–23; and Giovanni Dosi and Richard Nelson, "An Introduction to Evolutionary Theories in Economics," *Journal of Evolutionary Economics*, 4 (1994).

57. Colin Crouch and Henry Farrell, "Breaking the Path of Institutional Development? Alternatives to the New Determinism," *Rationality & Society* 16 (2004); Kathleen Thelen, *How Institutions Evolve: The Political Economy of Skills in Germany, Britain, the United States, and Japan* (New York: Cambridge University Press, 2004); and Jack Knight, *Institutions and Social Conflict* (New York: Cambridge University Press, 1992).

58. Martin Van Creveld, *The Transformation of War* (New York: Free Press, 1991), 95; and David B. Ralston, *Importing the European Army: The Introduction of European Military Techniques and Institutions into the Extra-European World, 1600–1914* (Chicago: University of Chicago Press, 1990). For example, U.S. military advisors were intimately involved in supporting the creation of militia forces in Latin America. See S. Löfving, "Paramilitaries of the Empire: Guatemala, Colombia and Israel," *Social Analysis*, 48 (2004).

59. On typological theorizing, see Alexander George and Andrew Bennett, *Case Studies and Theory Development in the Social Sciences* (Cambridge, MA: MIT Press, 2005), Chapter 11.

60. Adelman, 206. See also Skocpol.

61. Chorley, 208–209.

62. On historical process tracing and counterfactual analysis, see George and Bennett, Chapter 10; Tim Büthe, "Taking Temporality Serious: Modeling History and the Use of Narrative as Evidence," *American Political Science Review,* 96 (2002); and Clayton Roberts, *The Logic of Historical Explanation* (University Park: Penn State University Press, 1996).

63. Evan Lieberman, "Causal Inference in Historical Institutional Analysis: A Specification of Periodization Strategies," *Comparative Political Studies,* 34 (2001).

64. John Gerring, *Case Study Research: Principles and Practices* (New York: Cambridge University Press, 2007), 116–120; and George and Bennett, 80, 120–121.

## Chapter 2: Indonesia

1. Clifford Geertz, "The Integrative Revolution: Primordial Sentiments and Civil Politics in the New States," in *The Interpretation of Cultures: Selected Essays* (New York: Basic Books, 2000).

2. On the various interpretations of the New Order, see Dwight King, "Indonesia's New Order as a Bureaucratic Polity, a Neopatrimonal Regime, or a Bureaucratic Authoritarian Regime: What Difference Does It Make?" in Benedict Anderson and Audrey Kahin, eds., *Interpreting Indonesian Politics* (Ithaca, NY: Cornell University

Press, 1982); Donald K. Emmerson, "Understanding the New Order: Bureaucratic Pluralism in Indonesia," *Asian Survey*, 23 (1983); Harold Crouch, "Patrimonalism and Military Rule," *World Politics*, 31 (1979).

3. Ulf Sundhaussen, "The Military: Structure, Procedures, and Effects on Indonesian Society," in Karl D. Jackson and Lucian W. Pye, eds., *Political Power and Communications in Indonesia* (Berkeley: University of California Press, 1978), 60–61. See also Peter Britton, "The Indonesian Army: 'Stabiliser' and 'Dynamiser,'" in Rex Mortimer, ed., *The Showcase State: The Illusion of Indonesian's "Accelerated Modernisation"* (London: Angus and Robertson, 1973), 85.

4. Syarif Hidayat, "'Hidden Autonomy': Understanding the Nature of Indonesian Decentralization on a Day-to-Day Basis," in Maribeth Erb, Priyambudi Sulistiyanto, and Carole Faucher, eds., *Regionalism in Post-Suharto Indonesia* (New York: Routledge Curzon, 2006). See also Richard Tanter, "The Totalitarian Ambition: Intelligence and Security Agencies in Indonesia," in Arief Budiman, ed., *State and Civil Society in Indonesia* (Victoria, Australia: Center for Southeast Asian Studies, Monash University, 1994).

5. For perhaps the examples of these revisionism, see Benedict Anderson, ed., *Violence and the State in Suharto's Indonesia* (Ithaca, NY: Southeast Asia Program Publications, Cornell University, 2001); Jacque Bertrand, *Nationalism and Ethnic Conflict in Indonesia* (New York: Cambridge University Press, 2004); John Sidel, *Riots, Pogroms, and Jihad: Religious Violence in Indonesia* (Ithaca, NY: Cornell University Press, 2006).

6. Clifford Geertz, *Agricultural Involution: The Process of Ecological Change in Indonesia* (Berkeley: University of California Press, 1963), 47–48; Luc Nagtegaal, *Riding the Dutch Tiger: The Dutch East Indies Company and the Northeast Cost of Java, 1680–1743*, tr. Beverley Jackson (Leiden, The Netherlands: KITLV Press, 1996).

7. G. Carter Bentley, "Indigenous States of Southeast Asia," *Annual Review of Anthropology*, 15 (1986): 219–220; Michael Charney, *Southeast Asian Warfare, 1300–1900* (Leiden: Brill, 2004), 214–220. For more studies on precolonial Java, see Soemarsaid Moertono, *State and Statecraft in Old Java: A Study of the Late Mataram Period 16th to 19th Century* (Ithaca, NY: Cornell University Press, 1968); B. Schrieke, *Indonesian Sociological Studies* (Amsterdam: Royal Tropical Institute, 1955).

8. Gayl D. Ness and William Stahl, "Western Imperial Armies in Asia," *Comparative Studies in Society and History*, 19:1 (1977). On the Java War, see M. C. Ricklefs, *A History of Modern Indonesia, c. 1300* (Stanford, CA: Stanford University Press, 1993), 111–116. On the Aceh suppression, see Ricklefs, 144–147; Robert Cribb, *Gangsters and Revolutionaries: The Jakarta People's Militia and the Indonesian Revolution* (Honolulu: University of Hawaii Press, 1991), 31.

9. H. W. van den Doels, "Military Rule in the Netherland Indies," in *The Late Colonial State in Indonesia: Political and Economic Foundations of the Netherlands Indies, 1890–1942*, ed. Robert Crib (Leiden: KITLV Press, 1994), 59. According to Rick-

lefs, 68 percent of KNIL's Indonesian troops were Javanese, 20 percent Ambonese, and the remainder Sundanese, Madurese, Bugis, and assorted Malays (mainly Timorese) (Ricklefs, 131–147; David Chandler et al., *In Search of Southeast Asia* [Honolulu: University of Hawaii Press, 1987], 193–194; Elsbeth Locker-Scholten, "State Violence and the Police in Colonial Indonesia," in *Roots of Violence in Indonesia: Contemporary Violence in Historical Perspective*, eds. Freek Colombijn and J. Thomas Lindblad [Leiden: KITLV Press, 2002], 92–93.

10. J. S. Furnivall, *Netherlands India: A Study of a Plural Economy* (New York: Macmillan, 1944), 255; Heather Sutherland, *The Making of a Bureaucratic Elite: The Colonial Transformation of the Javanese Priyayi* (Singapore: Heinemann Educational, 1979), 130.

11. Harry J. Benda, "The Pattern of Administrative Reform in the Closing Years of Dutch Rule in Indonesia," *Journal of Asian Studies*, 25 (1966): 595–596; Donald K. Emmerson, "The Bureaucracy in Political Contact: Weakness in Strength," in Karl D. Jackson and Lucian W. Pye, eds., *Political Power and Communications in Indonesia* (Berkeley: University of California Press, 1978), 85–87.

12. Furnivall, 260.

13. F. W. Diehl, "Revenue Farming and Colonial Finances in the Netherlands East Indies, 1816–1925," in *The Rise and Fall of Revenue Farming: Business Elites and the Emergence of the Modern State in Southeast Asia*, eds. John Butcher and Howard Dick (New York: St. Martin's, 1993), 199–207.

14. Bernard H. M. Vlekke, *Nusantara: A History of the East Indian Archipelago* (Cambridge, MA: Harvard University Press, 1945), 325–375; L. de Long, *The Collapse of a Colonial Society: The Dutch in Indonesia during the Second World War* (Leiden, The Netherlands: KITLV Press, 2002), 19; Ricklefs, 172; Locker-Scholten, 48; Benda, "Administrative Reform," 594–596.

15. Adas argues for seeing the *jago* as a type of Hobsbawmian social bandit. Schulte-Nordholt provides an important corrective, pointing out the *jago*'s collusion with state officials. See Michael Adas, "From Avoidance to Confrontation: Peasant Protest in Precolonial and Colonial Southeast Asia," *Comparative Studies in Society and History*, 23 (1981); Henk Schulte Nordholt, "The *Jago* in the Shadow: Crime and 'Order' in the Colonial State in Java," *Review of Indonesian and Malaysian Affairs* 25 (1991).

16. Sutherland, 132–144; Onghokham, The Residency of Madiun Pryayi and Peasant in the 19th Century (PhD dissertation, Yale University, 1975); Michael Adas, "'Moral Economy' or 'Contested State': Elite Demands and the Origins of Peasant Protest in Southeast Asia," *Journal of Social History*, 13 (1980).

17. Cribb, *Gansters and Revolutionaries*, 18–21.

18. Ricklefs, 178–179; Locker-Scholten, 47. See also Harry J. Benda, "The Communist Rebellions of 1926–1928 in Indonesia," *Pacific Historical Review*, 24 (1955);

and Ruth McVey, *The Rise of Indonesian Communism* (Ithaca, NY: Cornell University Press, 1965).

19. Cited in Locker-Scholten, 47.

20. Benda, "Administrative Reform," 591.

21. On Japan's relationship with local nationalism, see Paul Kratoska, ed., *Asian Labor in the Wartime Japanese Empire* (Singapore: Singapore University Press, 2006); Joyce C. Lebra, ed., *Japan's Greater East Asia Co-Prosperity Sphere in World War II: Selected Readings and Documents* (New York: Oxford University Press, 1975); Roman H. Myers and Mark R. Peattie, eds., *The Japanese Colonial Empire, 1895–1945* (Princeton, NJ: Princeton University Press, 1984).

22. Benedict Anderson, *Java in a Time of Revolution: Occupation and Resistance* (Ithaca, NY: Cornell University Press, 1972), 26–27, 237; Anthony Reid, *The Indonesian National Revolution, 1945–1950* (Hawthorne, Victoria: Longman, 1974), 15–17; George McT. Kahin, *Nationalism and Revolution in Indonesia* (Ithaca, NY: Cornell University Press, [1952] 2003), 101–131; Joyce C. Lebra, *Japanese-Trained Armies in Southeast Asia* (New York: Columbia University Press, 1977), Chapter 4.

23. For the low estimation and a note on Hizbollah's devolved structure, see Kahin, 163. For a higher estimate, see Reid, *Indonesian National Revolution*, 15–17. For an extended study of Indonesian Islamic groups under Japanese occupation and in the revolution, see Harry Benda, *The Crescent and the Rising Sun: Indonesian Islam under Japanese Occupation* (The Hague: W. van Hoeve, 1958); C. Van Dijk, *Rebellion under the Banner of Islam: The Darul Islam in Indonesia* (The Hague: Martinus Nijhoff, 1981), 68–78.

24. Anderson, *Java in a Time of Revolution*. See also the entry in Robert Cribb, *Historical Dictionary of Indonesia* (Metuchen, NJ: Scarecrow Press, 1992), 364.

25. George Kahin, *Nationalism and Revolution*. A more recent addition is Reid, *Indonesian National Revolution*. This narrative deals mainly with the events on Java, relying as well on Anderson's *Java in a Time of Revolution* and Cribb's *Gangsters and Revolutionaries*. To appreciate the diversity of experiences on the outer islands, see Audrey Kahin, ed., *Regional Dynamics of the Indonesian Revolution: Unity from Diversity* (Honolulu: University of Hawaii Press, 1985).

26. Kahin, *Nationalism and Revolution*, 140–142; Cribb, *Gangsters and Revolutionaries*, 43, 49–62; Reid, *Indonesian National Revolution*, 22–23; Van Dijk, 134–135.

27. Cited in Anderson, *Java in a Time of Revolution*, 235.

28. Cribb, *Gangsters and Revolutionaries*, 70–78, 94–119; Geoffrey Robinson, *Dark Side of Paradise* (Ithaca, NY: Cornell University Press, 1995), 157–158; Kahin, *Nationalism and Revolution*, 162–164; Harold Crouch, *The Army and Politics in Indonesia* (Ithaca, NY: Cornell University Press, 1988), 27; Ruth McVey, "The Post-Revolutionary Transformation of the Indonesian Army, Part I," *Indonesia*, 11 (1971): 136–137, 140–142; Van Dijk, 75; Anderson, *Java in a Time of Revolution*, 105–106.

29. Kahin, *Nationalism and Revolution*, 184–185; Cribb, *Gangsters and Revolutionaries*, 118–125.

30. Reid, *The Indonesian National Revolution*, 78–79; Salim Said, *Genesis of Power: General Sudirman and the Indonesia Military in Politics, 1945–49* (Singapore: Institute of Southeast Asian Studies, 1991). In other parts of the country, the process of appointing commanders was even more bottom up. See Audrey Kahin, "Introduction," in *Regional Dynamics of the Indonesian Revolution*, 16–17.

31. McVey, "Post Revolutionary Transformation, Part I," 133–136; Lebra, 170–171.

32. An example of this anarchic situation: In June 1946, radicals of the Barisan Banteg (Buffalo Legion) affiliated with the 3rd TKI Division kidnapped Sjahrir and several other ministers favoring a conciliatory negotiating posture with the Dutch. See Kahin, *Nationalism and Revolution*, 186–189.

33. Petra M. H. Groen, "Militant Response: The Dutch Use of Military Force and the Decolonization of the Dutch East Indies, 1945–50," *Journal of Imperial and Commonwealth History*, 21 (1993): 36.

34. Cited in Van Dijk, 71–72

35. Reid, *Indonesian National Revolution*, 113–115; Kahin, *Nationalism and Revolution*, 260–262; Raymond Kennedy, "Truce in Indonesia," *Far Eastern Survey* 17 (1948).

36. See Kahin, *Nationalism and Revolution*, 228–229, 326–331; Van Dijk, 85–126; Karl Jackson and Johannes Meoliono, "Participation in Rebellion: The Dar'ul Islam in West Java," in R. William Liddle, ed., *Political Participation in Modern Indonesia* (New Haven, CT: Yale University Press, 1973); C. A. O. van Nieuwenhuijze, "The Dar ul-Islam Movement in Western Java," *Pacific Affairs*, 23 (1950).

37. Kahin, *Nationalism and Revolution*, 260–262, 295; Ann Swift, *The Road to Madiun: The Indonesian Communist Uprising of 1948* (Ithaca, NY: Cornell University Press, 1989).

38. On the military dimensions of the offensive and the counterinsurgency campaigns, see Kahin, *Nationalism and Revolution*, 391–392, 407–416; Groen, 38–40. On the diplomatic dimensions, see Gelof D. Homan, "The Netherlands, the United States, and the Indonesian Question, 1948," *Journal of Contemporary History*, 25 (1990); and Robert J. McMahon, *Colonialism and Cold War: The United States and the Struggle for Indonesian Independence, 1945–49* (Ithaca, NY: Cornell University Press, 1981).

39. McVey, "Post-Revolutionary Transformation, Part I," 137.

40. Cribb, *Gangsters and Revolutionaries*, 156–158; Robert Cribb, "Military Strategy in the Indonesian Revolution: Nasution's Concept of 'Total People's War' in Theory and Practice," *War & Society*, 19 (2001); McKey, "Post-Revolutionary Transformation, Part I," 165–166.

41. Reid, *Indonesian National Revolution*, 135.

42. T. B. Simatupang, *Report from Banaran: The Experience during People's War*, tr. Benedict Anderson and Elizabeth Graves (Ithaca, NY: Cornell University Press, 1972), 62–63.

43. Simatupang, 62–63.

44. See Simatupang's analysis in his June 19, 1949, memo, "General Report from Banaran: Developments since December 19, 1948," in Simatupang, Chapter 8.

45. A complete recounting and analysis of political and economic development in Indonesia following independence is beyond the scope of this book. On the parliamentary period, see Herbert Feith, *The Decline of Constitutional Democracy in Indonesia* (Ithaca, NY: Cornell University Press, 1962); on the Suharto era, see Donald Weatherbee, *Ideology in Indonesia: Sukarno's Indonesian Revolution* (New Haven, CT: Yale University Press, 1966). On the New Order, see Michael Vatikiotis, *Indonesian Politics under Suharto: Order, Development and Pressure for Change* (New York: Routledge, 1993).

46. A general consensus now holds that the coup was in fact genuine, if badly executed, and that Suharto was an opportunist but innocent in the conspiracy. See Harold Crouch, "Another Look at the Indonesia 'Coup,'" *Indonesia* 15 (1973); Helen-Louise Hunter, *Sukarno and the Indonesia Coup: The Untold Story* (Westport, CT: Praeger, 2007).

47. McVey, "The Post-Revolutionary Transformation, Pt I," 131–132.

48. McVey, "The Post-Revolutionary Transformation, Pt I," 174–175; Ken Conboy, *Kopassus: Inside Indonesia's Special Forces* (Jakarta: Equinox Publishing, 2003); Bryan Evans III, "The Influence of the United States Army on the Development of the Indonesian Army (1954–1964)," *Indonesia*, 47 (1989).

49. McVey, "The Post-Revolutionary Transformation, Pt. I," 140–142; Sundhaussen, "The Military: Structure, Procedures, and Effects," 67–68; Ulf Sundhaussen, *The Road to Power: Indonesian Military Politics, 1945–1967* (New York: Oxford University Press, 1982), 13–15.

50. McVey, "The Post-Revolutionary Transformation, Pt I," 143–145, 154; Van Dijk, 181, 343–353. Crouch, *The Army and Politics*, 32–37; for an extensive discussion of political maneuvering within the military, see Sundhaussen, *The Road to Power*.

51. For a translation of Nasution's work, see Abdul Haris Nasution, *Fundamentals of Guerrilla Warfare* (New York: Praeger, 1965). For an discussion of Nasution's impact on Indonesian military doctrine, see C. L. M. Penders and Ulf Sandhaussen, *Abdul Haris Nasution: A Political Biography* (New York: University of Queensland Press, 1985); Robert Cribb, "Military Strategy in the Indonesian Revolution"; Barry Turner, Nasution: Total People's Resistance and Organicist Thinking in Indonesia (PhD dissertation, Swinburne University of Technology, Melbourne, 2005).

52. Mohammed Natsir, cited in Audrey Kahin, *Rebellion to Integration: West Sumatra and the Indonesian Polity, 1926–1998* (Amsterdam: Amsterdam University Press 1999), 221.

53. Robinson, *Dark Side of Paradise*, 225–226.

54. David Kilcullen, "Globalisation and the Development of Indonesian Counterinsurgency Tactics," *Small Wars and Insurgencies*, 17 (2006); Cribb, "From Total People's Defence to Massacre," in Colombijn and Lindblad, *Roots of Violence in Indonesia*, 238; Robinson, "People's War," 291–292.

55. Richard Tanter, "The Totalitarian Ambition: Intelligence and Security Agencies in Indonesia," in Arief Budiman, ed., *State and Civil Society in Indonesia* (Monash, Victoria, Australia: Center for Southeast Asian Studies, Monash University, 1994), 221–225; Hans Antlöv, *Exemplary Centre: Administrative Periphery: Rural Leadership and the New Order in Java* (Richmond, Surrey, UK: Curzon Press, 1995), 68-67, 151.

56. Geoffrey Robinson, "People's War: Militias in East Timor and Indonesia," *South East Asia Research*, 9 (2001): 289–290.

57. Harold Crouch, "The Generals and Business in Indonesia," *Pacific Affairs*, 48 (1975/76): 520–521; Crouch, *The Army and Politics*, 323; Lesley McCulloch, "*Trifungsi*: The Role of the Indonesian Military in Business," in Jörn Brömmulhörster and Wolf-Christian Paes, eds., *The Military as an Economic Actors: Soldiers in Business* (New York: Palgrave MacMillan, 2002), 107–112.

58. R. William Liddle, "Coercion, Co-Optation and the Management of Ethnic Relations in Indonesia," in Michael E. Brown and Sumit Ganguly, eds., *Government Policies and Ethnic Relations in Asia and the Pacific* (Cambridge, MA: MIT Press, 1997).

59. Evans, 36–39; Rieffel and Wirjasuputra, 106.

60. McCulloch, 101–102; McVey, "The Post-Revolutionary Transformation, Pt. II," 148–149; Alexis Rieffel and Aninda S. Wirjasuputra, "Military Enterprises," *Bulletin of Indonesian Economic Studies*, 8 (1972): 107–108.

61. Crouch, "Patrimonialism and Military Rule," 579; Crouch, *Army and Politics*, 275–280; Bruce Glassburner, "In the Wake of General Ibnu: Crisis in the Indonesian Oil Industry," *Asian Survey*, 16 (1976).

62. On Aceh, see Damien Kingsbury and Lesley McCulloch, "Military Business in Aceh," in Anthony Reid, ed., *Verandah of Violence: The Background to the Aceh Problem* (Seattle: University of Washington Press, 2006); Geoffrey Robinson, "*Rawan* Is as *Rawan* Does: The Origins of Disorder in New Order Aceh," *Indonesia*, 66 (1998). On West Papua, see Denise Leith, *The Politics of Power: Freeport in Suharto's Indonesia* (Honolulu: University of Hawaii Press, 2003). On Kalimantan, see Charles Victor Barber and Kirk Talbott, "The Chainsaw and the Gun: The Role of the Military in Deforesting Indonesia," *Journal of Sustainable Forestry*, 16 (2003); William Ascher, "From Oil to Timber: The Political Economy of Off Budget Development Financing in

Indonesia," *Indonesia* 65 (1998); J. F. McCarthy, "The Changing Regime: Forest Property and Reformasi in Indonesia," *Development and Change*, 31 (2000).

63. Rieffel and Wirjasuputra say that military enterprises are responsible for 30 to 60 percent of the military's revenue. Crouch quotes the official armed forces newspaper from 1970 as saying that the government budget covers only half of the military's operational expenses (Rieffel and Wirjasuputra, 106; Crouch, *Army and Politics*, 274; "Current Data on the Indonesian Military Elite, January 1, 1999–January 31, 2001," *Indonesia*, 71 [2001]: 135).

64. Donald Greenlees, "Indonesia Wants Its Army Out of Business," *International Herald Tribune*, May 4, 2005.

65. Harold Crouch, "Generals and Business in Indonesia," *Pacific Affairs*, 48 (1975/76), 536; R. William Liddle, "Soeharto's Indonesia: Personal Rule and Political Institutions," *Pacific Affairs*, 58 (1985), 79; John T. Sidel, "Macet Total Logics of Circulation and Accumulation in the Demise of Indonesia's New Order," *Indonesia*, 66 (1998), 192–193.

66. Loren Ryter, "Pemuda Pancasila: The Last Loyalist Free Men of Suharto's Order?" *Indonesia* 66 (1998); Robinson, "Origins of Disorder," 137–138, 149–150; Robinson, "People's War," 302–306; McCarthy, 98, 104–105; Kingsbury and McCulloch, 203–206; Crouch, *Army and Politics*, 285.

67. Herbert Feith and Daniel S. Lev, "The End of the Indonesian Rebellion," *Pacific Affairs*, 35 (1963): 38.

68. Friend, 60.

69. Cited in Rex Mortimer, *Indonesian Communism under Sukarno: Ideology and Politics, 1959–1965* (Ithaca, NY: Cornell University Press, 1974), 384.

70. Mortimer, *Indonesian Communism under Sukarno*, 366, 380–394; Reinhardt, 104; Crouch, *Army and Politics*, 86–87.

71. Crouch, *Army and Politics*, 147–151; Kenneth R. Young, "Local and National Influences in the Violence of 1965," in Cribb, *The Indonesian Killings*, 878–885.

72. Robinson, *Dark Side of Paradise*, 292–300; David Easter, " 'Keep the Indonesian Pot Boiling': Western Covert Intervention in Indonesia, October 1965–March 1966," *Cold War History*, 5 (2005): 64.

73. Robert Cribb, "Unresolved Problems in the Indonesian Killings of 1965–1966," *Asian Survey*, 42 (2002); Adrian Vickers, "Reopening Old Wounds: Bali and the Indonesian Killings: A Review Article," *Journal of Asian Studies*, 57 (1998).

74. Robinson, *Dark Side of Paradise*; Kenneth R. Young, "Local and National Influences in the Violence of 1965" in Robert Cribb, ed., *The Indonesian Killings of 1965–1966: Studies from Java and Bali* (Clayton, Victoria, Australia: Centre of Southeast Asian Studies, Monash University, 1990), 85.

75. Cited in Robison, *Dark Side of Paradise*, 296.

76. Andrée Feillard, *Islam et Armée Dans L'Indonésie Contemporaine*, Cahier d'Archipel No. 28 (Paris: L'Harmattan, 1995).

77. Crouch, *Army and Politics*, 267.

78. R. William Liddle, "Useful Fiction: Democratic Legitimation in New Order Indonesia," in *The Politics of Elections in Southeast Asia*, ed. R. H. Taylor (New York: Cambridge University Press, 1996).

79. Tim Kell, *The Roots of Acehnese Rebellion, 1989–1992* (Ithaca, NY: Cornell University Southeast Asia Program, No. 64, 1995), 74–77.

80. Kristin E. Schulze, "The Struggle for an Independent Aceh: The Ideology, Capacity, and Strategy of GAM," *Studies in Conflict & Terrorism*, 26 (2003); Edward Aspinall, *Islam and Nation: Separatist Rebellion in Aceh, Indonesia* (Stanford, CA: Stanford University Press, 2009).

81. Benedict R. O'G. Anderson, "Old State, New Society: Indonesia's New Order in Comparative Historical Perspective," *Journal of Asian Studies*, 42 (1983): 493. See also Dewi Fortuna Anwar, *Indonesia in ASEAN: Foreign Policy and Regionalism* (New York: St. Martin's, 1994), 18–19.

82. On wider regional affairs following World War II, see Christopher Bayly and Tim Harper, *Forgotten Wars: Freedom and Revolution in Southeast Asia* (Cambridge, MA: Belknap Press of Harvard University Press, 2007); Ronald H. Spector, *In the Ruins of Empire: The Japanese Surrender and the Battle for Postwar Asia* (New York: Random House, 2007); Anwar, 124.

83. See Ricklefs, 318–319. For more detailed of the superpower involvement in the PRRI/Permesta rebellions, see Matthew Jones, "'Maximum Disavowable Aid': Britain, the United States and the Indonesian Rebellion, 1957–58," *English Historical Review*, 114 (1999): 459; Audrey Kahin and George McT. Kahin, *Subversion as Foreign Policy: The Secret Eisenhower and Dulles Debacle in Indonesia* (New York: New Press, 1995); Andrew Roadnight, *United States Policy Towards Indonesia in the Truman and Eisenhower Years* (New York: Palgrave Macmillan, 2002); Kenneth J. Conboy and James Morrison, *Feet to the Fire: CIA Covert Operations in Indonesia 1957–1958* (Annapolis: Naval Institute Press, 1999).

84. Michael Leifer, *Indonesia's Foreign Policy* (Boston: George Allen & Unwin, 1983), 27–28.

85. On Sukarno's personalistic leadership and the importance of domestic politics on foreign policy, see Frederick P. Bunnell, "Guided Democracy Foreign Policy 1960–1965: President Sukarno Moves from Non-Alignment to Confrontation," *Indonesia*, 2 (1966); Jon M. Reinhardt, *Foreign Policy and National Integration: The Case of Indonesia* (New Haven, CT: Yale University Southeast Asian Studies Monograph Series No. 17, 1971).

86. Crouch, *The Army and Politics*, 81.

87. Liefer, 63–74; Peter Savage, "The National Liberation Struggle in West Irian: From Millenarianism to Socialist Revolution," *Asian Survey*, 18 (1978); c.f. U.S. Department of State, Central Files, 611.98/1-2561, "Telegram from the Embassy in Indonesia to the Department of State, January 26, 1961," *Foreign Relations of the United States, 1961–1963*, Volume XXIII (Washington, DC: U.S. Government Printing Office, 1994), 302–304; U.S. Department of State, Central Files 656.9813/4-1061, "Memorandum of Conversation, April 10, 1961," in FRUS 1961–1963, 345.

88. Cited in Liefer, 79. For the purposes of this analysis, I will treat Indonesia's involvement in the 1962 Azhari rebellion in Brunei as part of the same anti-Malaysian campaign because it represented, in microcosm, the features of the wider struggle. For more details on the abortive Brunei operations, see J. A. C. Mackie, *Konfrontasi: The Indonesian–Malaysia Dispute, 1964–1966* (New York: Oxford University Press, 1974), 120–122; Matthew Jones, *Conflict and Confrontation in South East Asia, 1961–1965: Britain, the United States, and the Creation of Malaysia* (New York: Cambridge University Press, 2002), Chapter 4.

89. Robert M. Cornejo, "When Sukarno Sought the Bomb: Indonesian Nuclear Aspirations in the Mid-1960s," *Nonproliferation Review*, 7 (2000).

90. Justus M. Van Der Kroef, *The Communist Party of Indonesia: Its History, Program and Tactics* (Vancouver: University of British Columbia Press, 1965), 289.

91. Crouch, *Army and Politics*, 71–75; Mackie, 210–215, 259–260; Anwar, 28–30, 43. For an interesting analysis of the evolution of the conflict, see the CIA's report in National Intelligence Estimate No. 54/55–63, "The Malaysian–Indonesian Conflict," Director of Central Intelligence, October 30, 1963. See also U.S. Department of State, INR/EAP Files Lot 90 D 165 Secret, "Special National Intelligence Estimate: Short-Term Prospects in the Malaysia/Indonesia Conflict, September 16, 1964," *Foreign Relations of the United States, 1964–1968, Volume XXVI* (Washington, DC: U.S. Government Printing Office, 2001), 158–160.

92. Lieffer, 99; Jones, *Conflict and Confrontation*, 239–242, in passim; John Subritzky, *Confronting Sukarno: British, American, Australian and New Zealand Diplomacy in the Malaysian–Indonesian Confrontation, 1961–5* (New York: St. Martin's Press, 2000), 132.

93. Easter, 64–65.

94. Sajidiman Surjohadiprodji, "The Defence of Indonesia," in K. K. Sinha, ed. *Problems of Defence of South and East Asia* (Bombay: Manktalas, 1969), 228; Crouch, *Army and Politics*, 339; Anwar, 134; Shaun Narine, "ASEAN and the Management of Regional Security," *Pacific Affairs*, 71 (1998).

95. For details on the U.S. support for Indonesia, see William Burr and Michael L. Evans, eds., *East Timor Revisited: Ford, Kissinger, and the Indonesian Invasion*. National Security Archive Electronic Briefing Book No. 62, December 6, 2001; retrieved on July 24, 2007, from: www.gwu.edu/~nsarchiv/NSAEBB/NSAEBB62/index.html.

96. Robert Lawless, "The Indonesian Takeover of East Timor," *Asian Survey*, 16 (1976); Jill Jolliffe, *East Timor: Nationalism & Colonialism* (New York: University of Queensland Press, 1978); John G. Taylor, *Indonesia's Forgotten War: The Hidden History of East Timor* (Atlantic Highlands, NJ: Zed, 1991).

97. For demographic study, see Ben Kiernan, "The Demographics of Genocide in Southeast Asia: The Death Tolls in Cambodia, 1974–79, and East Timor, 1975–80," *Critical Asian Studies*, 35 (2003). On the paternalistic but not racialist attitude of Indonesia's "civilizing mission" in East Timor, see Benedict Anderson, "Imagining East Timor," *Arena*, 4 (April–May 1993).

98. Savage, 990–991; Ralph R. Premdas and Kwasi Nyamekye, "Papua New Guinea 1978: Year of the OPM," *Asian Survey*, 19 (1979): 68–70; David Webster, "'Already Sovereign as a People': A Foundational Moment in West Papuan Nationalism," *Pacific Affairs*, 74 (2001/2): 520.

99. Jamie S. Davidson and Douglas Kammen, "Indonesia's Unknown War: The Lineages of Violence in West Kalimantan," *Indonesia*, 73 (2001); Nancy Lee Peluso, "Passing the Red Bowl: Creating Community Identity through Violence in West Kalimantan, 1967–1997," in Coppel, *Violent Conflicts.*

100. Samuel Moore, "The Indonesian Military's Last Year in East Timor: An Analysis of Its Secret Documents," *Indonesia*, 72 (2001): 16; Douglas Kammen, "Notes on the Transformation of the East Timor Military Command and Its Implications for Indonesia," *Indonesia*, 67 (1999); Robinson, "People's War," 300–301, 307–309.

101. Geoffrey Robinson, *"If You Leave US Here, We Will Die": How Genocide Was Stopped in East Timor* (Princeton, NJ: Princeton University Press, 2010), 57.

102. Human Rights Watch, "Backgrounder: The Indonesian Army and Civilian Militias in East Timor, April 1999"; retrieved on July 24, 2007, from http://hrw.org/press/1999/apr/etmilitia.htm. See also Michael G. Smith, *Peacekeeping in East Timor: The Path to Independence* (Boulder, CO: Lynne Rienner, 2003), 41–47, 68–76; Damien Kingsbury, ed., *Guns and Ballot Boxes: East Timor's Vote for Independence* (Clayton, Victoria, Australia: Monash University Asia Institute, 2000); Robinson, "People's War," 275–278; Moore, 30–43; Jarat Chopra, "The UN's Kingdom of East Timor," *Survival*, 42 (2000): 27–28.

103. Anwar, 134–135. See also Anthony L. Smith, *Strategic Centrality: Indonesia's Changing Role in ASEAN* (Singapore: Institute of Southeast Asian Studies, 2000), 8; Liefer, 169.

104. Jun Honna, "Military Ideology in Response to Democratic Pressure during the Late Suharto Era: Political and Institutional Contexts," *Indonesia*, 67 (1999); Siddharth Chandra and Douglas Kammen, "Generating Reforms and Reforming Generations: Military Politics in Indonesia's Democratic Transition and Consolidation," *World Politics*, 55:1 (2002).

105. Romain Bertrand, "'Behave Like Enraged Lions': Civil Militias, the Army, and the Criminalisation of Politics in Indonesia," *Global Crime*, 6 (2004): 336–339.

106. Tim Huxley, *Disintegrating Indonesia? Implications for Regional Security* (London: International Institute for Strategic Studies 2002); Ian Douglass Wood, "The Changing Contours of Organized Violence in Post-New Order Indonesia," *Critical Asian Studies*, 38 (2006).

107. Timo Kivimäki and Rubin Thorning, "Democratization and Regional Power Sharing in Papua/Irian Jaya: Increased Opportunities and Decreased Motivations for Violence," *Asian Survey*, 42 (2002); Gerry van Klinken, *Communal Violence and Democratization in Indonesia: Small Town Wars* (New York: Routledge, 2007).

108. Vedi R. Hadiz, "Indonesian Local Party Politics: A Site of Resistance to Neoliberal Reform," *Critical Asian Studies*, 36 (2004): 619; Van Klinken, 125.

109. Chandra and Kammen, 102, 116.

110. Erb, Sulistiyanto, and Faucher, *Regionalism in Post-Suharto Indonesia*; Van Klinken, 5; Bridget Welsh, "Local and National: Keroyokan Mobbing in Indonesia," *Journal of East Asian Studies*, 8 (2008).

111. Bertrand, "Civil Militias, the Army, and the Criminalisation of Politics in Indonesia," 337.

112. Elizabeth Fuller Collins, "Indonesia: A Violent Culture?" *Asian Survey*, 42 (2002); Tim Lindsey, "From Soepomo to Prabowo: Law, Violence, and Corruption in the Preman State," in Coppel, *Violent Conflicts in Indonesia*; Ryter, "Pemuda Pancisila."

113. Robinson, "People's War."

114. Mancur Olson, "Democracy, Dictatorship, and Development," *American Political Science Review*, 87 (1993).

## Chapter 3: Iraq

1. Kanan Makiya [Samir al-Khalil], *Republic of Fear* (Berkeley: University of California Press, 1998). See also Isam al-Khafaji, "War as a Vehicle for the Rise and Demise of a State-Controlled Society: The Case of Ba'thist Iraq," in Steven Heydemann, ed., *War, Institutions and Social Change in the Middle East* (Berkeley: University of California Press, 2000), 259.

2. Aqil al-Nasri, *Al-Jaysh wa al-Sultah fi'l-'Iraq al-Maliki, 1921–1958* (Beirut: Dar al-Hisad l'il Nasr wa al-Tawziya' wa al-Tiba'ah, 2000), 52.

3. For general histories of the Ottoman rule in Mesopotamia, see Hanna Batatu, *The Old Social Classes and the Revolutionary Movements in Iraq* (Princeton, NJ: Princeton University Press, 1978); Charles Tripp, *A History of Iraq* (New York: Cambridge University Press, 2000), 8–13; Tom Nieuwenhuis, *Politics and Society in Early Modern Iraq: Mamluk Pashas, Tribal Sheikhs, and Local Rule between 1802 and 1831* (Boston: Kluwer, 1982); Gökhan Çentinsaya, *Ottoman Administration of Iraq, 1890–1908* (New York: Routledge, 2006).

4. Albertine Jwaideh, "Aspects of Land Tenure and Social Change in Lower Iraq," in Tarif Khalidi, ed., *Land Tenure and Social Transformation in the Middle East* (Beirut: American University of Beirut Press, 1984). See also Yitzhak Nakash, *The Shi'is of Iraq* (Princeton, NJ: Princeton University Press, 1994), 92–93; Batatu, 87.

5. Çentinsaya, 62–63, 72–90; Longrigg's *Four Centuries of Modern Iraq* (Oxford, UK: Clarendon Press, 1925), 308–309; Stephen Longrigg, *Iraq, 1900 to 1950: A Political, Economic, and Social History* (London: Oxford University Press, 1953), 52–54; Tripp, 17–24; Zoë Preston, *The Crystallization of the Iraq State: Geopolitical Function and Form* (New York: Peter Lange, 2003), 116–120.

6. Erik Jan Zürcher, "The Ottoman Conscription System, 1844–1914," *International Review of Social History*, 43 (1998); Çentinsaya, 40–43; Longrigg, *Iraq, 1900 to 1950*, 29–31, 40–43.

7. Werner Ende, "Iraq in World War I: The Turks, the Germans and the Shi'ite Mujtahids' Call for Jihad," *Proceedings of the Ninth Congress of the Union Européenne des Arabisants et Islamisants* (Leiden: Brill, 1981); Tripp, 33–34; Nakash, 60–61, 94–96.

8. Toby Dodge highlights the liberal element in British imperial policy toward Iraq, Sluglett its Machiavellianism. See Toby Dodge, *Inventing Iraq: The Failure of Nation Building and a History Denied* (New York: Columbia University Press, 2003); Peter Sluglett, *Britain in Iraq: Contriving King and Country* (New York: Columbia University Press, 2007); D. K. Fieldhouse, *Western Imperialism in the Middle East, 1914–1958* (New York: Oxford University Press, 2006), 70–72.

9. For a clear overview of the events of 1920, see Phebe Marr, *The Modern History of Iraq* (Boulder, CO: Westview, 1985), 32–34; Amal Vinogradov, "The 1920 Revolution in Iraq Reconsidered: The Role of the Tribes in National Politics," *International Journal of Middle East Studies* 3 (1973): 132–133.

10. On the RAF in Iraq, see Dodge, Chapter 7; David Omissi, *Air Power and Colonial Control: The Royal Air Force, 1919–1939* (New York: St. Martin's, 1990); Priya Satia, *Spies in Arabia: The Great War and the Cultural Foundations of Britain's Covert Empire in the Middle East* (New York: Oxford University Press, 2008).

11. Vinogradov, 132–133; Sluglett, *Britain in Iraq*, 169–173; Longrigg, *Iraq, 1900–1950*, 106–107.

12. Tripp, 47; Reeva Spector Simon, "The View from Baghdad," in Reeva Spector Simon and Eleanor H. Tejirian, eds., *The Creation of Modern Iraq* (New York: Columbia University Press, 2004).

13. Report by His Majesty's High Commissioner on the Finances, Administration, and Condition of the 'Iraq for the Period From 1 October 1920 to 31st March 1922 [FO 371/8998] in *Iraqi Administration Reports 1914–1932*, Vol. 7 (London: Archives Edition, 1992); Report by His Majesty's High Commissioner on the Finances, Administration,

and Condition of 'Iraq for the Period from 1st April 1922 to 31st March 1923 [FO 371/10095] in *Iraq Administrative Reports*, Vol. 7.

14. Raja Husayn Husni Khattab, *Tasis al-jaysh al-'Iraqi wa-tatawwur dawrihi al-siyasi min 1921–1941* (Baghdad: University of Baghdad College of Arts, 1979), 41; Ernest Main, *Iraq: From Mandate to Independence* (London: George Allen & Unwin, 1935), 120–132.

15. Mohammed Tarbush, *The Role of the Military in Politics: A Case Study of Iraq to 1941* (Boston: Kegan Paul International, 1982), 84–87; Khattab, 95–98.

16. Nakash, 78–79, 110–114; Tarbush, 86.

17. Dodge, 134; John Darwin, *Britain, Egypt and the Middle East: Imperial Policy in the Aftermath of War, 1918–1922* (New York: Macmillan, 1981), 33.

18. Report by His Majesty's High Commissioner on the Finances, Administration, and Condition of the 'Iraq for the Period From 1 October 1920 to 31st March 1922 [FO 371/8998] in *Iraqi Administrative Reports*, Vol. 7; Sluglett, *Britain in Iraq*, 86–90, 182–183; Tripp, 61.

19. High Commissioner Henry Dobbs to the Colonial Secretary, October 20, 1928, [FO 371/13035] in Alan de L. Rush, ed., *Records of Iraq, 1914–1966*, Vol. 2 (London: Archives Edition, 2001), 373–378.

20. Peter P. J. Hemphill, "The Formation of the Iraqi Army, 1921–1933," in Abbas Kelidar, ed., *The Integration of Modern Iraq* (New York: St. Martin's Press, 1979), 94–95; Tarbush, 78–83.

21. Cited in Tarbush, 88–90.

22. Dodge, 142–143; Sluglett, 96–98. See the comment by Yasin al-Hashimi, Report by His Majesty's Government in the United Kingdom of Great Britain and Northern Ireland to the Council of the League of Nations on the Administration of Iraq for the Year 1929 in *Iraqi Administrative Reports*, Vol. 7.

23. Nakash, 115–121; Tripp, 61–63.

24. Tarbush, 86; Ibrahim al-Marashi and Sammy Salama, *Iraq's Armed Forces: An Analytical History* (New York: Routledge, 2008), 21.

25. Khattab, 36–40, 95–98; Longrigg, *Iraq, 1900 to 1950*, 166–167; Tarbush, 78–83; Reeva Simon, *Iraq between Two World Wars: The Creation and Implementation of a Nationalist Ideology* (New York: Columbia University Press, 1986), 107–108; Marr, 37.

26. Marashi and Salama, 21; Mark Heller, "Politics and the Military in Iraq and Jordan, 1920–1958: The British Influence," *Armed Forces and Society*, 4 (1977): 81.

27. Report by His Majesty's High Commissioner on the Finances, Administration, and Condition of the 'Iraq for the Period From 1 October 1920 to 31st March 1922 [FO 371/8998] in *Iraqi Administration Reports*, Vol. 7; Khattab, 33–34; *Tarikh al-Quwat al-Iraqiyyah al-Musallahah* (s.n., Baghdad, 1986), Vol. 2, 326–327, 335.

28. Report by His Majesty's High Commissioner on the Finances, Administration, and Condition of 'Iraq for the Period from 1st April 1922 to 31st March 1923 [FO

371/10095] in *Iraq Administrative Reports*, Vol. 7; Report by His Brittanic Majesty's Government to the Council of the League of Nations on the Administration of Iraq for the Year 1925 in *Iraqi Administrative Reports*, Vol. 7; Marashi and Salama, 21.

29. Air Staff Note, "Military Aspects of the Anglo-Iraqi Treaty," January 2, 1930 [Fo 371/14502] in *Records of Iraq*, Vol. 5, 256–260; Ernest Main, *Iraq: From Mandate to Independence* (London: George Allen & Unwin, 1935), 122; Hemphill, 98–99; Khattab 61–64; *Tarikh al-Quwat al-Iraqiyyah*, Vol. 17, 51.

30. *Tarikh al-Quwat al-Iraqiyyah*, Vol. 2, 329–230.

31. Secretary of State for Air, "Defence of Iraq," January 14, 1925 [CO 537/816], in *Records of Iraq*, Vol. 4; see also Air Staff Note, "Military Aspects of the Anglo-Iraqi Treaty" [FO 371/14205] in *Records of Iraq*, Vol. 5.

32. Marashi and Salama, 35.

33. Heller, 84–85; Dodge, 70–71; Eliezer Beeri, *Army Officers in Arab Politics and Society* (New York: Praeger, 1970), 329–330.

34. Special Report by His Majesty's Government in the United Kingdom of Great Britain and Northern Ireland to the Council of the League of Nations on the Progress of 'Iraq During the Period 1920–1931 in *Iraq Administrative Reports*, Vol. 10.

35. Marr, 37; Simon, *Iraq between the Two World Wars*, Chapter 4; Fieldhouse, 101–102.

36. Extract from Dispatch from the Iraqi Ministry of Defense to the High Commission, Baghdad, June 24, 1928 [CO 730/143/6] in *Records of Iraq*, Vol. 5, 346–348; Special Service Officer (Captain de Gaury), Baghdad, to Air Staff Intelligence, Hinaidi, July 22, 1930 [AIR 23/120] in *Records of Iraq*, Vol. 6, 233.

37. Hemphill, 96.

38. Cited in Batatu, 26.

39. Much of Western perspective on the Assyrian affair is drawn from the account of Lieutenant Colonel R. S. Stafford, who was administrative inspector in Mosul and Irbil at the time, a view that is seconded by Ernest Main. Khaldun S. Husry and later Phebe Marr offer important correctives. See J. S. Stafford, *The Tragedy of the Assyrian Minority in Iraq* (New York: Kegan Paul, 2004 [1933]); Khaldun S. Husry, "The Assyrian Affair of 1933 (I)," *International Journal of Middle East Studies*, 5 (1974) and "The Assyrian Affair of 1933 (II)," *International Journal of Middle East Studies*, 5 (1974); Marr, 57–58; Main, 151.

40. Husri, "The Assyrian Affair of 1933 (II)," 353, 356.

41. For a larger account of the uprisings and military response, see Marr, 62–67, and Tripp, 84–87. On the upgrading of the Iraqi army, see Khattab, 63–69; Marashi and Salama, 34; Nasry, 76. On the Shi'a response and the role of Ghita and the tribes, see Nakash, 120–125.

42. Batatu, 118–119.

43. For a detailed discussion of the many overt and covert military interventions in Iraqi politics, see George M. Haddad, *Revolution and Military Rule in the Middle East: The Arab States, Volume 2, Part 1: Iraq, Syria, Lebanon, and Jordan* (New York: Robert Speller & Sons, 1971); Be'eri, op. cit.

44. Nakash, 124; Khalil, 171.

45. Itamar Rabinowitch, "Oil and Local Politics: The French–Iraqi Negotiations of the Early 1930s," in Uriel Dann, ed., *The Great Powers in the Middle East* (London: Holmes & Meier, 1988), 181.

46. D. Cameron Watt, "The Saadabad Pact of 8 July 1937," in *The Great Powers*; Ahmad Abd al-Razzaq Shikarah, *Iraqi Politics 1921–41: The Interaction between Domestic and Foreign Policy* (London: Laam, 1987), 132–133.

47. Lawrence Pratt, "The Strategic Context: British Policy in the Mediterranean and the Middle East, 1936–1939," in *The Great Powers*, 19–20.

48. Daniel Silverfarb, *Britain's Informal Empire in the Middle East: A Case Study of Iraq, 1929–1941* (New York: Oxford University Press, 1986), 74–77; William Roger Louis, *The British Empire in the Middle East, 1945–1951* (New York: Oxford University Press, 1984), 324; Watt, 337–340.

49. Marr, 74; Silverfarb, *Informal Empire*, 83–84; Khattab, 52–85; Batatu, 27.

50. Shikara 151–157; David H. Finnie, *Shifting Lines in the Sand: Kuwait's Elusive Frontier with Iraq* (Cambridge, MA: Harvard University Press, 1992), 99–123.

51. For a review of key Arabic sources on the subject, see Ayad al-Qazzaz, "The Iraqi–British War of 1941: A Review Article," *International Journal of Middle East Studies*, 7 (1976).

52. Tarbush, 178–179; George Kirk, *The Middle East in the War* (New York: Oxford University Press, 1952), 70.

53. Lukasz Hirszowicz, *The Third Reich and the Arab East* (Toronto: University of Toronto Press, 1966), 161–172.

54. Mahmud al-Durah, *Al-Harb al-Iraqiyyah al-Baritaniyyah 1941* (Beirut: Dar al-Taliah, 1973), 257–277; *PAIFORCE: The Official Story of the Persia and Iraqi Command, 1941–1946* (London: His Majesty's Stationary Office, 1948), 20–22.

55. John Glubb, *The Story of the Arab Legion* (London: Hodder & Stoughton, 1950), 278–303.

56. Cornwallis to Eden, E/2431/195/93 in *Political Diaries of the Arab World*, ed. Robert Jarman (Slough, UK: Archive Edition, 1998).

57. Adil Hasan Ghunaym, *Tatawwur al-harakah al-qawmiyyah fi al-'Iraq* (Cairo: n.p., 1960), 29; Walid S. Hamdi, *Rashid Ali al-Gailani and the Nationalist Movement in Iraq: A Political and Military Study of the British Campaign in Iraq and the National Revolution of May 1941* (London: Darf, 1987), 176–177.

58. Daniel Silverfarb, *The Twilight of British Ascendancy in the Middle East: A Case Study of Iraq* (New York: St. Martin, 1994), 11–16, 93–98.

59. Cornwallis to Eden, June 23, 1943 [E/3585/489/93] in *Political Diaries*.

60. Louis, *The British Empire in the Middle East*; see Michael J. Cohen, *Fighting World War Three from the Middle East: Allied Contingency Plans, 1945–1954* (Portland, OR: Frank Cass, 1997); David R. Devereux, *The Formulation of British Defense Policy towards the Middle East, 1948–56* (New York: St. Martin's Press, 1990); Phillip Darby, *British Defence Policy East of Suez, 1947–1968* (New York: Oxford University Press, 1973).

61. Silverfarb, *Twilight of British Ascendancy*, 93–98, 102–106; Louis, 324–327; Matthew Elliot, *"Independent Iraq": The Monarchy and British Influence* (New York: Tauris Academic Studies, 1996), 52, 61; Marashi and Salama, 65–66.

62. Elliot, 61, 148–152; Zach Levey, "Britain's Middle East Strategy, 1950–51: General Brian Robertson and the 'Small' Arab States," *Middle Eastern Studies*, 40 (2004): 62–64; Darwin, 65-67; Amitzur Ilan, *The Origin of the Arab-Israeli Arms Race: Arms, Embargo, Military Power and Decision in the 1948 Palestine War* (New York: New York University Press, 1996), 27–33.

63. David Tal, *The War in Palestine, 1948: Strategy and Diplomacy* (New York: Routledge, 2004), 158–163; Howard M. Sacher, *Europe Leaves the Middle East, 1936–1954* (New York: Knopf, 1972), 531–532; Eppel, 154–170; Ilan, 30.

64. Salih Juburi, *Mihnat filastin wa-asraruha al-siyasiyya wa al-askariyya* (Beirut: Dar al-Kutub, 1970), 142–144; Trevor Depuy, *The Elusive Victory: The Arab-Israeli Wars, 1947–1974* (Fairfax, VA: HERO Books, 1984), 18–19; Ilan, 120, Table 5 and Table 6.

65. Joshua Landis, "Syria in the Palestine War," in Avi Shlaim and Eugene Rogan, eds., *The War for Palestine: Rewriting the History of 1948* (Cambridge, UK: Cambridge University Press, 2001); Edgar O'Ballance, *The Arab-Israeli War, 1948* (Westport, CT: Hyperion, 1956), 40.

66. Diplomatic records also suggest that at Quwaqji may even have coordinated with the Zionist force to block reinforcements to the Mufti's forces at the battle of Kastel. See Depuy, 12–13; Avi Shlaim, "Israel and the Arab Coalition in 1948," in *The War for Palestine*, 85–86; O'Ballance, 84.

67. Dan Kurzman, *Genesis 1948: The First Arab-Israeli War* (New York: World Publishing, 1970), 206.

68. Sir H. Mack to Mr. Bevin, Iraq: Annual Review for 1948, January 7, 1949 [E 773/1011/93] in *Political Diaries*, Vol. 7.

69. Charles Tripp, "Iraq and the 1948 War: A Mirror of Iraq's Disorders," in *The War for Palestine*.

70. Eppel, 191; Kurzman, 333; O'Ballance, 115–118, 137–138.

71. Kenneth Pollack, *Arabs at War: Military Effectiveness, 1948–1991* (Lincoln: University of Nebraska Press, 2002), 115.

72. Longrigg, *Iraq, 1900 to 1950*, 382–383.

73. Nadav Safran, *From War to War: The Arab–Israeli Confrontation, 1948–1967* (New York: Pegasus, 1969).

74. Longrigg, *Iraq: From 1900 to 1950*, 360–365; Samira Haj, *The Making of Iraq, 1900–1963: Capital, Power and Ideology* (Albany: State University of New York Press, 1997), 5–6.

75. Uriel Dann, *Iraq under Qassem: A Political History, 1958–1962* (New York: Praeger, 1969), 24–26; Mufti, 99–108; Marr, 156–158.

76. Cited in Batatu, 847.

77. Batatu, 848; Dann, 105; Sluglett and Sluglett, 63, 69.

78. Dann, 167–169, 175; British Consulate-General Basra, Monthly Summary Report-March 1959, in *Political Diaries*, Vol. 8; Monthly Summary April 1959, 32.

79. Sluglett and Sluglett, 53, 62–63; Dann, 105–107, 118–120.

80. Basra Monthly Summary, May 1959, 40; Fortnightly Political Summary No. 7, March 26–April 1959; Dann, 210–201.

81. Iraq Political Summary No. 9, April 21–May 8, 1959; Iraq: Political Summary No. 11, May 26–June 8, 1959.

82. Dann, 224–225; Sluglett and Sluglett, 71–73.

83. Dann, 289–290, 303.

84. Sluglett and Sluglett, 90.

85. Batatu, 968–971, 984–985.

86. Cited in Sluglett and Sluglett, 85.

87. Sluglet and Sluglett, 86; Batatu, 1011–1012.

88. Be'eri, 198–199; Marashi and Salama, 95.

89. Monthly Summary Report April 1963; Consular-General Basra, Monthly Summary March 1963 in *Political Diaries*, Vol. 8, 610–612; C. J. H. Keith, Monthly Summary Report, June 1963, in *Political Diaries*, Vol. 8, 606–609; C. J. H. Keith, Monthly Summary Report, 4 August 5, 1963, in *Political Diaries*, Vol. 8, 632–641.

90. Mufti, 164; Marashi and Salama, 95–96.

91. Mufti, 127.

92. Sluglett and Sluglett, 93–94.

93. Khafaji, "War as a Vehicle," 264; Mufti, 126, 137; Marr, 201.

94. For an extensive discussion of the nationalization, see Michael Brown, "The Nationalization of the Iraqi Petroleum Company," *International Journal of Middle East Studies*, 10 (1979).

95. Al-Khafaji, "War as a Vehicle," 264–265; Marashi and Salami, 79–82; British observes noted that, despite the inflow of Soviet weaponry, the Iraqi "forces are still based on British organization." See Dispatch No. 1 (1011/1/61), British Embassy, Baghdad, January 2, 1961 in *Political Diaries*, Vol. 8, 448–467.

96. Martin Van Bruinesses, "Kurds, States, and Tribes" in Faleh Abdul Jabar and Hosham Dawod, eds., *Tribes and Power: Nationalism and Ethnicity in the Middle East* (London: Saqi, 2003), 172–173.

97. Sluglett and Sluglett, 80–81.

98. Van Bruinesses, "Kurds, States, and Tribes," 172–173; Sluglett and Sluglett, 81.

99. John S. Wagner, "Iraq: A Combat Assessment," in Richard Gabriel, ed., *Fighting Armies: Antagonists in the Middle East* (Westport, CT: Greenwood, 1983), 65.

100. David McDowall, *A Modern History of the Kurds* (New York: I. B. Tauris, 1996), 312.

101. Pollack, 179.

102. *Genocide in Iraq: The Anfal Campaign against the Kurds* (Washington DC: Human Rights Watch, 1993), 36–37, 329; McDowall, 1996, 347, 529; Martin Van Burinessen, "The Kurds between Iran and Iraq," *Middle East Report*, 141 (July–August 1986).

103. McDowall, 355; *Genocide in Iraq*, 38–39.

104. *Genocide in Iraq*, 46–50; MacDowall, 352.

105. *Genocide in Iraq*, 12–14, 53, 343–346.

106. See Bengio, *Saddam's Word*; Michael Lezenberg, "The Anfal Operations in Iraqi Kurdistan," in Samuel Totten, William S. Parsons, and Israel W. Charny, eds., *Century of Genocide: Critical Eyewitness Accounts* (New York: Routledge, 2004), 382–383.

107. *Genocide in Iraq*, 261–262; Ofra Bengio, *Saddam's Word: Political Discourse in Iraq* (New York: Oxford University Press, 1998), 189.

108. *Genocide in Iraq*, 44–48.

109. See, for instance, Director General Security of Irbil to Security Directorate of Shaqlawa, June 11, 1987, in *The Bureaucracy of Repression: The Iraqi Government in Its Own Words* (Washington, DC: Human Rights Watch, 1994), 62–63; *Genocide in Iraq*, 138–139, 161–166.

110. Cited in Joost Hiltermann, *A Poisonous Affair: America, Iraq, and the Gassing of Halabja* (New York: Cambridge University Press, 2007), 129.

111. *Genocide in Iraq*, 75.

112. See the instructions to resettle only the mothers—as opposed to the entire families—of Kurds whose fathers, sons, or husbands served either as soldiers or in the NDB. See First Corps instruction, September 16, 1987, in *Bureaucracy of Repression*, 78–82.

113. Faleh Abd al-Jabbar, "Why the Revolt Failed," *Middle East Report* (May–June 1992), 11; Kerim Yeldiz, *The Kurds in Iraq: Past, Present, and Future* (Ann Arbor, MI: Pluto Press, 2007), 35; McDowwal, 371–372; Dilip Hiro, *Desert Shield to Desert Storm: The Second Gulf War* (New York: Routledge, 1992), 404–406.

114. Diya' al-Din al-Majma'i, *Hurub Saddam* (London: Dar al-Hikmah, 2006), 67–69.

115. Batatu, 1088; see also Faleh A. Jabar, "The Iraqi Army and Anti-Army: Some Reflections on the Role of the Military" in Toby Dodge and Steven Simon, eds., *Iraq at the Crossroads: State and Society in the Shadow of Regime Change* (New York: Oxford University Press, 2003), 100–101.

116. Khalil, 29–32; Sluglett and Sluglett, 113–118.

117. Sluglett and Sluglett, 120–121; Efraim Karsh and Inari Rautsi, *Saddam Hussein: A Political Biography* (New York: Grove Press, 2002), 66.

118. Marashi and Salama, 117; Sluglett and Sluglett, 133; Shahram Chubin and Charles Tripp, *Iran and Iraq at War* (London: I. B. Tauris, 1989), 21.

119. Marashi and Salama, 120–121; Pollack, 167.

120. Wagner, 68; Jabar, "The Iraqi Army and Anti-Army," 116–118; Marashi and Salama, 122–123.

121. Hiltermann, 26; Anthony Cordesman, *Weapons of Mass Destruction in the Middle East* (Washington, DC: Brassey's, 1991), 60; Shai Feldman, *Nuclear Weapons and Arms Control in the Middle East* (Cambridge, MA: MIT Press, 1997), 135.

122. Jabar, "The Iraqi Army and Anti-Army," 81, 116–118; Khalil, 25–28.

123. Taha Yasin Ramadan, *Al-Jaysh ash-Sha'bi wa at-Tajriba an-Namuthaj* (Baghdad: Popular Army General Command, 1987), 62.

124. Batatu, 1094–1095; Sluglett and Sluglett, 184–185, 206–207; Khalil, 31.

125. Ramadan, 121–126.

126. Khalil, 31; Marashi and Salama, 125–126; Wagner, 73; Bengio, 151.

127. See Ramadan, 36–45.

128. *Al-Jaysh al-Shabi*, 1 (July 1977). For further analysis of the ideological discourse surrounding PA, see Bengio, 150–152.

129. Ramadan's analysis describes the war fighting both as both a "difficult" and "great" test of the PA. Predictably, his assessment vindicates the PA's performance in the war (Ramadan, 28, 59).

130. John Bulloch and Harvey Morris, *The Gulf War: Its Origins, History and Consequences* (London: Methuen, 1989), 53; Chubin and Tripp, 28, 54–55; Marashi and Salama, 132.

131. Pollack, 201.

132. Cited in Chubin and Tripp, 58; see also Dilip Hiro, *The Longest War: The Iran–Iraq Military Conflict* (London: Grafton Books, 1989), 89.

133. Ofra Bengio, "Iraq" in Colin Legum, Haim Shaked, and David Sihon, eds., *Middle East Contemporary Survey, 1979–80* (New York: Holmes & Meier, 1981), 507–508; Pollack, 201, 207–208.

134. *Al-Jaysh ash-Sha'bi*, 8 (February 1981). Due to the incomplete nature of Library of Congress's collection of this journal, it is impossible to thoroughly analyze changes in PA's official discourse longitudinally. It suffices to note that this sporadic collection continues this trend into the late 1980s.

135. Ofra Bengio, "Iraq," in Itamar Rabinovich and H. Shaked, eds., *Middle East Contemporary Survey, 1984–85* (New York: Holmes & Meier, 1987), 465; Marion Farouk-Sluglett, Peter Sluglett, and Joe Stork, "Not Quite Armageddon: Impact of the War on Iraq," *MERIP Reports*, 125/126 (1984). The forced induction of personnel into the PA continued after the war. See Roger Bartram, "Reflections on Human Rights Issues in Prewar Iraq," *Journal of Palestine Studies*, 20 (1991).

136. Ofra Bengio, "Iraq" in Ami Ayalon and Haim Shaked, eds., *Middle East Contemporary Survey, 1988* (Boulder, CO: Westview, 1990), 516.

137. Marashi and Salama, 155–156; Pollack, 219; Bengio, "Iraq," in *Middle East Contemporary Survey, 1984–85*, 463.

138. al-Khafaji, "War as a Vehicle," 272–281.

139. Amatzia Baram, "Neo-Tribalism in Iraq: Saddam Hussein's Tribal Policies, 1991–1996," *International Journal of Middle Eastern Studies*, 29 (1997): 1–3. See also Jabar, "The Iraqi Army and Anti-Army," 100–101; Adeed Dawisha, "'Identity' and Political Survival in Saddam's Iraq," *Middle East Journal*, 53 (1999); Batatu, 1048.

140. Jabar, "The Iraqi Army and Anti-Army," 92–97; Baram, "Neo-Tribalism," 10–12, 16–18.

141. Dawisha, "'Identity' and Political Survival," 62.

142. Jabar, "The Iraqi Army and Anti-Army," 96.

143. Cited in Baram, "Neo-Tribalism," 17–18.

144. Cordesman, *The Iraq War: Strategy, Tactics, and Military Lessons* (Westport, CT: Praeger, 2003), 17, 96; Marashi and Salama, 195–196; Amatzia Baram, *Building toward Crisis: Saddam Husayn's Strategy for Survival* (Washington, DC: Washington Institute for Near East Policy Policy Paper No. 47, 1998), 48–49. This idea of spontaneous mass resistance to the Americans was already present in 1991. See Kanan Makiya, *Cruelty and Silence: War, Tyranny, Uprising, and the Arab World* (New York: Norton, 1993), 70.

145. Juan Cole, "The United States and Shi'ite Religious Factions in Post-Ba'thist Iraq," *Middle East Journal*, 57 (2003): 548, 554.

146. Nir Rosen, *In the Belly of the Green Bird: The Triumph of Martyrs in Iraq* (New York: Free Press, 2006), 17–19, 33.

147. Amatzia Baram, "Who Are the Insurgents? Sunni Arab Rebels in Iraq," U.S. Institute of Peace Special Report No. 134, Washington DC, April 2005; retrieved on December 3, 2009, from: www.usip.org/files/resources/sr134.pdf.

148. Bing West, *The Strongest Tribe: War, Politics, and the Endgame in Iraq* (New York: Random House, 2008), 24; Eric Herring and Glen Rangwala, *Iraq in Fragments: The Occupation and its Legacy* (Ithaca, NY: Cornell University Press, 2006), 88–91, 112.

149. George Packer, *The Assassin's Gate: America in Iraq* (New York: Farrar, Straus, and Giroux, 2005), 323–325; Dan Murphy, "Shi'ites Taxing Thin U.S. Forces," *Christian Science Monitor*, April 8, 2004.

150. Ali A. Allawi, *The Occupation of Iraq: Winning the War, Losing the Peace* (New Haven, CT: Yale University Press, 2007), 276–279; Thomas E. Ricks, *Fiasco: The American Military Adventure in Iraq* (New York: Penguin, 2006), 243–245.

151. David Ucko, "Militias, Tribes, and Insurgents: The Challenge of Political Re-integration in Iraq," *Conflict, Security, and Development*, 8 (2008): 343–348; Cordesman, *Iraq's Insurgency and the Road to Civil Conflict* (Westport, CT: Praeger, 2008), 58–59; 82; Allawi, 316–320.

152. Ken Silverstein, "The Minister of Civil War," *Harper's* (August 2006); Kimberly Kagan, *The Surge: A Military History* (New York: Encounter Books, 2009), 7.

153. Hashim, 303, 306.

154. Kagan, 11, 40–41; Larry Diamond, *Squandered Victory: The American Occupation and the Bungled Effort to Bring Democracy to Iraq* (New York: Times Books, 2005), 218–228; Cordesman, *Iraq's Insurgency,* 297; Allawi, 447-450.

155. Cordesman, *Iraq's Insurgency,* 284–285, 514–516.

156. David Killcullen, *The Accidental Guerrilla: Fighting Small Wars in the Midst of a Big One* (New York: Oxford University Press, 2009); Michael R. Gordon, "The Former-Insurgent Counterinsurgency," *New York Times*, September 2, 2007; William S. McCallister, "Sons of Iraq: A Study in Irregular Warfare," *Small Wars Journal*, September 8, 2008.

157. Alisa Rubin and Stephen Farrell, "Awakening Councils by Region," *New York Times*, December 22, 2007; see also Kagan, *in passim*.

158. Adeed Dawisha, *Iraq: A Political History from Independence to Occupation* (Princeton, NJ: Princeton University Press, 2009), 272.

159. Ned Parker, "Machiavelli in Mesopotamia: Nouri al-Maliki Builds the Body Politic," *World Policy Journal* 26 (2009): 18–22; Anthony J. Schwarz, "Iraq's Militias: The True Threat to Coalition Success in Iraq," *Parameters* 37 (2007); Kagan, 70–77, 139.

160. Jawad Kathim, "Baghdad tu'akid at-tizameha difa' murtabat as-sahwa," *Al-Hayat*, April 15, 2009; Hadi Jasim, "Baghdad: 'Ansar Sahwa al-fadhil yu'bashiroon 'amalahum ma' al-jaysh," *Ash-Sharq al-Awsat*, April 1, 2009.

161. Cordesman, *Iraq's Insurgency,* 519.

162. "Maliki yutalib Kurdistan b'ihtiram al-hitt al-azraq," *Al-Hayat*, November 31, 2008; Steven Lee Myers, "Rivalries in Iraq Keep G.I.s in the Field," *New York Times*, January 26, 2010.

163. Kagan, 40–41, 54–55; Cordesman, *Iraq's Insurgency,* 594–601.

164. Sharon Behn and Sara A. Carter, "Iraqi Militias Feeling Pushback," *Washington Times*, April 12, 2008; Stephen Farrell and James Glanz, "More Than 1,000 in Iraq's Force Quit Basra Fight," *New York Times*, April 4, 2008; Solomon Moore, "Secret Iraqi Dealings Show Problems in Arms Order," *New York Times*, April 12, 2008; Kenneth Katzman, "Iraq: Politics, Elections, and Benchmarks," Congressional Research Service Report to Congress, August 21, 2009.

165. For a summary of the origins and growth of the tribal councils, see Yassin Muhammed Sadiqi, "25 Elf min rijal-ha yandhmoon ila quwat al-'amn," *Al-Hayat*, August 6, 2008; Scott Weiner, "Maliki Makes a Play for the Southern Tribes," Institute for the Study of War Backgrounder No. 37, November 6, 2008; Alissa J. Rubin, "Clash in Iraq Over a Plan for Councils Intensifies," *New York Times*, December 4, 2008.

166. Sami Zubaida, "The Fragments Imagine the Nation: The Case of Iraq," *International Journal of Middle East Studies*, 34 (2002): 214.

167. For a discussion of the centripetal forces keeping Iraq together, see Reider Visser and Gareth Stransfield, eds., *An Iraqi of its Regions: Cornerstone of a Federal Democracy* (New York: Columbia University Press, 2008).

168. Anthony Cordesman and Adam Mausner, *Withdrawal from Iraq: Assessing the Readiness of Iraqi Security Forces* (Washington, DC: Center for Strategic and International Studies, 2009), 151.

169. "Turkey Says 41 Rebels Killed in Iraq Offensive," AFP, February 25, 2008; "Baghdad yahither min saddamat bayn al-jaysh al-turki wa peshmerga," *Ash-Sharq al-Awsat*, February 26, 2008, in Arabic.

170. Timothy Williams and Sa'ad Al-Izzi, "Iran Claims an Oil Field It Seized from Iraqis," *New York Times*, December 20, 2009.

171. Ernesto Londoño and Leila Fadel, "U.S. Failure to Neutralize Shiite Militia in Iraq Threatens to Snarl Pullout," *Washington Post*, March 4, 2010.

172. "Iraqi Officer: The Current Iraqi Army Is Closer to a Gendarmerie Than a Regular Army," *Ash-Sharq al-Awsat*, May 17, 2007; Abdel-Wahhab al-Qassab, "Rebuilding the Iraqi Army (A Preliminary View)," in Khair el-Din Haseeb, ed., *Planning Iraq's Future: A Detailed Project to Rebuild Post-Liberation Iraq* (Beirut: Center for Arab Unity Studies, 2006), 197–198.

## Chapter 4: Iran

1. See Ervand Abrahamian, *A History of Modern Iran* (New York: Cambridge University Press, 2008), 18. See also Richard Cottam, *Nationalism in Iran* (Pittsburgh, PA: University of Pittsburgh Press, 1979).

2. Michael Axworthy, "The Army of Nader Shah," *Iranian Studies*, 40 (2007).

3. John Gerring, *Case Study Research: Principles and Practices* (New York: Cambridge University Press, 2007), 116–120; Alexander George and Andrew Bennett, *Case Studies and Theory Development in the Social Sciences* (Cambridge, MA: MIT Press, 2005), 80, 120–121.

4. David B. Ralston, *Importing the European Army: The Introduction of European Military Techniques and Institutions into the Extra-European World, 1600–1914* (Chicago: University of Chicago Press, 1990).

5. Mark Katz, ed. *Revolution: International Dimensions* (Washington, DC: CQ Press, 2000), Part I.

6. Steven Ward, *Immortal: A Military History of Iran and Its Armed Forces* (Washington, DC: Georgetown University Press, 2009), 62–72; Stephanie Cronin, "Building a New Army: Military Reform in Qajar Iran," in Roxane Farmanfarmaian, ed., *War and Peace in Qajar Persia: Implications Past and Present* (New York: Routledge, 2008), 65–67.

7. Cited in Abrahamian, *History of Modern Iran*, 22; for more on the Qashqai under the Qajar, see Lois Beck, *Qashqai of Iran* (New Haven, CT: Yale University Press, 1986), 60–90.

8. Willem Floor, "The Luti: A Social Phenomena in Qajar Persia," *Die Welt Des Islam*, 13 (1971); Vanessa Martin, *The Qajar Pact: Bargaining, Protest, and the State in Nineteenth Century Persia* (New York: I. B. Tauris, 2005), Chapter 6.

9. Quoted in Guity Nashat, *The Origins of Modern Reform in Iran, 1870–80* (Urbana: University of Illinois Press, 1982), 55.

10. Nashat, 66–71; James A. Bill, "Modernization and Reform from Above: The Case of Iran," *Journal of Politics*, 32 (1970); A. Reza Sheikholeslami, "The Patrimonial Structure of Iranian Bureaucracy in the Late Nineteenth Century," *Iranian Studies*, 11 (1978).

11. Abrahamian, *History of Modern Iran*, 36–37.

12. Stephanie Cronin, *The Army and the Creation of the Pahlavi State in Iran, 1910–1926* (New York: I. B. Tauris, 1997), 54–57.

13. Abrahamian, *History of Modern Iran*, 52–53; Gene Garthwaite, *Khans and Shahs: A Documentary Analysis of the Bakhtiari in Iran* (New York: Cambridge University Press, 1983), 114–115; Ward, 92–97.

14. Ashgar Fathi, "The Role of 'Rebel' in the Constitutional Movement in Iran," *International Journal of Middle Eastern Studies*, 10 (1979); Mansour Bonakdarian, "A World Born through the Chamber of a Revolver: Revolutionary Violence, Culture, and Modernity in Iran, 1906–1911," *Comparative Studies of South Asia, Africa, and the Middle East*, 25 (2005).

15. Initially, Italy was approached to provide expert advisors for the gendarmerie, but they demurred under pressure from Britain and Russia. See Cronin, *Army and the Creation of the Pahlavi State*, 16–19.

16. Cronin, *Army and the Creation of the Pahlavi State*, 8, 21–23.

17. Ward, 109–111; Abrahamian, *History of Modern Iran*, 58–60.

18. Abrahamian, *History of Modern Iran*, 62.

19. Abrahamian, *History of Modern Iran*, 67; Michael Zirinsky, "Imperial Power and Dictatorship: Britain and the Rise of Reza Shah, 1921–1926," *International Journal of Middle East Studies*, 24 (1992).

20. Cronin, *Army and the Creation of the Pahlavi State*, 200.

21. Stephanie Cronin, *Tribal Politics in Iran: Rural Conflict and the New State, 1921–1941* (New York: Routledge, 2007), 22–29, 52–53; Cronin, *Army and the Creation of the Pahlavi State*, 98–102, 206; Ward, 135–137; Abrahamian, *History of Modern Iran*, 93.

22. Cronin, *Army and the Creation of the Pahlavi State*, 109–110, 137–139; Banani, 54.

23. M. Reza Ghods, "Iranian Nationalism and Reza Shah," *Middle Eastern Studies*, 27 (1991).

24. Ward, 142–147; Cronin, *Army and the Creation of the Pahlavi State*, 125–136, 208; Banani, 55–57.

25. Cronin, *Tribal Politics in Iran*, 31–33; Cronin, *Army and the Creation of the Pahlavi State*, 120–122, 210–214; Nikki R. Keddie, *Modern Iran: Roots and Results of Revolution* (New Haven, CT: Yale University Press, 2003), 91, 102.

26. Cronin, *Tribal Politics in Iran*, 69.

27. Abrahamian, *History of Modern Iran*, 67–69; Keddie, 93–94.

28. Ann Tibbitts Schultz, *Buying Security: Iran Under the Monarchy* (Boulder, CO: Westview Press, 1989), 53.

29. Tareq Y. Ismael, *Iran and Iraq: Roots of Conflict* (Syracuse, NY: Syracuse University Press, 1982), 31; Will Swearingen, "Geopolitical Origins of the Iran–Iraq War," *Geographical Review*, 78 (1988).

30. D. Cameron Watt, "The Saadabad Pact of 8 July 1937," in Uriel Dann, ed., *The Great Powers in the Middle East* (London: Holmes & Meier, 1988).

31. For details of the invasion, see Richard Steward, *Sunrise at Abadan: The British and Soviet Invasion of Iran, 1941* (New York: Praeger, 1988); Ward, Chapter 6.

32. Ervand Abrahamian, *Iran between Two Revolutions* (Princeton, NJ: Princeton University Press, 1982), 169–176; Beck, *Qashqai of Iran*, 143–148.

33. Moyara de Moraes Reuhsen, "Operation 'Ajax' Revisited, 1953," *Middle Eastern Studies*, 29 (1993); Mark Gasiorowski, "The 1953 Coup d'Etat in Iran," *International Journal of Middle East Studies*, 19 (1987); Beck, *Qashqai of Iran*, 153–154; Osamu Miyata, "The Tudeh Military Network during the Oil Nationalization Period," *Middle Eastern Studies*, 23 (1987).

34. Ruhollah Ramazani, *Iran's Foreign Policy, 1941–1972: A Study of Foreign Policy in Modernizing Nations* (Charlottesville: University of Virginia Press, 1975), 72–73, 158–163; Mark J. Gasiorowski, *U.S. Foreign Policy and the Shah: Building a Client State in Iran* (Ithaca, NY: Cornell University Press, 1991), 53–56; Ward, 171–177.

35. Gasiorowski, *U.S. Foreign Policy and the Shah*, 95, 109–113, 121; Ramazani, 278–285.

36. The literature on the impact of oil on Iran's economy and its connection to military modernization is enormous. For a basic outline, see Abrahamian, *History of Modern Iran*, 123–134. For more detail, see Morteza Gharebaghian, "Oil Revenue and the Militirisation of Iran," *Social Scientist*, 15 (1987); and Robert Looney, "The Role of Military Expenditures in Pre-Revolutionary Iran's Economic Decline," *Iranian Studies*, 21 (1988).

37. Victor J. Croizat, "Imperial Iranian Gendarmerie," *Marine Corps Journal* (October 1975): 30; see also Gasiorowski, *U.S. Foreign Policy and the Shah*, 114–117.

38. Abrahamian, *History of Modern Iran*, 133; Fred Halladay, *Iran: Dictatorship and Revolution* (New York: Penguin, 1979), 214. See also Lawrence Brenner, "Iran's Educational Revolution: Military Style," *Comparative Educational Review*, 10 (1966); Reinhold Loeffler, "Tribal Order and the State: The Political Organization of Boir Ahmad," *Iranian Studies*, 11 (1978).

39. Darius Rejali, *Torture and Modernity: Self, Society, and State in Modern Iran* (Boulder. CO: Westview, 1994), 104; Michael Rubin, *Into the Shadows: Radical Vigilantes in Khatami's Iran, Washington Institute for Near East Policy* (Washington, DC: Washington Institute for Near East Policy Paper No. 56, 2001), 13–14.

40. Guilain Denoeux, *Urban Unrest in the Middle East: A Comparative Study of Informal Networks in Egypt, Iran, and Lebanon* (Albany: SUNY Press, 1993), 127–128; Willem Floor, "The Political Role of Lutis in Iran," in Michael Bonine and Nikki Keddie, eds., *Modern Iran: The Dialectics of Continuity and Change* (Albany: SUNY Press, 1981), 92.

41. Halladay, 267–268; Schultz, 17–20; Ramazani, 348–350, 400.

42. Donald Vought, "Iran," in Richard Gabriel, ed., *Fighting Armies: Antagonists in the Middle East: A Combat Assessment* (Westport, CT: Greenwood, 1983), 96–97.

43. William Hickman, *Ravaged and Reborn: The Iranian Army* (Washington, DC: Brookings Institution, 1982), 2–3.

44. Schultz, 22–25; Ward, 195–199; Ramazani, 361–368.

45. Leonard Spector, *Nuclear Ambition: The Spread of Nuclear Weapons, 1989–1990* (Boulder, CO: Westview, 1990), 203–206.

46. Quoted in Ramazani, 360.

47. Gasiorowski, *U.S. Foreign Policy and the Shah*, 113; Ward, 201–210; Sepehr Zabih, *The Iranian Military in Revolution and War* (New York: Routledge, 1988), 9–12.

48. Ramazani, 411–413, 435–438; David McDowall, *A Modern History of the Kurds* (New York: I. B. Tauris, 2004), 337–338.

49. Halliday, 273; Ward, 204–205.

50. The idea of the "king's dilemma" is raised in Samuel Huntington, *Political Order in Changing Societies* (New Haven, CT: Yale University Press, 2006), 177–191.

51. Ferydoon Firoozi, "Iranian Censuses 1956 and 1966: A Comparative Analysis," *Middle East Journal*, 24 (1970); Mohammed Kamiar, "Population Size, Distribution, and Growth in Iran," *Population Geography*, 7 (1985).

52. Abrahamian, *Iran between Two Revolutions*, Chapter 10.

53. Keddie, 219–222; Maziar Behrooz, *Rebels with a Cause: The Failure of the Left in Iran* (New York: I. B. Tauris, 1999), 51–69; Ervand Abrahamian, *The Iranian Mojahedin* (New Haven, CT: Yale University Press, 1989), 137–139.

54. On the cycles of protests in Iran, see Charles Kurzman, *The Unthinkable Revolution in Iran* (Cambridge, MA: Harvard University Press, 2004). For an explanation of the shah's decision making, see Marvin Zonis, *Majestic Failure: The Fall of the Shah* (Chicago: University of Chicago Press, 1991).

55. Misagh Parsa, *Social Origins of the Iranian Revolution* (New Brunswick, NJ: Rutgers University Press, 1989), 116, 224–227, 240–242; Saïd Arjomand, *The Turban for the Crown: The Islamic Revolution in Iran* (New York: Oxford University Press, 1988), 120–124, 135–136; Shaul Bakash, *Reign of the Ayatollahs: Iran and the Islamic Revolution* (New York: Basic Books, 1984), 56; Assef Bayat, "Workers Control after the Revolution," *MERIP Reports* 113 (1983): 19.

56. Arjomand, *Turban for the Crown*, 126; Abrahamian, *Iranian Mojahedin*, 171–175; Ward, 225–226.

57. Amir Taheri, *Khomeini and the Islamic Revolution* (Bethesda, MD: Adler & Adler, 1985), 251–252; Parsa, 291–294.

58. Arjomand, *Turban for the Crown*, 135; Bakash, 56.

59. Cited in Bakash, 57–60. See also Abrahamian, *Iranian Mojahideen*, 49–52.

60. Cited in Abrahamian, *History of Modern Iran*, 163.

61. Deneoux, 129. See also Moojan Moomen, *An Introduction to Shi'i Islam: The History and Doctrine of Twelver Shi'ism* (New Haven, CT: Yale University Press, 1987), 199.

62. Rejali, 104, 111; Rubin, 24–26. For more details on the incorporation of hojjatiyah into following the revolution, see Mahmoud Sadri, "Hojjatiya," *Encyclopedia Iranica Online*, retrieved on March 2, 2010, from www.iranica.com/.

63. Bakash, 67, 77, 121–123, 145–146; Taheri, 249–255; Arjomand, *Turban for the Crown*, 141–143.

64. William Hickman, *Ravaged and Reborn: The Iranian Army, 1982* (Washington, DC: Brookings Institution, 1982), 13–14.

65. Ward, 226–230; Kenneth Katzman, *The Warriors of Islam: Iran's Revolutionary Guard* (Boulder, CO: Westview Press, 1993), 31–33.

66. Bakash, 63–64, 144–145; Katzman, 41, 51–57, 149.

67. Ward, 244–246; Gregory Rose, "The Post-Revolutionary Purge of Iran's Armed Forces: A Revisionist Assessment," *Iranian Studies*, 17 (1984).

68. Ward, 227–229, 238–240; Shahram Chubin and Charles Tripp, *Iran and Iraq at War* (Boulder, CO: Westview Press, 1988), 33; Hickman, 8–10.

69. On IRGC's role in worker suppression, see Parsa, 267–273; Bayat, "Workers Control after the Revolution," 33. On MEK, see Abrahamian, *Iranian Mojahideen*, 213–220; Bakash, 157–158.

70. On involvement in the ethnic minorities, see Parsa, 258–264; Beck, Chapter 12.

71. Katzman, 28; MacDonald, 269; Ward 230–233.

72. Bakash 100–101, 224–225; Arjomand, *Turban for the Crown*, 171–173.

73. Bakash, 69–70; Alvin Rubinstein, "The Soviet Union and Iran Under Khomeini," *International Affairs*, 57 (1981).

74. On exporting the revolution to the Arab world, see Marvin Zonis and Daniel Brumberg, *Khomeini, the Islamic Republic of Iran, and the Arab World* (Cambridge, MA: Harvard Middle East Paper No. 5, 1987). On territorial claims to Bahrain, see David Menashri, "Iran" in Colin Legum, Haim Shaked, and Daniel Dishon, eds., *Middle East Contemporary Survey, 1978–79* (London: Holmes and Meier, 1980), 538–541.

75. Quoted in Chubin and Tripp, 35; see also Ward, 243–244.

76. Hickman, 19; Chubin and Tripp, 36.

77. Bakash, 127; Ward, 249–255.

78. Takeyh, 90–91, 100–102.

79. Cited in Rouleau, 6.

80. Ward, 258–260; Anthony Cordesman, *The Iran-Iraq War and Western Security, 1984–1987* (London: Jane's, 1987), 68–69, 104–105; Katzman 131; Chubin and Tripp, 46–48.

81. Hiro, 96.

82. Ward, 247; Katzman, 104–106.

83. Ward, 246; Katzman, 89–92; Zabih, 217–218.

84. Zabih, 140–141.

85. Zabih, 190–192; Cordesman, *The Iran-Iraq War and Western Security*, 92–96; Hiro, 132.

86. David Menashri, "Iran," in Colin Legum, Haim Shaked, and Daniel Dishon, eds., *Middle East Contemporary Survey, 1981–2* (London: Holmes and Meier, 1984), 533–543.

87. Katzman, 85.

88. Ward, 246, 263.

89. Chubin and Tripp, 128–130; Katzman, 65.

90. Ward, 281–283.

91. Katzman, 101; Chubin and Tripp, 74.

92. Katzman, 81–88, Ward, 247; Arjomand, *Turban for the Crown*, 165.

93. Katzman, 67–69; Ward, 227, 246.

94. Cordesman, *The Iran-Iraq War and Western Security*, 124, 128–129; Zabih, 218–219.

95. Gideon Gera, "The Iraqi-Iranian War," in Colin Legum, Haim Shaked, and Daniel Dishon, eds., *Middle East Contemporary Survey, 1988* (Boulder, CO: Westview, 1990), 212–213; David Menashri, "Iran," *Middle East Contemporary Survey, 1988, 477*; Ward, 297.

96. Bakash, 129.

97. Dilip Hiro, *The Longest War: The Iran–Iraq Military Conflict* (New York: Routledge, 1991), Appendix II.

98. F. Adelkhah, J.-F. Bayart, and O. Roy, *Thermidor en iran* (Brussels: Complexe, 1993); M. C. Wells, "Thermidor in the Islamic Republic of Iran: The Rise of Muhammed Khatami," *British Journal of Middle Eastern Studies*, 26 (1999).

99. Dan Brumberg, *Reinventing Khomeini: The Struggle for Reform in Iran* (Chicago: University of Chicago Press, 2001); Saïd Arjomand, *After Khomeini: Iran under His Successors* (New York: Oxford University Press, 2009).

100. Cited in Menashri, "Iran," *Middle East Contemporary Survey, 1988*, 477.

101. Cited in Katzman, 93.

102. Cited in Spector, 210–211.

103. Katzman, 91–92; 103–106, 120–122; Ward, 304.

104. H. E. Chehabi, "Iran and Lebanon After Khomeini," in H. E. Chehabi, ed., *Distant Relations: Iran and Lebanon in the Last 500 Years* (New York: I. B. Tauris, 2007).

105. Arjomand, *After Khomeini*, 136–142; David Menashri, "Iran" in Ami Ayalon, ed., *Middle East Contemporary Survey, 1992* (Boulder, CO: Westview, 1995), 399, 424.

106. Katzman, 91–92; 103–106, 120–122; Arjomand, *After Khomeini*, 59, 136–142; Ward, 304.

107. Wehrey, 25–29, 44.

108. On the bonyad, see Ali Rashidi, "The Process of De-Privatisation in Iran after the Revolution of 1979," in T. Coville, ed., *The Economy of Islamic Iran: Between State and Market* (Tehran: Institut Francais de Recherche en Iran, 1994); Ali A. Saeidi, "The Accountability of Para-Governmental Organizations (Bonyads): The Case of Iranian Foundations," *Iranian Studies*, 37 (2004); Suzanne Maloney, "Agents or Obstacles? Parastatal Foundations and Challenges for Iranian Development," in Parvin Alizadeh, ed., *The Economy of Iran: Dilemmas of an Islamic State* (New York: I. B. Tauris, 2000).

109. Arjomand, *After Khomeini*, 60–61, 153–155.

110. Menashri, "Iran," in *Middle East Contemporary Survey, 1992*, 413–418; Asef Bayat, "Squatters and the State: Back Street Politics in the Islamic Republic," *Middle East Report*, 191 (1994).

111. Hossein Aryan, "Mass Mobilization: The Rise of Iran's Paramilitary Enforcer," *Jane's Intelligence Review* (July 2008): 38–41; Wilfred Buchta, *Who Rules Iran? The Structure of Power in the Islamic Republic* (Washington, DC: Washington Institute for Near East Policy, 2000), 66–67; Ward, 307.

112. For more details, see Rubin, *Into the Shadows*.

113. Wehrey, 7; Katzman, 155.

114. Elain Sciolino, "Iran Protests Spread to 18 Cities; Police Crack Down at University," *New York Times*, July 13, 1999.

115. Douglas Jehl, "Despite Police Dismissals, Iran Protests is the Angriest Yet," *New York Times*, July 12, 1999.

116. Buchta, 147–148; Ward, 323.

117. Ward, 323–324; Cordesman and Klieker, 74–78.

118. Janet Afary, "The Sexual Economy of the Islamic Republic," *Iranian Studies*, 42 (2009): 11; Arjomand, *After Khomeini*, 150–153.

119. Caitlin Talmadge, "Closing Time: Assessing the Iranian Threat to the Strait of Hormuz," *International Security*, 33 (2008).

120. Mohsen Milani, "Tehran's Take," *Foreign Affairs*, 88 (2009).

121. Aryan, 40.

122. Aryan, 38–41; Ali Alfoneh, "What Do Structural Changes in the Revolutionary Guard Mean?" (Washington, DC: American Enterprise Institute Public Policy Research No. 7, 2008); retrieved on February 5, 2010, from: www.aei.org/docLib/20080923_23487MEO07_g.pdf.

123. Babak Rahimi, "The Role of the Revolutionary Guards and the Basij Militias in Iran's 'Electoral Coup'" TerrorismMonitor, Vol. VII, No. 21 (July 1, 2009), Jamestown Foundation; retrieved on February 2, 2010, from www.jamestown.org/uploads/media/TM_007_58.pdf; Suad Jafarzadeh, "Basij Militia Turns Strong Arm against Dissent," *Washington Times*, June 28, 2009.

124. "Mousavi's Defying Statement to the Iranian Nation"; retrieved on February 2, 2010, from: www.pbs.org/wgbh/pages/frontline/tehranbureau/2009/06/mousavis-defying-statement-to-the-iranian-nation.html.

125. "Mousavi's 15th Statement: The 30th Anniversary of the Formation of the Basij"; retrieved on February 2, 2010, from: http://khordaad88.com/?p=790#more-790.

126. Iranian reformist website www.tagheer.com, in Persian 1200 on November 29, 2009 in BBC Worldwide Monitoring.

127. Mehr news agency, Tehran, in English on October 2, 2009, in BBC Worldwide Monitoring.

128. Brian Murphy, "Iran Rewards Basij Militias with Clout," Associated Press, February 10, 2010.

129. E'temad newspaper supplement, printed in Iran, on November 10, 2009, in BBC Worldwide Monitoring.

130. Etemad, Tehran, in Persian, November 23, 2009, page 2, in BBC Worldwide Monitoring.

131. Mardom-Salari website, Tehran, in Persian, October 5, 2009, in BBC Worldwide Monitoring.

132. Voice of the Islamic Republic of Iran, Tehran, in Persian, November 25, 2009, in BBC Worldwide Monitoring.

133. Borzou Daragahi, "Iran's Top Leader Tell Militias Not to Step In," *Los Angeles Times*, January 10, 2010.

134. Steven Ward says directly that "only the Iraqi invasion and subsequent failure of the regime to translate its ideological fervor into victory saved the Artesh and

undermined the idea that professional military forces were unnecessary." Katzman notes counterfactually that "absent an external threat to the authority of the new regime, the regular military might well have been expendable as an organization." See Ward, 304; Katzman, 27–28.

135. Brumberg, 33–38.

## Chapter 5: Learning to Live with Militias

1. Joel Migdal, *Strong Societies and Weak States: State–Society Relations and State Capabilities in the Third World* (Princeton, NJ: Princeton University Press, 1988), 18. See also Robert Bates, *When Things Fell Apart: State Failure in Late-Century Africa* (New York: Cambridge University Press, 2008), 147–148.

2. Neil J. Mitchell, *Agents of Atrocity: Leaders, Followers, and the Violation of Human Rights in Civil War* (New York: Palgrave Macmillan, 2004); Stanley Cohen, *States of Denial: Knowing about Atrocities and Suffering* (Malden, MA: Polity Press, 2001), 108–109.

3. For a recent example of literature emphasizes the state's indispensability, see Ian Loader and Neil Walker, *Civilizing Security* (New York: Cambridge University Press, 2007); Ashraf Ghani and Clare Lockhart, *Fixing Failed States: A Framework for Rebuilding a Fractured World* (New York: Oxford University Press, 2008).

4. For a larger comparison of regions, see Ariel Ahram, "Origins and Persistence of State-Sponsored Militias," *Journal of Strategic Studies* (forthcoming).

5. Christopher Bayl and Tim Harper, *Forgotten Wars: Freedom and Revolution in Southeast Asia* (Cambridge, UK: Belknap Press, 2007); Joyce C. Lebra, *Japanese-Trained Armies in Southeast Asia: Independence and Volunteer Forces in World War II* (New York: Columbia University Press, 1977).

6. Etel Solingen, "Pax Asiatica versus Bella Levantina: The Foundations of War and Peace in East Asia and the Middle East," *American Political Science Review*, 101 (2007).

7. Miguel A. Centeno, *Blood and Debt: War and the Nation-State in Latin America* (University Park: Pennsylvania State University Press, 2002).

8. Jeffrey Herbst, *States and Power in Africa: Comparative Lessons in Authority and Control* (Princeton, NJ: Princeton University Press, 2000). See also Robert Jackson and Carl Rosberg, "Why Africa's Weak States Persist: The Empirical and the Juridical in Statehood," *World Politics*, 35 (1982): 19.

9. Vadim Volkov, *Violent Entrepreneurs: The Use of Force in the Making of Russian Capitalism* (Ithaca, NY: Cornell University Press, 2002). For a comparison of Africa and Soviet Eurasia, see Mark Beissinger and Crawford Young, eds., *Beyond State Crisis? Postcolonial Africa and Post-Soviet Eurasia in Comparative Perspective* (Baltimore: Johns Hopkins University Press, 2002).

10. Christoph Zürcher, *The Post-Soviet Wars: Rebellion, Ethnic Conflict, and Nationhood in the Caucasus* (New York: New York University Press, 2007); Kathleen

Collins, *Clan Politics and Regime Transition in Central Asia* (New York: Cambridge University Press, 2006); Jesse Driscoll, Exiting Anarchy: Militia Politics after the Post-Soviet Wars (PhD dissertation, Stanford University, 2009); Charles King, "The Benefits of Ethnic War: Understanding Eurasia's Unrecognized States," *World Politics*, 53 (2001).

11. Mehran Kamrava, "Military Professionalization and Civil–Military Relations in the Middle East," *Political Science Quarterly*, 115 (2000).

12. Yezid Sayigh, *Armed Struggle and the Search for State: The Palestinian National Movement, 1949–1993* (New York: Oxford University Press, 1997); Oren Barak, *The Lebanese Army: A National Institution in a Divided Society* (Albany: SUNY Press, 2009).

13. Ian Lustick, "The Absence of Middle Eastern Great Powers: Political 'Backwardness' in Historical Perspective," *International Organization*, 51 (1997).

14. Robert Rotberg, "The New Nature of Nation-State Failure," *Washington Quarterly*, 25 (2002): 93–94.

15. Thráinn Eggertsson, "The Old Theory of Economic Policy and the New Institutionalism," *World Development*, 25 (1997).

16. Louise Andersen, "What to Do: The Dilemma of International Engagement in Fragile States," in Louise Andersen, Bjørn Møller, and Finn Stepputat, eds., *Fragile States and Insecure People? Violence, Security, and Statehood in the Twenty-First Century* (New York: Palgrave Macmillan, 2007); Brennan Kraxberger, "Failed States: Temporary Obstacles to Democratic Diffusion or Fundamental Holes in the World Political Map?" *Third World Quarterly*, 28 (2007).

17. Barak Mendelsohn, "Bolstering the State: A Different Perspective on the Jihadi Movement," *International Studies Review*, 11 (2009).

18. Jane Channa, *Security Sector Reform: Issues, Challenges and Prospects* (New York: Oxford University Press, 2002).

19. James D. Fearon and David Laitin, "Neotrusteeship and the Problem of Weak States," *International Security*, 28:4 (2004); Stephen Krasner, "Sharing Sovereignty: New Institutions for Collapsed and Failing States," *International Security*, 29 (2006).

20. Robert Rauchhaus, "Principal-Agent Problems in Humanitarian Intervention: Moral Hazards, Adverse Selection, and the Commitment Dilemma," *International Studies Quarterly*, 53 (2009).

21. Cited in Geoffrey Robinson, *"If You Leave Us Here, We Will Die": How Genocide Was Stopped in East Timor* (Princeton, NJ: Princeton University Press, 2010), 86.

22. Christine Fair and Peter Chalk, *Fortifying Pakistan: The Role of U.S. Internal Security Assistance* (Washington, DC: U.S. Institute of Peace Press, 2006); Shuja Nawaz, *Crossed Swords: Pakistan, the Army, and the War Within* (New York: Oxford University Press, 2008); Mark Mazetti, Jane Perlez, Eric Schmitt, and Andrew Lehren, "Pakistan Aids Insurgency in Afghanistan, Reports Asserts," *New York Times*, July 25, 2010.

23. Alex de Waal, *Famine Crimes: Politics and the Disaster Relief Industry* (Bloomington: Indiana University Press, 1997), 124–125; for a more recent example, see Jeffrey Gettleman and Neil MacFarquhar, "Somalia Food Aid Bypasses Needy, U.N. Study Says," *New York Times*, March 9, 2010.

24. Stephen David, *Catastrophic Consequences: Civil Wars and American Interests* (Baltimore: Johns Hopkins University Press, 2008), 159.

25. Max Manwaring, *A "New" Dynamics in the Western Hemisphere Security Environment: The Mexican Zetas and Other Private Armies*, U.S. Army War College Strategic Studies Institute Monograph (September 2009), available at www.strategicstudies institute.army.mil/pubs/display.cfm?pubID=940 (October 15, 2009). On Mexico, see Patrick O'Day, "The Mexican Army as Cartel," *Journal of Contemporary Criminal Justice*, 17 (2001). On Colombia, see Russell Crandall, *Driven by Drugs: U.S. Policy Toward Colombia* (Boulder, CO: Lynne Rienner, 2008).

26. Eric Heinze, "Nonstate Actors in the International Legal Order: The Israeli–Hezbollah Conflict and the Law of Self-Defense," *Global Governance*, 15 (2009).

27. Channa, 41–48; Chris Smith, "Security-Sector Reform: Development Breakthrough or Institutional Engineering," *Conflict, Security, and Development*, 1 (2001); Eric Scheye and Gordon Peake, "To Arrest Insecurity: Time for a Revised Security Sector Reform Agenda," *Conflict, Security, and Development*, 5 (2005).

28. Simon Chesterman, *You, the People: The United Nations, Transitional Administration, and State-Buildiing* (New York: Oxford University Press, 2004), 239–242.

29. Alan Kuperman, "The Moral Hazard of Humanitarian Intervention: Lessons from the Balkans," *International Studies Quarterly*, 52 (2008).

30. James Rielly and Bates Gill, "Sovereignty, Intervention, and Peacekeeping: The View from Beijing," *Survival*, 42 (2000); Ramesh Thakur, *The United Nations, Peace, and Security* (New York: Cambridge University Press, 2006), 264.

31. David M. Edelstein, *Occupational Hazards: Success and Failure in Military Occupations* (Ithaca, NY: Cornell University Press, 2008); Kimberly Marten Zisk, *Enforcing the Peace* (New York: Columbia University Press, 2004), 64, 96–97.

32. On the comparison between the U.S. and British occupations of Iraq, see Toby Dodge, *Inventing Iraq: The Failure of Nation Building and a History Denied* (New York: Columbia University Press, 2003).

33. Douglass C. North, "The New Institutional Economics and Third World Development," in John Harris, Janet Hunter, and Colin Lewis, eds., *The New Institutional Economics and Third World Development* (New York: Routledge, 1995); Shahar Hameiri, "Failed States or a Failed Paradigm?: State Capacity and the Limits of Institutionalism," *Journal of International Relations and Development*, 10 (2007).

34. Michael Klare, "The Deadly Connection: Paramilitary Bands, Small Arms Diffusion, and State Failure," in Robert I. Rotberg, ed., *When States Fail* (Princeton, NJ: Princeton University Press, 2004), 117.

35. Sherrill Stroscheim, "Making or Breaking Kosovo: Application of Dispersed State Control," *Perspectives on Politics*, 6 (2008): 657–658.

36. "Negotiations Break Down in Stand Off with Pirates," *New York Times*, April 11, 2009.

37. Yochi Dreazen, "U.S. to Fund Afghan Militias, Applying Iraq Tactics," *Wall Street Journal*, December 23, 2008.

38. Amin Saikal, "Afghanistan's Weak State and Strong Society," in Simon Chesterman, Michael Ignatieff, and Ramesh Thakur, eds., *Making States Work: State Failure and the Crisis of Governance* (New York: United Nations University Press, 2005), 205.

39. Ahmed Rashid, "A Deal with the Taliban?" *New York Review of Books*, 57 (February 25, 2010); Fotini Christia and Michael Semple, "Flipping the Taliban," *Foreign Affairs* 88 (2009).

40. *U.S. Army & Marine Corps Counterinsurgency Field Manual* (Chicago: University of Chicago Press, 2007), 110–113.

41. Seth Kaplan, *Fixing Fragile States: A New Paradigm for Development* (Westport, CT: Praeger, 2008), 53–55.

42. Edward N. Luttwak, "Give War a Chance," *Foreign Affairs*, 78 (1999); see also Suzanne Werner and Amy Yuen, "Making and Keeping Peace," *International Organization*, 59 (2005); Chester Crocker, "A Poor Case for Quitting," *Foreign Affairs*, 79 (2000); Sergio De Mello, "Enough Is Enough," *Foreign Affairs*, 79 (2000).

43. Michael Colaresi and Sabine C. Carey, "To Kill or to Protect: Security Forces, Domestic Institutions, and Genocide," *Journal of Conflict Resolution*, 52 (2008); R. J. Rummel, *Death by Government* (New Brunswick, NJ: Transaction, 1994).

44. Arthur Jay Klinghoffer, *International Dimensions of Genocide in Rwanda* (New York: New York University Press, 1998), 80–91.

45. Matthew Krain, "State-Sponsored Mass Murder: The Onset and Severity of Genocides and Politicides," *Journal of Conflict Resolution*, 41 (1997); Barbara Harff, "No Lessons Learned from the Holocaust? Assessing Risks of Genocide and Politicides since 1955," *American Political Science Review*, 97 (2003).

46. "Fixing a Broken World," *The Economist*, January 29, 2009.

47. Chris Clapham, "Sovereignty and the Third World State," *Political Studies*, 47 (1999); Herbst, Chapter 9; William Reno, *Warlord Politics and African States* (Boulder, CO: Lynne Rienner, 1998); Ken Menkahus, "Government without Governance in Somalia: Spoilers, State Building, and the Politics of Coping," *International Security*, 31 (2006).

48. On economic development in the absence of states, see Avinash K. Dixit, *Lawlessness and Economics: Alternative Modes of Governance* (Princeton, NJ: Princeton University Press, 2004).

49. James C. Scott, *Seeing Like a State: How Certain Schemes to Improve the Human Condition Have Failed* (New Haven, CT: Yale University Press, 1998), 340.

50. S. Neil MacFarlane and Yuen Foon Khong, *Human Security and the U.N.: A Critical History* (Indianapolis: Indiana University Press, 2006), 245–246; see also Marlies Glasius, "Human Security from Paradigm Shift to Operationalization: Job Description for a Human Security Worker," *Security Dialogue*, 39 (2008).

51. David Kilcullen, *The Accidental Guerrilla: Fighting Small Wars in the Midst of a Big One* (New York: Oxford University Press, 2009), xvi.

52. John A. Nagl, "Forward to the University of Chicago Press Edition," in *U.S. Army & Marine Corps Counterinsurgency Field Manual*, xv; on the history of American counterinsurgency, see John Fishel and Max G. Manwaring, *Uncomfortable Wars Revisited* (Norman: University of Oklahoma Press, 2006).

53. Anthony James Joe, *Resisting Rebellion: The History and Politics of Counterinsurgency* (Lexington: University of Kentucky Press, 2004), 113; Austin Long, *On "Other War": Lessons from Five Decades of RAND Counterinsurgency Research* (Santa Monica, CA: RAND, 2006), 54, 71; Ian F. W. Beckett, *Modern Insurgencies and Counter-Insurgencies: Guerrillas and Their Opponents since 1750* (New York: Routledge, 2001), 24–25.

54. Mancur Olson, "Democracy, Dictatorship, and Development," *American Political Science Review*, 87 (1993). See also Zachariah Cherian Mampilly, Stationary Bandits: Understanding Rebel Governance (PhD dissertation, University of California, Los Angeles, 2007).

55. Suzette Heald, "Controlling Crime and Corruption from Below: Sungusungu in Kenya," *International Relations*, 21 (2007); Mark Bradbury, *Becoming Somaliland* (Bloomington: Indiana University Press, 2008).

56. Cited in MacFarlane and Khong, 7; see also R. J. Rummel, *Death by Government* (New Brunswick, NJ: Transaction, 1994); Mark Cooney, "From Warre to Tyranny: Lethal Conflict and the State," *American Sociological Review*, 62 (1997).

57. Paul Collier, *Wars, Guns, and Votes: Democracy in Dangerous Places* (New York: Harper Collins, 2009), Chapter 4; Rachel Stohl and Suzette Grillot, *The International Arms Trade* (Malden, MA: Polity Press, 2009).

58. Leonard Wantchenkon, "The Paradox of 'Warlord' Democracy: A Theoretical Investigation," *American Political Science Review*, 98 (2004); Larry Diamond, *Developing Democracy: Toward Consolidation* (Baltimore: Johns Hopkins University Press, 1999), 138–140; Marina Ottaway, "Rebuilding State Institutions in Collapsed States," *Development and Change*, 33 (2002).

# INDEX